ABUNDANT LIFE 365

Devotions to **Empower Your Every Day**

Ashley & Carlie Terradez

Published by Harrison House Publishers
Shippensburg, PA 17257

ISBN 13 TP: 9781667511092
ISBN 13 eBook: 9781667511108
ISBN 13 HC: 9781667511122
ISBN 13 LP: 9781667511139

For Worldwide Distribution.
1 2 3 4 5 6 7 8 / 30 29 28 27 26 25

ABUNDANT LIFE 365

Devotions to **Empower Your Every Day**

Table of Contents

The thief does not come except to steal, and to kill, and to destroy. I have come that they may have life, and that they may have it more abundantly.

John 10:10

W hat does the abundant life mean? Well, the word *abundant* means a great quantity, more than adequate, oversufficient, abounding, and richly supplied, as with resources. This obviously means more than enough things, but it is so much more!

The word *life* is translated from the Greek word *zōē*. It has a much deeper meaning that the one we gain from the English word and goes far beyond simple physical existence. It refers to a quality of life that comes from God Himself. It's not just about being alive biologically but experiencing a life God intended for us—abundant, vibrant, and victorious.

Whenever we examine our lives, it is very easy for us to attribute every circumstance—both good and bad—to God. However, this verse very clearly distinguishes between things that are good and things that are evil. Is the circumstance you are considering of death and destruction? Is something being stolen from you? If so, it is from the enemy! On the other hand, if it is something good, a blessing, abundant health or prosperity: that is from God.

God is only good, and the devil is only bad. This is the litmus test by which we should evaluate each circumstance in which we find ourselves! If something is being stolen, killed, or destroyed, you can trust in God to deliver you from that situation. His plans for you are good, and only good.

Every day in this devotional, we will look at a scripture that will focus on an aspect of the abundant life Jesus came for you to have! Keep your eyes on Jesus and see your life transform into abundance in every area!

For assuredly, I say to you, whoever says to this mountain, "Be removed and be cast into the sea," and does not doubt in his heart, but believes that those things he says will be done, he will have whatever he says.

Mark 11:23

When God created the universe, He used the creative power of His words. He simply said, *"Let there be..."* and whatever He said came to be in the physical realm! Then, when He created mankind, He said, *"Let Us make man in Our image, according to Our likeness..."* (Genesis 1:26). Then He gave humanity dominion over the earth.

God gave us authority over natural creation, and the way we exercise that authority is through our words—just as He does. In this verse, Jesus reveals that the power of our words is real and active.

He literally tells us we can have whatever we say! If there is a mountain in our way—an obstacle that is keeping us from moving into the good things God has in store for us, we can speak to them and say, "Get outta here!"

However, we must believe in our hearts that what we say will come to pass. If we doubt, or do not have complete confidence in the power and authority we have been given, then our words will not have the power God has intended for them to have.

This is why when we say, "Oh, this is killing me," we don't actually die. We don't truly believe the words we are speaking when we say things like that. This is also why we must be very intentional about the words we speak and teach ourselves to only speak words we truly mean.

In doing so, we can train our hearts and minds to believe the words we speak. As we speak out in faith, we will begin to see the things we say begin to manifest in our physical lives.

So we may boldly say: "The Lord is my helper;
I will not fear. What can man do to me?"

Hebrews 13:6

C an you see the boldness, the fearlessness, in this statement? The author of Hebrews was standing strong in trust in our God, who is always on our side and never lets us down! In any situation, we can stand firm, knowing that God is for us, and never against us. His presence in our lives gives us the courage to stand unshaken, even in the face of difficulty.

Our faith and confidence in God give us boldness. When something (or some*one*) comes against us, we can immediately stand up and say, "No! The Lord is my helper; no weapon formed against me shall prosper (Isaiah 54:17)." God is always present to help us, no matter what—or who—tries to cause us harm. His strength within us is greater than any attack we may face.

Often, when we are confronted with challenges in this life— in our health, our finances, our relationships, our workplaces— our first response is a natural one: fear. It is easy to become intimidated when we forget that God stands with us in every situation. *Yet, if God is on our side, what do we have to be afraid of?*

There are promises throughout the Word of God which give us solutions to any challenge that may come our way. In fact, that is the focus throughout this entire devotional! Every day, we will examine a scripture which assures us of some aspect of abundant life God has promised us.

So, whether the enemy is cancer or bankruptcy, rumors or natural storms, lies or strife, the answer is still the same: "The Lord is my helper; I will not fear! What can man do to me? "

God is not a man, that He should lie, Nor a son of man, that He should repent. Has He said, and will He not do? Or has He spoken, and will He not make it good?

Numbers 23:19

This verse is a powerful reminder that God is infinitely more trustworthy than imperfect mankind—He never lies, and He never changes His mind. When He says something, He means it, and when He makes a promise, He keeps it! This truth about God is the bedrock of our trust in Him.

God's Word is *always* reliable! In a world where promises are often broken and words can lose their meaning, God's Word stands strong and unchanging. We've all experienced times when someone didn't follow through on what they said, leaving us disappointed or hurt. But with God, it's completely different. What He says, He will do. We can count on it, no matter what's going on around us. This isn't just a comforting idea; it's a reality we can hold onto in every part of our lives.

When God fulfills His promises, He doesn't just meet the minimum requirements—He goes above and beyond! His works are good, high-quality, and often more than we could have ever expected. God doesn't do things halfway. When He moves in our lives, it's always with excellence and love.

Every one of God's promises are "Yes" and "Amen" (2 Corinthians 1:20). There's no hesitation in His commitment to us. Every promise He makes is guaranteed! Therefore, we can live with hope and confidence, knowing that God is true to His Word and perfect in everything He does.

So today, put your trust in Him. He's the faithful God who always keeps His promises, and He is working everything out for your good!

January 5

Your words were found, and I ate them, and Your word was to me the joy and rejoicing of my heart; for I am called by Your name, O Lord God of hosts.

Jeremiah 15:16

I magine finding a food or drink that is so nourishing that not only gives you physical strength but also brings joy and rejoicing to your heart every day. That's exactly what the Bible is for us—a source of spiritual food that sustains us, brings joy, increases wisdom and knowledge, and deepens our relationship with our Creator!

Just like how we need food to fuel our physical bodies, we need God's Word for fuel as well. When Jeremiah says, *"Your words were found, and I ate them,"* he's expressing a deep hunger we all have for something more. Many people never know exactly *what* they are missing, but the Word is what we need! And when we dive into the Word, it's like a feast for our souls. When we "eat" or absorb His Word, it becomes a part of us, shaping our thoughts, actions, and even our emotions. It gives us the strength to face whatever challenges come our way.

But it doesn't stop there. God's Word doesn't just sustain us; it also fills our hearts with joy. Picture the joy of a child receiving a long-awaited gift. That's the kind of joy God's Word brings when we truly engage with it. It's more than just words on a page; it's the voice of the Creator of the universe speaking directly to us, reminding us that we are known, loved, and called by name.

Think about that for a moment—God knows your name! The One who created everything, who holds the stars in place, knows you personally. That's a reason to rejoice! Every time we open our Bibles, we're reminded of this truth. So, let's keep feasting on God's Word, finding strength, joy, and the deep assurance that we are called and cherished by Him.

January 6

And do not be conformed to this world, but be transformed by the renewing of your mind, that you may prove what is that good and acceptable and perfect will of God.

Romans 12:2

Life is full of influences, isn't it? Everywhere we turn, something is trying to shape how we think, act, and live. But instead of conforming to the world's way of doing things, we are called to be transformed by the renewing of our minds.

Imagine your mind as a garden. If left unattended, weeds—representing the world's distractions—will take over. But when you immerse yourself in the Word of God, it's like planting seeds that bring forth good fruit. Renewing of your mind leads to real, lasting transformation!

Delving into Scripture engages you in a process that reshapes how you think and view the world. Instead of seeing things the way the world does, you begin to see things from God's perspective. This enables you to believe God's promises and receive them so they can begin to manifest in your everyday life.

When the Bible speaks of "proving" God's will, it refers to having tangible evidence of His goodness in your life. It's not simply *telling* people about God's love and favor, although that *can* be part of it. Instead, proving His will is when your life is a living advertisement of His goodness, love, and favor that others can see and experience for themselves.

As you allow God's Word to renew your mind, expect to see a transformation that speaks volumes! Your life will become a testimony to the power of His Word, offering clear evidence of His will to those around you. Keep nurturing that garden of your mind and watch how God's goodness flourishes in your life and extends to inspire those around you!

And let us not grow weary while doing good, for in due season we shall reap if we do not lose heart.

Galatians 6:9

Have you ever felt drained while waiting for a change in your life, whether it's healing, finances, or another breakthrough? Do you ever get discouraged because it feels like you are the only person around you who is doing the right things? Maybe it is in the realm of faith, or even just the integrity and morality—or lack thereof—of friends, family, or coworkers. It can be challenging when you're believing God and trying to do what's right, yet results seem so distant!

Although this is a feeling all of us can relate to, Galatians 6:9 reminds us that our efforts in doing good are not in vain. The journey might seem long, but don't forget that God's promises are unfaltering. Even if we can't see immediate results, God is always at work behind the scenes.

Trusting God—especially when faced with a lack of *physical* evidence anything is changing—can be difficult, but do not lose heart! Your continued faith and integrity are seeds which are being planted. They are significant and powerful, even if the outcome isn't visible yet.

The only way to truly fail is to give up! Keep your faith strong and continue doing good, knowing that your breakthrough is on its way. God's timing is perfect, and His plan for you is unfolding. Stay hopeful and patient; the best is yet to come!

Remember that your efforts are not your own. If you are feeling drained, you may be relying too much on your own ability rather than leaning on Jesus. He encouraged us that His yolk is easy, and His burden is light (Matthew 11:30). Keep believing, and trust that God will fulfill His promises in due season. You're on the right path, and your perseverance *will* lead to the harvest you've been waiting for.

Let him who stole steal no longer, but rather let him labor, working with his hands what is good, that he may have something to give him who has need.

Ephesians 4:28

Paul is speaking here directly to those who have lived in ways that were not honoring to God, specifically to those who have stolen or taken what is not theirs. But the message goes far beyond that alone. This is about rejecting behavior that will harm others, or ourselves, and instead choosing a way of life that is beneficial for everyone.

The transformation Paul describes isn't just about stopping a bad habit of kleptomania! No, this is about replacing a lifestyle of laziness and dependency with something good. We are called to good, honest, and meaningful work. This kind of work is a blessing to us as a way to support our own families. However, there is a greater purpose than simply working for our own natural supply.

Paul doesn't say to work just to build wealth or to accumulate more for ourselves. It isn't to gather into barns so we can retire and relax. After all, God is the one who provides for our needs, isn't He? Actually, the end goal is to have something to give to *others*—to those in need. When we understand this simple truth, our focus shifts from self-centeredness to a heart of generosity. When we labor in a way that pleases God, we become a source of blessing to those around us.

So today, let's reflect on our own lives. Are we taking or giving? Are we working with integrity, to both benefit ourselves and bless others? Let's commit to being people who, through our work and our lives, are able to give to those in need. That's the kind of prosperity God desires for each of us.

And His name, through faith in His name, has made this man strong, whom you see and know. Yes, the faith which comes through Him has given him this perfect soundness in the presence of you all.

Acts 3:16

This verse summarizes the story of a man who was made completely whole through faith in Jesus. The man who was healed was known to those around him as someone who had been crippled from birth! Yet, through faith in Jesus' name, he experienced *"perfect soundness,"* a complete and undeniable restoration and healing of his physical body.

Faith in Jesus is not just a mental agreement with who He is; it's a powerful, life-changing force! When we place our trust in Him, that faith brings healing and wholeness to every part of our being—spirit, soul, and body. It can even change the natural, physical reality around us! But here's something even *more* amazing: the very faith we need comes from Jesus Himself. He is the author and finisher of our faith (Hebrews 12:2). This means that not only does He initiate our faith, but He also brings it to a place of fullness and completion.

We often think that we need to muster up faith *on our own*, but this scripture reveals that *our faith is a gift from Jesus!* The strength to believe, to trust, and to hope in God's promises comes directly from Him. As we rely on Jesus, He supplies us with the faith needed to receive His promises. When we are weak, He is strong, and through Him, we can experience the fullness of His healing, restoration, and blessing.

Rest in the truth that Jesus is both the source and the sustainer of your faith! Whatever you are facing, trust in His name and allow His faith to work in you, bringing you to a place of perfect soundness and peace.

*Who Himself bore our sins in His own body on the tree,
that we, having died to sins, might live for
righteousness—by whose stripes you were healed.*

1 Peter 2:24

This verse is a powerful summary of the Gospel. It tells us that Jesus bore our sins in His own body on the cross, a selfless act that not only secured our forgiveness but also empowered us to live a new life. Often, we focus on the latter part of the verse—*"by His stripes, you were healed"*—and rightly so, as it speaks to the physical and emotional healing that Jesus provides. However, there is a deeper truth here that we can't forget, or we will miss out on a huge part of the benefits we receive through salvation!

The verse begins with the promise that, because Jesus bore our sins, we have died to them. This is more than just a theological statement; it's a practical reality! Our old sinful nature was crucified with Christ, and now we have the supernatural ability to live righteously. This means that the power of sin has been broken in our lives. We are no longer slaves to our old habits, thoughts, and desires. Instead, we have been given the grace to live in a way that honors God. When temptation arises, we can stand firm, knowing that sin has no authority over us anymore.

This is a promise for godly living, a reminder that our salvation is not just about avoiding hell but about living a life that reflects the character of Christ. We can be physically and emotionally well because we are spiritually alive in Him. Our healing extends to every part of us—spirit, soul, and body. Let's not disregard the first part of the verse but embrace it fully, understanding that Jesus' sacrifice empowers us to live in righteousness. Through His stripes, we are healed—body, soul, and spirit, fully restored in Him.

My son, give attention to my words; incline your ear to my sayings. Do not let them depart from your eyes; keep them in the midst of your heart; for they are life to those who find them, and health to all their flesh.

Proverbs 4:20-22

God's Word is more than just good advice—it's life-changing wisdom. God, as a loving Father, asks us to pay attention and listen carefully to His words. Why? Because His Word has the power to transform every area of our lives. It brings change in our soul, our bodies, our relationships, and our ways of doing things. Instead of seeing the world through purely natural eyes, we begin to experience life from God's perspective.

Imagine God's Word as a prescription. It's like taking "Gos-pills," medicine for your spirit, soul, and body. Just as we take physical medicine for health, God sent His Word to heal and strengthen us in every aspect of life—whether it's our bodies, relationships, emotions, or even finances. When we read, meditate on, and speak the Word, it starts working from the inside out, producing real, lasting change.

It's not enough to simply hear the Word once and walk away. The New Living Translation says, *"Don't lose sight of them. Let them penetrate deep into your heart."* That means the Word has to sink in and take root. Just like any good medicine, it works best when you stay consistent and take it regularly. As you feed on scripture, you'll notice it bringing life and healing to the situations you're facing—whether it's a tough season at work, a strain in your family, or a health challenge.

God's Word has the power to change things. Take it daily. Let it bring life and health to you in ways you never imagined!

January 12

But if the Spirit of Him who raised Jesus from the dead
dwells in you, He who raised Christ from
the dead will also give life to your mortal bodies
through His Spirit who dwells in you.

Romans 8:11

What an amazing reminder of the power of God living inside each of us! If you're born again, the very Spirit who raised Jesus from the dead dwells in you. Think about that for a moment! That's not just a nice thought—it's a powerful truth. The same power that conquered the grave is active in your life today!

This means that His Spirit brings life to your body, not only in the spiritual sense but also physically. God's healing power is available to you, flowing through your mortal body. You can stand in faith for healing and strength, knowing that the Spirit of God is giving life to you. And even more than that, you can release this power into the lives of others. Whether through prayer or encouragement, the Spirit within you enables you to share God's life and power with the people around you.

Sometimes life can feel overwhelming, and the tasks in front of us seem impossible. But here's the good news: God's Spirit in you isn't just for big miracles like healing. He also provides the strength, energy, and ability to tackle the everyday challenges you face. This is a continuous, ongoing, life-sustaining presence of the Holy Spirit which lives within you and is constantly giving life to your body! Whether it's at work, in your family, or in ministry, the Spirit of God equips you with everything you need to fulfill your purpose.

So, trust the Spirit within you. Lean into His power. Whatever you're facing today, remember that the same Spirit that raised Jesus from the dead is alive and active in you!

January 13

A merry heart does good, like medicine,
but a broken spirit dries the bones.

Proverbs 17:22

There's something truly powerful about laughter and joy. Studies have shown that laughter has both physical and mental health benefits. When you laugh, your body releases endorphins, which are the body's natural feel-good chemicals. These endorphins not only improve your mood but also act as pain relievers, helping to alleviate physical discomfort and promote overall well-being.

Laughter also reduces the level of stress hormones like cortisol and adrenaline. It shifts your focus away from negative emotions. Laughing lowers blood pressure, improves circulation, and boosts your immune system. Some studies even suggest that regular laughter can improve heart health by increasing blood flow and promoting healthy cardiovascular function!

No matter what you're facing today, take a moment to laugh! Sometimes, we get so caught up in the seriousness of life that we forget the power of a joyful heart. You might be dealing with stress at work, challenges at home, or even physical ailments. But you also have a God-given ability to release joy from deep within. It's a supernatural gift of the Spirit, just waiting to bubble up when you choose to release it.

Find ways to bring laughter into your life. Watch a funny video, call that friend who always makes you smile, or simply take time to reflect on God's goodness. Joy is contagious, and the more you focus on it, the more it grows. Let your merry heart heal you. Just as medicine works to make us feel better, joy brings healing to any dryness caused by this natural world.

So today, make a conscious effort to laugh a little! Let joy be your medicine and tap into the healing power of a merry heart.

He sent His word and healed them,
and delivered them from their destructions.

Psalm 107:20

God sees our needs long before we even cry out for help. If you're facing sickness, heartbreak, lack, or some other form of destruction, God's Word has the power to bring healing and deliverance to any situation!

Jesus *is* the Word who was sent to deliver you. He is the living expression of God's love and care for us. When Jesus died on the cross, He took on our pain, our suffering, and our broken-ness. He made a way for us to experience wholeness—physically, emotionally, and spiritually. Healing isn't just something He does; it's who He is.

What's even more amazing is that God sent His Word before you ever had a need. He knew the battles you'd face and the struggles that would try to pull you down. But in His infinite love and wisdom, He made a way for healing and deliverance long before you needed it.

This scripture isn't just about the past. It speaks to your immediate needs and anything you may face in the future. It reassures you that God has already provided what you need to overcome. His Word is alive and active, working in your life right now. Every promise in the Bible is guaranteed through Jesus. When you speak, believe, and act on the Word of God, you activate its power in your life.

No matter what kind of destruction you might be dealing with today, you can rest in the fact that God has already provided the answer. Jesus has already paid the price. You don't have to earn it or deserve it; you just have to receive it. Trust in the healing power of His Word and believe that God is faithful to deliver you.

Beloved, I pray that you may prosper in all things and be in health, just as your soul prospers.

3 John 2

This beautiful verse reminds us that God's heart for us is to prosper and be in health. But notice where it starts: with our souls. It's like the foundation of a house—everything else rests on it.

When John talks about prosperity, he's not just referring to financial or physical well-being, although those are absolutely included! He's talking about *a thriving soul*—our minds, wills, and emotions. If our inner world is in turmoil or disarray, it's going to be tough to see real change in our outer world. Think of it like trying to build a dream home on a shaky foundation; it's just not going to work out well.

Now, don't get discouraged if you're struggling in this area. The good news is that we're not left to figure it all out on our own. Psalm 23 assures us that God is the Restorer of our souls! He's got the expertise and the compassion to mend our brokenness. We don't have to muster up the strength to heal ourselves; we just need to rely on and trust in Him.

So, if you're feeling out of sorts or if life feels heavy, start by turning to God. Let Him work on your heart and mind. As He heals and restores your soul, you'll find that His peace and joy start to overflow into other areas of your life. Healing starts from the inside out.

Remember, your life and well-being are important to God. He's invested in the prosperity of your whole self—body, soul, and spirit. Embrace His promise of restoration and watch how it transforms everything around you!

January 16

Jesus said to him, "If you can believe, all things are possible to him who believes."

Mark 9:23

S it for a moment and think about what things you have considered impossible in your life. Maybe you've faced a situation where a miracle seemed necessary—like the restoration of a missing or damaged organ, a dream job that feels out of reach, or even debt that seems insurmountable. These scenarios can feel overwhelming and beyond our control. But here's the good news: Jesus assures us that *"all things are possible"* for those who believe.

It's important to remember that *"all things"* doesn't just mean the things that are easy or that we've seen happen to others before. It includes the things that seem beyond reason and defy reality. God's power isn't limited by our past experiences or our current limitations. His capacity to make things happen is without measure!

The key phrase here is *"If you can believe."* Belief—or faith—is not just a passive state but an active choice we make. We choose to trust in God's promises and His power to work in our lives, even when circumstances suggest that what we are believing for is impossible. This choice to believe opens the door to the miraculous. God loves to prove His power on behalf of his kids!

So today, reflect on where you need to apply this belief. Are there areas in your life where you're holding back faith because you've deemed them impossible? Invite God into those spaces, choosing to believe that He can make the impossible possible. In doing so, you align yourself with His limitless power and open your life to Him to do amazing things!

*But you have an anointing from the Holy One,
and you know all things.*

1 John 2:20

I n times of uncertainty, or when faced with important decisions, it's vital to remember that we have been given an
anointing from the Holy One. This divine anointing
equips our spirits with an understanding that surpasses our own
human knowledge. Even when we feel lost or unsure, our spirits
are still deeply connected to God's wisdom that knows what
we need to know.

One powerful way to tap into this divine insight is through
praying in the Spirit. When we do this, we're not relying on our
own understanding but opening ourselves up to the guidance
of the Holy Spirit. Praying in the Spirit can bring revelation to
areas of our lives where we might need clarity or insight. It's as
if we're accessing a hidden reservoir of knowledge that our
spirits are already familiar with, but that hasn't yet fully reached
our conscious minds!

Praying in the Spirit can be especially life-changing when we
seek direction, wisdom, or even improvement in our natural
skills. By connecting with the God's wisdom and power He has
made available to us, we can bridge the gap between that
imparted understanding from Him and our physical knowledge.
By praying in the Spirit, complex decisions become more
manageable and enhance our natural abilities.

So, don't forget that you've got an amazing anointing and
connection with God! When you're feeling unsure or stuck, just
pray in the Spirit and let that divine wisdom flow into your daily
life. It'll give you the clarity and confidence you need to handle
whatever comes your way. For more information regarding the
baptism of the Holy Spirit, request a free booklet on our website
at Terradez.com/booklet.

A fool vents all his feelings,
but a wise man holds them back.

Proverbs 29:11

Not every emotion or thought needs to be shared with others. It's easy to fall into the habit of constantly venting our frustrations or anxieties, thinking that it will make us feel better. However, sharing every feeling we have isn't the wisest approach!

When we focus on the negative aspects of our lives and speak about them constantly, we unintentionally give those things more power. Words can strengthen what we dwell on, and when we continuously verbalize our struggles, we allow them to gain a stronger grip on our minds. Instead of helping us move forward, this often keeps us stuck in a negative cycle.

Wisdom teaches us to choose carefully what feelings we speak aloud or share with others. Not only do our words have power to strengthen the negative circumstance, but they can also negatively affect those around us, even when that wasn't our intention! Sometimes, it's better to process our feelings directly with the Lord. By doing this, we not only protect ourselves from unnecessary drama but also focus on finding divine wisdom and solutions rather than magnifying the problem.

This doesn't mean bottling up emotions or ignoring what we feel. Instead, it's about learning to manage our emotions wisely. Before reacting, pause and ask yourself: *Will sharing this feeling improve my situation, or will it make things worse?* Often, the wisest course of action is to pray and seek peace before speaking. This takes strength and self-control, but these are gifts you have already been given, so you can do it!

Today, consider how you handle your emotions. Are you quick to vent, or are you practicing the wisdom of restraint? Sometimes silence speaks volumes.

This Book of the Law shall not depart from your mouth,
but you shall meditate in it day and night, that you may
observe to do according to all that is written in it.
For then you will make your way prosperous,
and then you will have good success.

Joshua 1:8

When we keep the promises of God before us—allowing them to consume our thoughts, color our words, and influence our decisions—something glorious happens: *"For **then** you will make your way prosperous, and **then** you will have good success."* Success isn't random or something left to chance—it's a natural outcome of living by the principles God has laid out for us.

The good news is that our success, happiness, prosperity, and health are not determined by outside forces—not the economy, the opinions of others, or even the enemy's schemes. They are rooted in God's Word, which never changes. When we align our lives with what He has spoken, we position ourselves to receive the fullness of His blessings. God has already made up His mind about us—He has destined us for victory!

This truth empowers us because world-overcoming faith is not something we have to manufacture on our own. It already lives within us through Jesus. He has made a way for us to walk in victory, no matter what comes our way. As we meditate on His Word and keep it at the forefront of our minds, we can trust that success will follow. It's not a question of if, but when. God's promises are sure, and He has already declared that we are chosen, set apart, and called to prosper.

Let this be your confidence as you walk through today!

January 20

*And they overcame him by the blood of the Lamb
and by the word of their testimony....*

Revelation 12:11

I n simple terms, this verse says that we overcome by what Jesus did for us on the cross and by what we are prepared to say about it! Find out what the Lord says about your situation and agree with that. This means purposefully agreeing with God's promises and speaking out those rather than confirming every negative thing around us. This isn't about ignoring problems, but rather aligning our words and beliefs with God's Word, not with our doubts or fears.

When our daughter was five years old, we moved to Colorado from the UK. It was a big adjustment in lots of ways and the change in altitude was no exception!

Shortly after arriving in the mountains, we took a family hike to spy out the land. We were at 9,500 feet and, coming from sea level, the lack of oxygen made climbing hills even more challenging. Yet on we trekked until the children spotted a grassy knoll that was begging to be climbed. As the children raced ahead, Hannah lagged behind as her little legs struggled to keep up. Finally, we all reached the top—us adults just barely.

We were sure that we would have to carry Hannah up that thing, but she did it all by herself. All the way up she was muttering something that we couldn't quite understand until she shouted it from the top as loud as she could: *"I can do all things through Christ who strengthens me!"* (Philippians 4:13).

That day, she learned how speaking the Word enabled her to overcome. What worked for Hannah will work for us too! Whatever mountain you're facing, speak life over it. Agree with God's promises and watch how He enables you to overcome.

Death and life are in the power of the tongue,
and those who love it will eat its fruit.

Proverbs 18:21

We can choose death or life by the words that we speak. The things we say hold the ability to build up or tear down, to bring life or death, both to others and to ourselves.

Your words shape your world. Jesus said that when we use the power of our words, they can have a tangible impact on the world around us (Matthew 21:21; Mark 11:23). This is how much power choosing life can have. When we speak words of life—encouragement, health, increase, truth, kindness—we create an environment that reflects God's love, power, and grace. On the other hand, words spoken carelessly or of death and destruction can harm relationships, discourage others, and curse your circumstances, leaving lasting damage.

This verse talks about "loving" the power of the tongue, meaning we should take the power of our words very seriously. We need to place value upon what we say. If we treasure the potential of our words, we will see the benefits, like peace, strengthened relationships, growth, and change in our circumstances.

If you feel that watching what you say is a challenge, you're not alone! It can be easy to slip into speaking negatively. But the good news is, we don't have to do it in our own strength. Psalm 141:3 is a perfect prayer: *"Set a guard, O Lord, over my mouth; keep watch over the door of my lips."*

Ask God daily to help you speak words that align with His Word. When you slip up, show grace to yourself and others, and just keep growing in this area.

Let's choose life with our words today!

January 22

A man's stomach shall be satisfied from the fruit of his mouth; from the produce of his lips he shall be filled.

Proverbs 18:20

At first glance, it may seem odd to connect words with hunger, but this verse highlights the truth that our words can create either abundance or lack in our lives.

If you're experiencing lack—whether it's financially, emotionally, or spiritually—pause and consider: What have you been speaking over your life and situation? The words we speak, whether positive or negative, have the power to shape our reality. Have you been speaking life, hope, and blessings, or have you been dwelling in doubt and negativity?

This proverb encourages us to treasure the words that come from our mouths. When we intentionally speak words of life, encouragement, and success, we are planting seeds that will produce a harvest of abundance. Just as a farmer plants crops with the expectation of reaping a full harvest, we can also expect to see fruitful results when we plant words of blessing and faith!

Imagine your words as seeds. Every time you speak positively—about your family, finances, health, or dreams—you're watering and fertilizing your future. It's not just about surviving; it's about thriving and being filled. God has given us the incredible gift of speech, and with it, we have the ability to shape our lives for the better. Your words will grow, and then you will be filled by the harvest they produce!

So today, be mindful of what you say. Speak words that align with God's promises and watch how those words can fill up your life, both spiritually and physically.

But the fruit of the Spirit is love, joy, peace, longsuffering [patience], kindness, goodness, faithfulness, gentleness, self-control. Against such there is no law.

Galatians 5:22-23

The fruit of the Spirit—love, joy, peace, patience, kindness, goodness, faithfulness, gentleness, and self-control—are like a bouquet of qualities that bloom in our lives when we let the Holy Spirit work in us. It's not at all about *trying harder* to be more patient or more kind! The secret is that the same Spirit who raised Jesus from the dead, as Romans 8:11 reminds us, is living inside of you, empowering you every day!

Think about that for a minute: The power that conquered death is the same power that enables you to love when it's hard, to show patience when you want to snap, and to keep your peace when the world around you is chaotic. It's not about *your* strength, but *His* strength operating in and through you.

We all have moments when our flesh wants to take over—when someone frustrates us, or life doesn't go as planned. In those moments, instead of trying to "be better" in your own strength, lean into the Holy Spirit. When you feel like you're about to lose control, pause and ask Him to help you respond with love. Love is the foundation of all the other fruits. Through love, joy rises up, peace settles in, and self-control becomes second nature!

So today, as you face whatever comes your way, remember you don't have to do it alone. In John 15:5, Jesus said, *"I am the vine, you are the branches. He who abides in Me, and I in him, bears much fruit: for without Me you can do nothing."* The Spirit inside you is ready to bring out the fruit that reflects God's nature. You just have to tap into His power and let Him produce the fruit from the inside out!

For God has not given us a spirit of fear,
but of power and of love and of a sound mind.

2 Timothy 1:7

How amazing is this? If you've ever felt plagued with fear or anxiety, this verse is a reminder that fear does not come from God. Fear is not part of your spiritual DNA as a believer!

The moment you accepted Christ, you were born again with a spirit of power, love, and self-control—a sound mind. So, when fear comes knocking at the door of your heart, remember that it has no claim on you. God has already equipped you with the courage and strength to overcome it. Your spirit is not afraid because it is empowered by God Himself, filled with His love, and anchored in His wisdom.

If you're feeling anxious, start drawing from your spirit, where God's power resides. Speak against the worry tormenting your mind. You don't have to sit with your fears or let them control you. Instead, you can cast them down by replacing them with the promises found in God's Word. If you're worried about finances, for example, remind yourself that God promises to provide for your every need. If you're afraid of failure, remember that God says He has plans to prosper you, not to harm you.

By focusing on these truths, you'll find that your mind is no longer consumed by fear, but filled with the soundness and peace that God has already placed within you. You're stronger than you think, because God's power, love, and sound mind are already yours! Trust in that, and walk boldly, with confidence, in every day of your life, in any circumstance.

Finally, brethren, whatever things are true, whatever things are noble, whatever things are just, whatever things are pure, whatever things are lovely, whatever things are of good report, if there is any virtue and if there is anything praiseworthy—meditate on these things.

Philippians 4:8

Philippians 4:8 is a call to refocus! It's so easy to let our thoughts drift toward everything that's wrong—stress at work, problems at home, and any uncertainties about the future. But what we often forget is that dwelling on those negative things gives them power. The more we focus on what's going wrong, the more we'll start to see it dominate our thoughts, and eventually, our lives.

Our minds are powerful, and the things we choose to meditate on can shape our reality. If we constantly fixate on negativity, we'll start to experience more of it. But here's the good news: the opposite is also true! When we meditate on what is true, noble, just, pure, lovely, and praiseworthy, we begin to see more of those things in our lives.

Paul is challenging us to shift our thinking, to actively choose what we meditate on. Realistically, sometimes, it feels like there's nothing good to think about. Maybe life is tough, and you're struggling to see anything worth celebrating. In those moments, meditate on Jesus. He embodies everything in Philippians 4:8. His life, His words, and His love are true, noble, just, and pure. The depth and reward of the sacrifice He made for you should be enough to redirect negativity to thankfulness!

So, what are you meditating on today? If your thoughts are dragging you down, remember that you have the power to redirect them. Focus on the good and watch how it begins to reshape your perspective and your life.

January 26

For as he thinks in his heart, so is he.

Proverbs 23:7

Our thoughts have a profound influence on the direction of our lives. What we think about ourselves and our circumstances truly matters because our thoughts shape our reality!

Have you heard the phrase, "You are what you eat?" Well, this verse is saying, "You are what you think!" If you constantly think of yourself as a failure or believe nothing will ever go right, that mindset affect your actions, your attitude, and how you approach life. Your thoughts become a self-fulfilling prophecy. If you walk around thinking you're a loser, you'll start acting like one, and pretty soon, you'll start seeing evidence of it all around you. But the good news is, that works in reverse, too!

The Bible calls us to renew our minds. When you begin to shift your thoughts from negativity to hope, from failure to possibility, things start to change. That doesn't mean life instantly becomes perfect, but you'll start to notice differences in how you handle challenges, how you see yourself, and how you respond to the world around you.

When you think of yourself as someone who can grow, someone who has purpose, and someone loved by God, you'll find yourself living more in alignment with those truths. Your behavior will begin to follow the path your mind is taking.

So, next time you find yourself stuck in negative thinking, pause and remember that what you think shapes what you experience. Speak life over yourself, believe that God is working in you, and watch how your circumstances begin to reflect the change in your heart! Your thoughts matter more than you know—because how you think in your heart is who you will become.

*But now He has obtained a more excellent ministry,
inasmuch as He is also Mediator of a better covenant,
which was established on better promises.*

Hebrews 8:6

As we continue through this year-long devotional, we will read many promises from the Old Testament. Sometimes, reading those promises, you might think, *Well, that was to Abraham, or Isaac, or the Israelites. Those promises don't apply to me.* However, nothing could be further from the truth! As New Covenant believers, we can claim the promises of the Old Covenant, too! We have a *better* covenant with even *greater* promises, and Jesus affirmed that He came not to abolish the Law but to fulfill it (Matthew 5:17). This means the blessings promised to God's people in the Old Testament still apply to us today!

In the Old Covenant, God's promises were conditional, based on perfect obedience. Deuteronomy 28, for example, outlines blessings for those who obey and curses for those who don't. Realizing they fall short, many believers feel unworthy of these promises.

The truth is, the Law was holy but incomplete, unable to provide salvation or lasting blessing because of human weakness (Romans 8:3-4). The Israelites couldn't perfectly follow the Law, leading to repeated consequences. Humanity needed a Savior, not just a set of rules.

Jesus accomplished what the Law couldn't. By living sinlessly and sacrificing Himself, He redeemed us from every curse of the Law (Galatians 3:13). His righteousness now qualifies us for God's promises, as He fulfilled every requirement on our behalf (2 Corinthians 5:21).

Now, as believers, we're made righteous **in Christ**, enabling us to claim **all** God's promises, even those in the Old Covenant!

*Every place that the sole of your foot will tread upon
I have given you, as I said to Moses.*

Joshua 1:3

D o you feel that you are at the bottom of the totem pole at work? Is a neighbor in your apartment building or neighborhood completely insufferable? Are you in the middle of a situation where you feel that you have no power to influence change?

It's easy to feel powerless in such situations, but God says He has given the land to you! This verse isn't just about physical land; it's a powerful reminder of the spiritual authority you carry. Wherever you go, spiritually speaking, you have been given authority and power. Even if it feels like you're stuck in a situation with little natural control, God has granted you a spiritual authority that surpasses any earthly obstacle.

This doesn't mean you should assert this authority by being domineering or arrogant with the people around you. Instead, it's about recognizing the power you have in the spiritual realm. Take authority over spirits of gossip, or strife, or evil. Imagine setting up a protective boundary around your home, where no harmful force can penetrate. You have the authority to declare that no weapon formed against you will prosper!

So, next time you face a challenging situation, remember you have a divine backing. Take a moment to pray, speak against any negativity, and claim your spiritual authority. It's not about dominating others but about standing firm in the power God has given you. You're the head, not the tail; above, and not beneath. You're not powerless! Greater is He who is in you than he who is in the world (1 John 4:4). You are spiritually equipped to handle and overcome any challenge that comes your way.

Then the LORD said to me, "You have seen well, for I am ready to perform My word."

Jeremiah 1:12

God is ready—no hesitation, no waiting for a "better" time. He's not idle or pacing around in worry or indecison, wasting time. When it comes to His promises, He's already set to bring them to pass in your life. But sometimes, it can feel like there's a delay, and that's where doubt can creep in. Yet, God is steady, faithful, and always on time. If things seem slow, it's not because He's holding out on you or waiting until you've got everything perfectly lined up.

Our world is messy, full of flawed people, challenging circumstances, and sometimes, even our own inner roadblocks. These things can hinder or obscure the work God's doing. But remember, none of these obstacles are bigger than God's power or His willingness to see His promises fulfilled in your life! Instead of giving in to frustration or disappointment, take any delays or challenges as an invitation to trust Him more. Lean in, knowing He is as committed to His Word as He has always been.

Think of the Israelites standing at the Red Sea with the enemy closing in behind them. God was ready to part the waters; all it took was Moses' raised staff and their step of faith. When you pray, ask God to remove any roadblocks, whether they're caused by other people, spiritual opposition, or even hidden parts of your own heart.

He's not only able but more than willing to help you navigate these challenges. His readiness to act on His promises isn't just a possibility—it's reality. All He asks is that you come to Him in faith, asking for His guidance and intervention. Trust Him to make His Word alive in your life today!

January 30

What then shall we say to these things? If God is for us, who can be against us? He who did not spare His own Son, but delivered Him up for us all, how shall He not with Him also freely give us all things?

Romans 8:31-32

Ever feel like the odds are stacked against you, and you're up against a mountain you just can't seem to climb? It's in those moments when you might start wondering, "Is God really on my side?" But let's take a moment to flip the script and remember: *If God is for me, who can be against me?*

Imagine this: the Creator of the universe, who made everything from the tiniest atom to the vast galaxies, is on your side. The same God who spoke the stars into existence is rooting for you! It's like having a superhero in your corner, only this superhero created everything and knows exactly how to tackle every problem you're facing.

Now, think about this. God didn't just give us a little help; He gave us His own Son, Jesus. Let that sink in for a moment. If God was willing to give up something as precious as His Son, the most valuable gift He could offer, how could He possibly withhold anything else good from us? That's right—He won't!

Whatever you need today, whether it's strength, wisdom, peace, finances, or healing, God's got it covered! He's not holding back, waiting for you to earn it or somehow repay Him. Everything He offers is freely given, out of unconditional love and grace.

So, when life feels tough and you're facing obstacles, remember this: God's not just passively watching. He's actively giving, supporting, and loving you through every challenge. Embrace that truth and let it fill you with hope and confidence. God has what you need, and He's with you through every storm!

Have I not commanded you? Be strong and of good courage; do not be afraid, nor be dismayed, for the Lord your God is with you wherever you go.

Joshua 1:9

What a comforting promise! No matter where life takes you, God is right there with you. It's like having the ultimate backup, always ready to support you, no matter the situation!

Think about it—if God is on your side, what's there to be afraid of? Fear has a sneaky way of opening the door to the very things we're anxious about. When we let fear take over, we're really just setting ourselves up for trouble. But if we embrace strength and courage, we're choosing to trust in God's promises and His presence. It's like saying, "Hey, I believe that God's got this under control, so I don't need to worry."

Being strong and courageous isn't about being completely without fear—it's about trusting that even when we're scared or unsure, God is with us. He's not just watching from a distance; He's walking right alongside us, guiding us through every challenge. And this trust allows God to work in ways we might not even see or understand.

So, next time you're faced with a challenge or feeling overwhelmed, remember this: God is with you, and that's a game changer. Let that truth fill you with courage and push out the fear. When you hold onto that strength and confidence in God's presence, you're not just facing your challenges—you're opening up space for God to act in powerful ways. By trusting Him, you invite His strength to carry you through, turning obstacles into opportunities for His power to shine.

Delight yourself also in the Lord,
and He shall give you the desires of your heart.

Psalm 37:4

A t first glance, this might sound like a promise of instant fulfillment of all our personal wishes. But let's dig a little deeper to find out what this verse really means.

True delight in the Lord isn't about getting everything we want; it's about a transformation of our hearts. The Hebrew word for *delight* actually means to be soft and pliable. Imagine your heart as a lump of clay. When you surrender to God, saying, "Lord, mold me, shape me, and use me as You wish," you're letting Him work on that clay. In this process, He gently forms your desires to align with His own.

As you grow in your relationship with God, something beautiful happens. Your desires start to shift. What you once thought you wanted might no longer hold the same allure. Instead, you'll find that you start craving what He wants for you. It's not that your dreams vanish; rather, they become infused with His purpose. You begin to desire the things that truly matter to Him and, consequently, to you.

This is what happened when we began our own ministry. We had been perfectly content to serve another and really didn't *want* to launch out on our own! However, as we delighted ourselves in the Lord, He changed our hearts, and Terradez Ministries was born!

So, when you read this verse, think of it as an invitation to open your heart fully to God. Let Him soften you, shape you, and guide your desires. The more you surrender to His will, the more you'll find that your deepest yearnings align with His grand, perfect plan. He will cause you to desire to go where He wants you to go, say what He wants you to say, and become exactly who He created you to be!

You will keep him in perfect peace,
whose mind is stayed on You,
because he trusts in You.

Isaiah 26:3

Have you ever found yourself overwhelmed by life's challenges? Maybe it's a troubling doctor's report, persistent pain, a struggling bank account, or a child going through a tough time. It's so easy to be consumed by these issues, letting them rob us of our peace. When we focus on our problems, it's like being caught in a storm where everything feels out of control.

But here's the thing: when we shift our gaze from the storm to the One who calms the storm, our perspective changes. God wants us to look to Him, to trust in His promises even when everything around us seems uncertain. Imagine your mind as a sailboat. If your sail is set toward the storm, you're bound to be tossed around. But if you adjust your sail toward the wind, you'll find direction and stability.

When we choose to focus on God's promises, we're saying, "Lord, despite what my eyes see and my heart feels, I trust in Your Word. You said You would provide peace, and I'm standing firm on that." This doesn't mean the troubles disappear, but it does mean that amidst the turbulence, you'll find an unshakable peace that only God can give. Just like when Peter trusted in Jesus to walk on the water, when you keep your eyes on Jesus, you can see the impossible!

So, next time you feel your peace has been shaken, remember this verse. Turn your gaze back to God, let His promises anchor you, and watch as His perfect peace floods your heart, no matter the storm you're facing.

February 3

Christ has redeemed us from the curse of the law, having become a curse for us (for it is written, "Cursed is everyone who hangs on a tree").

Galatians 3:13

If you've ever read through the Old Testament, you know it's *packed* with promises from God. But often, those promises are tied to conditions. Things like, "If you fully obey the Lord...then you will be blessed." The bar is set high, and it can feel intimidating. Many believers today read those conditions and start feeling disqualified. We see where we've fallen short, how we haven't met every "if" in those verses. Maybe you've even wondered if, instead of receiving the blessings, you deserve the curses listed for those who missed the mark.

Yet, here's the powerful truth: Jesus saw that impossible standard and did something incredible: He took on every curse and consequence for our failures and shortcomings when He went to the cross. Think about that—every curse outlined in Deuteronomy for failing to uphold the law was placed on Him. And He didn't just take the curses; He fulfilled every requirement of the law *perfectly* on our behalf. That's why His sacrifice isn't just about forgiveness; it's about freedom from the pressure of God's standard of perfection!

In Romans 8:3-4, we're reminded that Jesus did what we could never do. He lived perfectly under the law so that we don't have to. Now, we're not held back by our imperfections but are covered by His righteousness. So, instead of disqualifying yourself, remember that *Jesus* qualified you. You don't have to earn God's promises of abundant life; they're given freely because of what He's already done!

34

Then great multitudes came to Him, having with them the lame, blind, mute, maimed, and many others; and they laid them down at Jesus' feet, and He healed them. So the multitude marveled when they saw the mute speaking, the maimed made whole, the lame walking, and the blind seeing; and they glorified the God of Israel.

Matthew 15:30-31

I magine the scene: crowds of people, some who couldn't walk, others who couldn't see or speak, all pressing forward, each with a desperate need. They brought their brokenness right to Jesus, and without hesitation, He healed every single one of them. It's easy to gloss over the miracle when we read it on the page, but picture it—someone who's been unable to walk since birth suddenly standing up, someone whose eyes have only known darkness now blinking in amazement at colors and faces they're seeing for the first time. This wasn't a quiet healing event; it was explosive, real, and life-changing!

What's even more incredible is that there was no condition beyond Jesus' power. People who were missing limbs were restored! Imagine the hope and joy in that moment—no matter what shape or depth of hurt they brought, Jesus could and would make them whole. There's not a single need we could bring to Him today that falls outside His ability or compassion. He was able then, and He is able now!

These healings weren't just for the sake of health alone; they were a sign pointing back to God's heart. The crowd didn't just walk away with restored bodies; they left marveling at the goodness and power of God. When we experience the abundant life, whether physical, emotional, or spiritual, it's not just a gift for us. It's a moment where God is glorified, and others see His love and power at work. Every blessing brings glory to God, who loves to make us whole!

Trust in the Lord with all your heart,
and lean not on your own understanding;
in all your ways acknowledge Him,
and He shall direct your paths.

Proverbs 3:5-6

Have you ever faced a mountain so big it feels like there's no way around it? When you're up against a challenge, don't just rely on your own smarts or natural ability to reason your way through it, over it, or around it. It's easy to think we've got the best plan, but God's understanding is way beyond ours.

Imagine you're on a hike, and you come across a boulder that seems impossible to climb over. Your instinct might be to find a way around it or just give up. But if you listen to a guide who knows the terrain, they might lead you through a path you didn't even see—one that's safer and quicker. That's what trusting in God is like. He sees the whole landscape, not just the boulder right in front of you.

Sometimes, when you're following His direction, it might look like you're going in the opposite direction of what seems logical or best. It might even feel like you're taking a step back instead of moving forward. But remember, God's ways and thoughts are higher than ours. His guidance often doesn't make sense to our natural minds, but it's always the most effective way to get to victory.

So, when you're facing that giant obstacle, don't panic! Trust in God's path, even if it doesn't make logical sense. Look for His peace as your compass and let Him guide you through. He'll lead you to where you need to be, often in ways you could never have imagined! Trust Him fully, and you'll find the best way through your challenge.

February 6

Bless the Lord, O my soul; and all that is within me, bless His holy name! Bless the Lord, oh my soul, and forget not all His benefits: who forgives all your iniquities, who heals all your diseases, who redeems your life from destruction, who crowns you with lovingkindness and tender mercies, who satisfies your mouth with good things, so that your youth is renewed like the eagle's.

Psalm 103:1-5

Our hearts should always have an attitude of praise and thanksgiving, no matter what's going on around us. David encouraged himself to bless the Lord with every part of his being. This isn't just a casual "thank you" but a deep, soul-level gratitude that recognizes how blessed we truly are.

Think about it: God forgives all our sins. Every single one! He's not holding grudges or tallying up our mistakes; He's wiping the slate clean. And if that's not enough, He's also healing every disease, whether it's physical, emotional, or spiritual. He's the ultimate healer.

But there's more! He redeems us from destruction. Life can be tough, and we might feel like we're on the edge, but God pulls us back from the brink and sets us on solid ground. He showers us with His endless love and compassion.

And let's not forget this: He satisfies our mouths with good things. Imagine that—a banquet of blessings and goodness that keeps our spirits refreshed and our bodies rejuvenated with the vitality of youth!

So, how can we ever doubt His goodness? When we remember all these benefits, it's clear that He's always there, ready to come through for us in every circumstance. Even when life gets tough, let's keep our hearts full of praise and thanksgiving, recognizing the incredible ways God continues to bless us.

*So Jesus answered and said to them, "Assuredly,
I say to you, if you have faith and do not doubt, you will
not only do what was done to the fig tree, but also if you
say to this mountain, 'Be removed and be cast into
the sea,' it will be done."*

Matthew 21:21

F aith is like a spark that ignites a powerful authority within us—a gift Jesus freely gave, empowering us to speak to the seemingly immovable obstacles in our lives. When Jesus tells us we can command mountains to be cast into the sea, He's not just using a metaphor. He's reminding us that we're not powerless against life's challenges. He's inviting us to stand before each mountain with the confidence that, through Him, we can see it removed.

What mountains are you facing today? Maybe it's fear, a chronic illness, or a habit you feel trapped by. It might be a relationship that's wearing you down, a financial struggle that seems unending, or a constant battle with feelings of inadequacy. In faith, we're invited to speak to each one of these mountains with authority, knowing that if we believe, they will be moved!.

Jesus didn't come simply to rescue us from our sins but to show us an abundant life, full of strength, purpose, and possibilities. When we truly understand that we're equipped to face and overcome challenges, we step into a life that's defined not by our limitations but by His limitless strength. This isn't about never encountering difficulties; it's about having the confidence to face them head-on, knowing that God has given us authority to overcome.

The mountains may seem large, but remember—the power within you is even greater!

*And whatever things you ask in prayer,
believing, you will receive.*

Matthew 21:22

F aith is at the heart of answered prayer! It is so important to trust God when we pray. If we don't believe that God will grant what we are asking Him for, why would we even ask? When we come to God in prayer, fully believing that He's able to do what we're asking, we position ourselves to see Him move in powerful ways. It's not just about the things we ask for, but the confidence we have in the One we're asking. He's a good Father who knows how to give good gifts.

But here's the thing—how often do we forget to ask? James 4:2 flat out tells us that we don't *have* because we don't *ask*! We carry around worries, burdens, and hopes, but sometimes we don't bring them to God. Maybe we're afraid our requests are too small, or we just assume He already knows what we need. (And that part is true: He *does* know what you need before you even ask Him.)

However, God still wants us to come to Him with everything. When we ask—believing that He'll answer—we give Him the opportunity to show up in ways we might not expect. Prayer is also the number one way we communicate and connect with our Creator, Father, Helper, Healer, Provider, and Friend. Why would we neglect such a powerful relationship?

So, take a moment to think: What have you been holding onto that you haven't brought before God? Have you been asking? He's ready and waiting to hear from you! Approach Him in prayer with faith, trusting that He *will* respond. Let's not miss out on the blessings He wants to pour into our lives by simply forgetting to ask.

Blessed be the God and Father of our Lord Jesus Christ, the Father of mercies and God of all comfort, who comforts us in all our tribulation, that we may be able to comfort those who are in any trouble, with the comfort with which we ourselves are comforted by God.

2 Corinthians 1:3-4

God is the ultimate source of comfort. He doesn't just offer temporary relief; He's always right there in the middle of our hardest moments, even when it doesn't feel like it at first, providing tangible peace. Whether we're facing loss, disappointment, or confusion, He remains present, ready to wrap us in His love. What's even more amazing is that this comfort isn't just for us to keep. It's designed to flow through us to others.

Even though in this fallen world we will experience hardships, God brings us through these times and uses them to help us empathize with others. Maybe you've walked through a season of grief, and now, when someone else is struggling, you're able to say, "I get it. I've been there, too." God can take our wounds and transform them into wisdom, enabling us to offer the same comfort we've received to those who are hurting.

When God brings us through difficult seasons, we become a living testimony of His faithfulness. We're equipped with the tools to encourage others because we've lived through them ourselves. The comfort you received is not wasted. Rather, it is multiplied as you offer it to someone in need.

So today, thank God for being the Father of all comfort and ask Him to help us be sensitive to those around us who might need encouragement. Because when we've been comforted by God, we are uniquely positioned to extend that same grace to others!

*How God anointed Jesus of Nazareth with the
Holy Spirit and with power, who went about doing good
and healing all who were oppressed by the devil,
for God was with Him.*

Acts 10:38

The life of Jesus was marked by His powerful and compassionate works, revealing to us God's heart for freedom and healing. Jesus wasn't selective in His love; He healed *all* who came to Him. Every sickness, every form of brokenness—anything that stole wholeness from a person—was dealt with by Jesus as an oppression, a byproduct of the devil's influence in a world corrupted by sin. That's not to say that every illness is a direct attack from Satan himself, but it's a result of the enemy's work in this world. God sees every form of oppression as something He's ready to counter with His love and power!

Yet, here is an even greater encouragement: the same Holy Spirit that anointed Jesus to bring healing is available to us today. Jesus took His authority and, through His death and resurrection, extended it to those who believe in Him! That's incredible, because it means that while the devil may be the "god" of this world, he's no match for the authority and power we have through Christ. Notice, that lowercase "g" is no accident. Satan's power is limited, and through Jesus, we're given a power that triumphs over any authority he might claim!

So, the next time you face something that tries to hold you back, remember the Spirit who empowered Jesus is now empowering you. Healing, strength, and freedom aren't just things Jesus did in the past—they're realities we get to live in today. Let that inspire your faith to stand boldly, using your authority, knowing that God is with you, just as He was with Jesus.

*And let the peace of God rule in your hearts, to which
also you were called in one body; and be thankful.*

Colossians 3:15

L etting peace guide our hearts is such a powerful concept. The Amplified Bible translates this word "rule" as
"act as an umpire." Imagine peace as an umpire, calling
the shots in your life. When you're unsure, anxious, or caught
up in stress, that peace is right there saying, "Let it go," or,
"Move forward, you're good." It's a freeing thought, right? Instead of being ruled by the ups and downs of emotions or
circumstances, you're led by peace, making decisions from a
place of calm and assurance.

What if you started living this way—allowing peace to make
the final calls? When a situation comes your way, instead of
reacting with worry, you could pause and listen for that internal
voice of peace. It could be something as simple as choosing
how to spend your morning or as big as deciding the next step
in your career. Either way, peace keeps you grounded, steering
you away from making decisions based on fear or anxiety.

It's also important to remain in a state of gratitude. When
you're thankful, it's hard for fear, doubt, or negativity to take
root because thankfulness rewires your perspective. Instead of
obsessing over what's missing, gratitude shifts your focus to
what's already present and good in your life. It can be as simple
as noticing the sunshine or a kind word from a friend.

As you start giving thanks for even the smallest things, peace
naturally grows. It begins to crowd out anxiety and stress, cre-
ating an atmosphere of calm and contentment in your heart.
Gratitude doesn't just change your day—it changes your whole
mindset, allowing peace to act as umpire in your life more *and*
every day.

Your word I have hidden in my heart,
that I might not sin against you.

Psalm 119:11

Hiding God's Word in our hearts is one of the most powerful ways we can change, not just in our behavior but within our character. Romans 12 reminds us that transformation happens when we renew our minds. How do we do that? By getting the Word of God inside us, allowing it to take root in our hearts. It's not a magic formula; it's a process, one that grows as we spend time meditating on Scripture.

It's easy to think that if we just try hard enough, we can overcome our struggles and stop falling into sin. But will-power only gets us so far. In fact, the more we "try" to change ourselves, the more challenging and discouraging it can become! Using our own effort—apart from the grace of God—causes frustration when we keep falling into the same habits of sin or negative behaviors. Focusing on the sin strengthens its power!

However, *real* change comes when God's Word starts to shape our thoughts and desires. As we meditate on His truth, we're less drawn to sin because our hearts begin to reflect God's heart. The pull of sin weakens when we have a stronger pull toward God's ways. This comes effortlessly when we are focusing on His Word and His nature already at work on the inside!

When we fill our hearts with His truth, there's less room for everything else. When we study the Bible, pray, and reflect on God's promises, we're replacing old, destructive habits with something better. The more we hide His Word inside, the more it changes us from the inside out.

This isn't about striving harder, but about inviting God's Word to transform us. As His Word takes root, we'll find ourselves naturally walking away from the things that once held us in bondage to sin.

Now may the God of hope fill you with all joy and peace in believing, that you may abound in hope by the power of the Holy Spirit.

Romans 15:13

God is the source of all hope! He isn't just a distant observer of our lives—He actively fills us with joy and peace as we choose to trust in the promises He has laid out for us. Think about that for a moment: the Creator of everything wants to deposit good things into our hearts and lives. But they don't come automatically! As we dig into His Word, as we cling to His promises even when things don't make sense, that's when He starts to fill us up with this joy and peace that the world can't match.

Now, if you're going through a rough patch and feeling like joy or peace are out of reach, it's easy to wonder, "What's wrong with me?" But it's not about what you can do on your own. God has already placed the Holy Spirit inside you, and that's the game-changer! The Holy Spirit isn't just sitting still. He's active, ready to release those very things you feel are missing—whether it's joy, peace, or even faith. You don't have to work it up by yourself or figure it all out. Tapping into the Spirit within you in faith allows those blessings to flow freely. Sometimes, it's just a matter of asking God to stir those things up within you, to remind you that His power is more than enough.

Hope is so important. It's not wishful thinking or crossing your fingers that things will work out. It's rooted in the promises of God, and He never disappoints. So, when things seem uncertain, fix your eyes on what He's promised. Putting hope and trust in Him won't let you down. In time, those promises will come to pass because God always keeps His Word. Just keep trusting, keep believing, and watch what He will do!

Moses was one hundred and twenty years old when he died. His eyes were not dim nor his natural vigor diminished.

Deuteronomy 34:7

What a life Moses had! At one hundred and twenty, he was still vibrant, seeing clearly and moving with strength, right to the very end. It's incredible, isn't it? He wasn't frail or struggling but was able to hike up a mountain in his final act of faith and obedience. When it was time, he didn't die because of sickness or age but simply because he had fulfilled his purpose.

This is an inspiring glimpse into the fullness God has in mind for us. Yes, our bodies will age, but the covenant we have through Jesus is even richer than what Moses experienced. Hebrews 8:6 reminds us that the promises available to us are rooted in an even greater foundation—a new and better covenant! God has more for us in health, strength, and purpose, right up to our final breath.

So often, we get caught up in the world's view of aging—seeing it as a slide into weakness. But Moses' story speaks a better truth. You don't have to settle for less than the abundant life! Strength, vitality, and purpose can continue as long as we're here. When our time comes, we can go with peace, knowing we've completed our work. But that doesn't mean we have to expect sickness or decline to define our final years.

With the power of Christ's covenant, live with expectation that God has good plans—not of sickness or weakness. And until your last day on earth comes, you can trust Him to be your strength and health, filling each day with purpose, clear vision, and the vigor to follow Him. So, keep pressing forward, trusting in His promises, and know that God's plan includes you living abundantly, right up until He calls you home!

*To know the love of Christ which passes knowledge; that
you may be filled with all the fulness of God.*

Ephesians 3:19

The love of Christ is beyond human comprehension. It's
not something we can analyze or fully understand with
our limited minds. We could spend our entire lives
trying to figure it out and still only scratch the surface. His love
isn't just a feeling or a fleeting emotion; it's eternal, deep, and
beyond anything we can grasp with our limited understanding.

But here's the beautiful part: while our minds might struggle
to comprehend it, our hearts can know God's love through the
revelation of the Holy Spirit. As we draw closer to Jesus, deepening our relationship with Him, the Holy Spirit opens our eyes
and reveals this incredible love to us.

It's like peeling back layers, one at a time, as we journey
deeper into intimacy with Him. Suddenly, things we once knew
only in theory become real. As the Holy Spirit works in us, He
reveals the breadth, length, depth, and height of Christ's love in
new and more tangible ways.

And as we grow in that understanding, as we allow His love
to sink into the very core of our being, something powerful happens: we become filled. Not just with a little peace or a brief
sense of joy, but with the very fullness of God. This includes
His nature, His faith, His hope, His joy: all the gifts of the Spirit
He has given us. It includes creativity, spiritual gifts, health and
wholeness, prosperity: *anything* that we can associate with
Him.

Different aspects of His fullness—the abundant life—that we
knew were true, but hadn't yet seen, begin to come to pass in
our lives. And through it all, we continue to grow, to experience
more of His fullness, letting His love lead us into the abundant
life more and more in every way!

February 16

Your ears shall hear a word behind you, saying,
"This is the way, walk in it," whenever you
turn to the right hand or to the left.

Isaiah 30:21

When we come to a crossroad in life—decisions about jobs, relationships, or direction—we often find ourselves asking, "What now, Lord?" In these moments, the comforting truth is that God promises to guide us. It's not about making the "perfect" decision; it's about leaning into His presence while staying confident in knowing He desires to lead us more than we even want to be led.

Sometimes we doubt whether we'll hear God clearly, but the promise here is that He *will* speak in ways we can understand. He speaks personally and intimately, guiding us when we're unsure whether to take a left or right. This is the assurance of knowing He loves us deeply and desires our good. God isn't playing games with our future. He wants us to know His will, and He's not hiding it from us!

We don't have to strain to hear Him either. God is always speaking; it's just a matter of tuning in. Sometimes, that word comes through scripture, sometimes through the gentle nudging of the Holy Spirit in prayer, and sometimes through wise counsel from those around us. It could even be in the quiet, inner *knowing* that comes when we listen.

So, instead of stressing over whether you've missed His voice or overcomplicating His guidance, you can rest in the promise that if you seek Him, you will hear Him. God is always ready to direct your steps, and as you stay open, listening, and trusting, He will faithfully lead you to where He wants you to go.

To discover more about how to tune into God's frequency and hear His voice more clearly, we recommend our 31-Day Devotional entitled *Hearing God*.

February 17

He sent them to preach the kingdom of God
and to heal the sick.

Luke 9:2

I magine being one of the twelve, standing there as Jesus calls you by name and gives you a mission. He didn't just ask them to go out and talk; He sent them with power, with purpose. They weren't merely speakers or messengers. Healing the sick wasn't just a side act, and preaching about the kingdom of God wasn't just filling time with religious talk or philosophy. Jesus was announcing that everything His followers did would declare, "God's kingdom is right here, with you!" The disciples' lives became a demonstration of that message.

But Jesus didn't stop with just twelve. Soon after, He sent seventy more, giving them the same authority to heal and proclaim the kingdom of God. But there is something very important we must remember: the mission didn't end with them! This call wasn't just a limited assignment for a chosen few. Jesus never even *hinted* that His miracles would stop when the twelve or seventy left the scene. In fact, these verses are our reminder that this power and purpose are for *everyone* who believes.

So, if someone tells you that signs and wonders ended back then, it's worth asking, "Which ones?" Because God's mission continues through us—through those who believe (Mark 16:17-18). You and I are called to walk in the same Spirit, to live like God's kingdom is alive and active—because it is! All of us have the opportunity to share His kingdom with those around us, not just in words but through our actions, prayers, and faith. Remember, the same Spirit that empowered the twelve and the seventy empowers you today. Go out and live as if the kingdom has truly come near—because through you, *it has*.

And when they had prayed, the place where they were assembled together was shaken; and they were all filled with the Holy Spirit, and they spoke the word of God with boldness.

Acts 4:31

There's something powerful about being filled with the Holy Spirit. This verse gives us a clear picture of what happens when believers gather in prayer and welcome God's presence. The Spirit of God literally shook the place where they were praying! And this wasn't just some minor rumble—it was a sign that God was moving, waking them up to His power and purpose. When we pray and truly open ourselves to His presence, He disrupts our routine, breaks through our comfort zones, and stirs us to action.

When we are filled with the Holy Spirit, something incredible happens: we find ourselves speaking the Word of God with a boldness we didn't have before. It's not about being naturally brave or eloquent. Instead, it's about letting God's Spirit move through us, giving us the words and the courage to say what needs to be said and do what needs to be done. There's a shift in our hearts that turns fear into courage and hesitation into confidence. After he experienced this, Peter spoke with an eloquence that was completely out of character because it was the Spirit of God in him giving him the words to speak.

And here's the really exciting part: when we speak with that Spirit-empowered boldness, people take notice. The words we say aren't just empty chatter—they carry weight. God confirms His message through us, often backing it up with signs and wonders. The Spirit doesn't just send us out; He equips us and makes sure that what we say has an impact. So, when the Holy Spirit shakes you up, trust that He's setting the stage for something powerful. Speak boldly and watch how God moves!

*To this end I also labor, striving according to
His working which works in me mightily.*

Colossians 1:29

Have you ever found yourself pushing through life, giving everything you've got, only to feel like you're running on fumes? It's like that feeling of being all out of energy, your reserves drained, yet there's still so much more to do. That's because when we rely only on our own strength, there's a limit to what we can handle. Human effort is like a fuel tank; you can only go so far before you're empty. That emptiness is real, and it can lead to frustration, burnout, and exhaustion.

But here's the good news: when we shift from working out of our own strength to depending on Christ's power, everything changes. His strength is limitless, where ours falls short. We aren't meant to do life on our own, pushing through with grit and willpower alone. Jesus is with us, not just as a backup plan for when we're exhausted, but as the source of power that works within us every single day.

The New Living Translation says, *"That's why I work and struggle so hard, depending on Christ's mighty power that works within me."* Imagine tapping into His strength, allowing it to flow through you, fueling everything you do. The struggles don't disappear, but suddenly you're not carrying the weight alone. Jesus's power becomes the driving force, enabling you to keep going without reaching the bottom of your tank.

This isn't just about surviving tough days—it's about *thriving*, knowing that you have an endless source of strength that comes from Him! Let Christ's power work mightily in you, filling you up and sustaining you far beyond what human effort could ever achieve.

*God also bearing witness both with signs and wonders,
with various miracles, and gifts of the Holy Spirit
according to His will.*

Hebrews 2:4

The amazing thing about God is that He doesn't just speak through His Word and leave it at that—He shows up in real ways to back it up. Imagine hearing a powerful message that resonates deeply with your spirit, aligning perfectly with Scripture, and then witnessing God move in supernatural ways. That's what it means when God bears witness through signs and wonders. It's His way of saying, "Yes, this is Me. Yes, I'm with you, and I want you to see it."

When miracles happen following the proclamation of His Word, it's a divine stamp of approval. It's God showing us that not only does He hear, but He responds. It's not random; it's intentional, and it's always rooted in His agreement with the truth being shared. Sometimes we feel like we need constant reminders of God's presence, but He is so faithful in showing up. His miraculous works aren't just about big moments; they're about Him agreeing with His Word and revealing His glory!

Then there are the gifts of the Holy Spirit, which are powerful and life-changing. They're given to us, but not by our own choosing. We can ask for them, we can (and should) desire them, but ultimately, God decides how and when these gifts are distributed. It's a reminder of His sovereignty, His perfect timing, and His grace. So, while we should absolutely seek the gifts of the Spirit, we must also trust that He knows exactly what we need and when we need it.

Live expectantly, trusting that God will continue to show Himself in incredible ways—according to His will. His power and His presence are not distant concepts; they are real, personal, and available to you every day!

*For as the heavens are high above the earth, so great is
His mercy toward those who fear Him; as far as the east
is from the west, so far has He removed our
transgressions from us.*

Psalm 103:11-12

Imagine standing on the shore of a vast ocean, looking out over the horizon, with no end in sight. That's just a glimpse of how immense God's mercy is toward us. His love and compassion reach so high above us—like the heavens towering over the earth—that it's beyond what we can comprehend. And yet, this mercy is as real as the air we breathe.

Now think about setting off on a journey eastward. You could travel endlessly, never coming to a place where it stops being "east." That's what God's forgiveness is like! Through Jesus' sacrifice, our sins aren't just tucked away; they're removed to a place so far, they can never be brought back against us. We might struggle to forget our failures, but God, in His mercy, has already cast them away as far as the east is from the west.

Sometimes, we hold on to guilt or shame, feeling that we need to pay for our mistakes over and over. But God's forgiveness isn't partial or temporary—it's complete. He's not asking us to punish ourselves or constantly try to earn His acceptance. Instead, He wants us to live freely, knowing that His mercy has covered us fully.

So today, remember this boundless mercy and let it shape the way you walk through your day. Release the burden of guilt, because God has already removed it! Walk with confidence in His love, knowing that when He sees you, He sees you through the lens of His forgiveness and mercy. In Christ, you are set free, welcomed, forgiven, and loved beyond measure!

*Surely He has borne our griefs and carried our sorrows;
yet we esteemed Him stricken, smitten by God, and
afflicted. But He was wounded for our transgressions he
was bruised for our iniquities; the chastisement for our
peace was upon Him. And by His stripes we are healed.*

Isaiah 53:4-5

Sometimes, we think we have to carry our pain and sickness alone or even think we should just "accept" them as our lot in life. But Isaiah 53 paints a different picture—one of a Savior who steps into our deepest hurts to bring true healing. The Hebrew word for *griefs* in this scripture is *choli*, which doesn't just mean sadness or disappointment; it refers to sickness as well. Jesus carried our *choli*, taking on every form of grief, sickness, wound, and disease for us on the cross.

Isaiah also says He "carried our sorrows." In Hebrew, *makob* is used here, referring to all forms of pain, both physical and emotional. That means Jesus didn't just carry our visible wounds; He took on every hidden ache, every heartbreak, and every layer of grief. He knows those parts of us that hurt the most because He felt them firsthand.

Then there's "healed"—*raphe*. This word goes beyond just the idea of feeling better; *raphe* speaks of being restored, made whole, mended from within. When Jesus bore the stripes on His back, He took every necessary step for our *raphe*, a complete cure that extends to our souls (mind, will, and emotions) *and* physical bodies.

This is about receiving total wholeness because of what Jesus has already done for us! So, as you go through your day, remember that your pain—your *choli*, your *makob*—has already been carried, and your *raphe* is His promise to you. Let yourself rest in that assurance. Jesus bore it all so that you can live in wholeness and peace!

53

*Therefore I say to you, whatever things you ask when
you pray, believe that you receive them,
and you will have them.*

Mark 11:24

There's something incredible in these words from Jesus. He tells us to pray for literally anything. There's no limit to what we can bring before God! We're invited to pray boldly, knowing there's no ceiling on what we can ask for. But there's a key to seeing these prayers fulfilled: we need to believe that we receive what we've asked for *while* we're praying! That belief—the quiet confidence that it's already ours—opens the door to God's answers.

The believing and receiving occur first. Before we ever see a hint of it in the physical world, we're instructed to believe. Then the physical "having" of it comes. But first, God asks us to lean in and receive by faith, trusting Him completely. So, we're invited to take God at His word—to trust so deeply that we don't just wait passively. Instead, we're encouraged to rejoice, plan, and even act as if the prayer has already been answered.

This approach isn't pretending or wishful thinking. It's aligning our hearts with the promises of God, knowing that when He speaks, things start to happen, whether we see it yet or not. So, step out in faith today. Rejoice in what God has promised, make plans as though the answer is already on its way, and take action in the direction of that prayer.

James said we don't have because we aren't asking (James 4:2). So, ask, believe, receive, and let your confidence in God's faithfulness move you forward, even before you see it come to pass in the physical realm. This is living in the flow of God's promises, expecting His hand to shape your reality in ways beyond what you can imagine!

However, when He, the Spirit of truth, has come, He will guide you into all truth; for He will not speak on His own authority, but whatever He hears He will speak; and He will tell you things to come.

John 16:13

There's nothing like having someone you can truly rely on—someone who always tells you the truth, never steers you wrong, and speaks with your best interest in mind. That's exactly who the Holy Spirit is. He doesn't guess or speculate. Everything He says flows straight from the heart of the Father, full of purpose, clarity, and love for you. When it feels like everything around you is shifting and it's hard to know what to believe, the Holy Spirit is right there—steady, dependable, and ready to lead you, especially in those moments when you feel unsure or overwhelmed.

That means when the Holy Spirit speaks to your spirit, you can trust what you're hearing. It's not just a good idea or a passing thought—it's insight from Heaven, hand-delivered by the One who knows the beginning from the end. In a noisy world full of mixed messages, having the Spirit of truth as your guide changes everything. He's not just around to give you comfort—He's here to lead you forward.

And it's not always in big, dramatic moments. Sometimes it's a quiet knowing. A sense of peace about something that didn't make sense before. A little light breaking through confusion. Maybe even a glimpse into what's ahead. The Holy Spirit delights in showing you what you couldn't know on your own—not to overwhelm you, but to empower you!

So stay close. Lean in. And listen. He's not holding back. He's speaking, and He wants to guide you into the fullness of all He has prepared for you. This is part of walking in the abundant life—being led, day by day, by the Spirit of truth.

So when Jesus had received the sour wine, He said, "It is finished!" And bowing His head, He gave up His spirit.

John 19:30

With His dying breath on the cross, Jesus declared, *"It is finished."* Those words reverberate through eternity, with a power that changed everything! When Jesus took His final breath, He wasn't just ending His life on earth—He was completing the mission He came to fulfill. Every healing, every miracle, and every act of love He had poured out had a single purpose: to accomplish what we could never achieve ourselves. And when He said it was finished, it was. Fully. Finally.

This isn't a work-in-progress salvation, where every mistake we make demands a fresh sacrifice. No, Jesus' one act on the cross was enough. That moment secured eternal life and wholeness for anyone who believes. It sealed your salvation, your forgiveness, your blessing, your favor, your success, and even your healing. He's not climbing back up on that cross each time you feel unworthy, defeated, or sick. He already carried it all, finished it all, and declared it done! Now, all that's left for us to do is receive it.

You don't have to earn what's already been given! When Jesus said it was finished, He meant you don't have to strive for perfection anymore. Whatever sin, shame, pain, or fear you're holding, you can lay it down. You are free to live in the fullness of His sacrifice, experiencing His healing and salvation every day. Trust in the power of His final words—*"It is finished"* means your redemption, your wholeness, and your relationship with Him are completely secure. You don't have to do anything but believe and receive. Let those words echo in your heart today: it is finished, and you are loved, healed, and whole because of Him.

If it is possible, as much as depends on you,
live peaceably with all men.

Romans 12:18

L iving at peace with everyone sounds great, right? But anyone who's been out in the world for more than five minutes knows it's not always easy. Some people are just... difficult! Still, we're called to do our part. That means, when it comes to peace, we're responsible for our role in any situation. We don't get to control other people's responses, but we are accountable for our own choices and attitudes. If there's a way to avoid drama or keep things calm, we need to try.

This doesn't mean we compromise our values or tiptoe around others just to keep the peace. Instead, it means letting God guide us in handling each situation. Every interaction is different, and some people—let's be real—are just set on stirring up trouble. In those moments, trying to stay peaceful can feel like an impossible task. But that's where seeking God's wisdom comes in. He can show us how to respond (or not respond) in a way that maintains our own peace—even when others try to rattle us.

Of course, sometimes, despite our best efforts, peace just isn't possible. There will always be people who, no matter what you say or do, seem determined to create conflict. When that happens, remember that peace doesn't always mean agreeing or being best friends with everyone. Sometimes, it means setting boundaries and accepting that not every relationship can be harmonious.

Don't let those people steal your peace, either! Keep your eyes on Jesus and stay in His peace. God sees your heart and knows the effort you're making. If you're doing your part to live peaceably, you can rest knowing that you're honoring Him, even if others choose a different path.

For He made Him who knew no sin to be sin for us, that we might become the righteousness of God in Him.

2 Corinthians 5:21

I magine Jesus, pure and blameless, untouched by the stain of sin, willingly taking on the sin of the world. He, who was completely righteous and without sin, took on the full weight of all the wrongs, failings, and flaws of humanity. Jesus didn't just carry sin; He *became* sin on that cross, embodying everything we've done or ever will do that falls short. He didn't deserve it, but He took it on anyway.

This means that our very nature, once bound up in brokenness and sin, can now be transformed! In Jesus, we find freedom because the sin that kept us separate from God was nailed to the cross with Him (Colossians 2:13-14). When He died, our sin nature died too (Romans 6:6-7). It's like a complete trade-off, an exchange that defies logic. His death wasn't just an act of love; it was the very act that allows us to step into God's presence without shame or condemnation.

Trusting in what Jesus did is more than just believing in His sacrifice. It's about letting go of that old identity—characterized by sin—and embracing a new one. We are no longer defined by our past or by a "sinner" label; instead, we're marked by His righteousness. In *becoming sin*, Jesus made it possible for us to *become righteous*, to be seen by God as clean, pure, and whole.

So, don't live under the weight of shame. Don't walk around thinking you're not good enough. You're free to live as a person made new. In Him, you've stepped out of darkness and into the light, clothed in His righteousness. Today, you can stand tall, fully assured of His love, knowing that His grace has made you brand-new!

*For you know the grace of our Lord Jesus Christ, that
though He was rich, yet for your sakes He became poor,
that you through His poverty might become rich.*

2 Corinthians 8:9

J esus, rich beyond measure, chose to become poor for
our sake. His sacrifice wasn't just about spiritual poverty;
it was about exchanging everything He had, including
the comforts of physical wealth, to bring us out of lack. The
Greek word for *rich* here, *plousios*, refers to material wealth and
abundance, not only a fullness of spirit. Jesus surrendered all
His richness as God so that we could inherit abundance in
every area of life.

Before we knew Him, we were truly poor—yes, spiritually,
but also in our ability to access the wholeness and provision
God intended for us. Yet, the moment we receive Him, our entire reality changes! We're no longer poor in any way Instead,
we inherit His fullness. This richness encompasses every part of
us—our soul, our relationships, and yes, even our physical resources. His act on the cross didn't just lift us spiritually; it
opened the way for physical blessings, giving us access to His
unlimited supply of provision.

As believers, we're no longer bound to a life of poverty, in
any sense! Jesus' poverty—His decision to step away from His
divine and physical wealth—was the foundation for our prosperity, rooted in God's kingdom. We're meant to live fully, to
experience His abundance in spirit, soul, and body. Poverty has
no place in our lives because we're not only saved; we're
enriched by His grace, carrying the fullness of abundant life He
came and died to give us.

Let this truth reshape how you believe and receive today:
aware that through His sacrifice, *plousios*—true wealth and
wholeness—has become yours!

He will not be afraid of evil tidings;
his heart is steadfast, trusting in the Lord.

Psalm 112:7

W e are located near the mountains in Colorado. Daily, we can look at towering mountains, each one rooted deep into the earth, standing tall and immovable despite the fiercest wind or heaviest snow or rain. That's the kind of solid, unshakable confidence this verse encourages us to have. A "steadfast" heart isn't just a nice idea; it's about choosing to be established, fixed, and securely determined in what God says about us and our lives. When our hearts are anchored in Him, we're not easily shaken, even when the storms of life try to knock us down.

Bad news and challenges come to everyone—financial stress, health issues, uncertainty about what's next. But we are grounded in God's love and promises, these things don't move us. Trusting in the Lord means keeping our focus on what His Word says: that we're loved, safe, provided for, and guided by the One who holds everything together.

Instead of letting fear take root, we can let the news—evil tidings—of the world pass by, knowing it doesn't have the power to uproot us. It doesn't mean we ignore reality; it means we're choosing a greater truth—a faith that declares God is in control, no matter what comes. His perfect love, after all, is what drives out fear.

The more we anchor ourselves in His love, the less space there is for anxiety to creep in. His promises are our security, our stability, and the foundation of our hearts. Today, plant yourself firmly in the truth of His Word so that any "evil tidings" are powerless to shake you. With a heart steadfast in Him, you're free to live boldly, knowing He's got you—surrounding you with His protection and favor—through it all.

...imitate those who through faith
and patience inherit the promises.

Hebrews 6:12

Waiting on God's promises isn't always easy, especially when it feels like nothing is happening. Imagine Abraham, holding on to God's promise for 25 years before Isaac was born. Or Noah, building an ark and trusting God's plan for 100 years before a single drop of rain fell! This kind of waiting wasn't passive; it was a journey filled with trust, *action*, and a deep faith that didn't waver, even when the wait stretched on and on.

Faith is holding onto God's Word, even when there's no sign of the promise coming to life. It's trusting that God's timing is perfect, even when it doesn't match our own. Patience isn't sitting back and wishing for change; it's the determination to keep believing, keep hoping, and keep moving forward. God's promises may take time to unfold, but they're always worth the wait. True faith isn't about seeing results immediately—it's about being steadfast in believing God is who He says He is, even when the outcome is unseen.

The great news is we aren't left to figure this out on our own! Throughout the Bible, and even today, there are countless examples of those who have trusted God through thick and thin, with incredible results.

Look around you—perhaps there are people in your life or church whose faith has carried them through long seasons of waiting. We have a list of testimonies on our website that can encourage you as well! Let their stories inspire you and remind you that God is faithful. He's done it before, and He'll do it again. He is no respecter of persons, but His power responds to your faith. Keep holding on, stay patient, and know that, like Abraham and Noah, you're in good company.

March 3

*"For I will restore health to you
And heal you of your wounds," says the Lord....*

Jeremiah 30:17

What an incredible promise! This is an invitation to believe that God's healing power is real, powerful, and available to you right now, regardless of your situation, no matter the cause, no matter the injury or disease. There is *nothing* too big for God to heal!

Because of what Jesus accomplished on the cross, you have access to this promise. Restoration and healing aren't things we hope for off in the distance—they're gifts you can embrace in faith today. Whatever has come against your body, even if it's been a long-standing issue or the result of an unexpected accident, God's healing power can bring complete restoration.

We have a story that is a vivid example of this truth. One day, while trying to save a bunny from her dog, Carlie broke her ankle when she accidentally stepped into a hole! At first, she had a vision of trying to hobble through the airport to the United States in a cast, on crutches. However, instead of panicking, she declared her healing right there in the field! With faith stirring in her heart, she didn't sit around waiting. Carlie got up and ran, trusting that God's promise would come through. Of course, at first, her ankle hurt! However, by the time she made it home, her ankle was *fully healed*.

This is the kind of faith and expectation God wants us to have. He's not just a healer of sickness but of all wounds—physical, emotional, and spiritual. So today, take hold of this promise for yourself. Let His words sink deep into your spirit, strengthening your faith. No matter what you've been through, believe that He can restore you completely. He's already done the work; all you have to do is receive it by faith!

The wise woman builds her house,
But the foolish pulls it down with her hands.

Proverbs 14:1

When we think of "building," we might picture the heavy lifting involved in constructing something solid, like a house. But there's more to it than that. Building a life—a family, a career, or our own character—takes intention and care. A wise person, someone after God's heart, looks for ways to strengthen, grow, and increase what they've been given. Wisdom calls us to be active participants in our lives, to seek God's guidance, and to stay grounded in His truth. This isn't a passive approach; it's one of actively building up what God has entrusted to us.

Sometimes, though, the biggest obstacle we face is ourselves. How often do we slip into self-criticism, doubt, or defeat? Instead of lifting ourselves up, we can tear ourselves down with our words, attitudes, or insecurities. We can become our own worst enemy, letting our thoughts chip away at the foundation God has helped us lay. But God calls us to something better!

Today, let's choose to speak life over ourselves. Declare, "I have wisdom from God. I have an anointing from the Holy One. I know what I need to know because God equips me for every challenge." These words are more than positive thinking; they are a declaration of the truth God has spoken over us. Our words have power, shaping our mindset and influencing our actions. Let's choose words that build up, strengthen, and encourage us on this journey of abundant life.

So today, instead of tearing ourselves down, let's remember that we are called to be builders. With God's wisdom and strength, we have the power to build something beautiful with our lives. Every decision, every word, and every step is a chance to create a life that reflects God's goodness and purpose for us.

...If you abide in My word, you are my disciples indeed. And you shall know the truth, and the truth shall make you free.

John 8:31-32

Life gets loud. It throws opinions, pressure, and confusion your way—so much so that it's easy to feel stuck or unsure of what's real. That's exactly why abiding in the Word matters. It's not just about reading a verse here and there; it's about staying connected to the truth long enough for it to take root. Jesus said it plainly: when you live in His Word, you'll know the truth—and that truth will bring freedom.

God's Word isn't just informative—it's transformational. It cuts through the fog and brings clarity right where you need it. Whether you're facing lies from the enemy, old habits that try to creep back in, or situations that make you question your next step, the truth found in Scripture exposes the lie and sets you back on solid ground. It's how you stop living by reactions and start walking with intention.

This freedom isn't some vague spiritual idea. It shows up in real ways. You stop carrying burdens you were never meant to bear. You make decisions with peace instead of fear. You stop striving to prove yourself because you already know who you are in Him. That's what truth does—it unlocks the life God intended for you all along.

If you feel tangled up or weighed down, don't run harder—lean in. Get back to the Word. Let it speak. Let it settle things in your heart and steady your steps. Because when you know the truth, you don't just think differently—you live differently. That's where freedom begins.

Because you have made the LORD, who is my refuge, even the Most High, your dwelling place, no evil shall befall you, nor shall any plague come near your dwelling.... "Because he has set his love upon Me, therefore I will deliver him; I will set him on high, because he has known My name. He shall call upon Me, and I will answer him; I will be with him in trouble; I will deliver him and honor him. With long life I will satisfy him, and show him My salvation."

Psalm 91:9-10; 14-16

When life feels like it's closing in, remember that God's promises are personal and powerful. Every time you call on Him, He will deliver you—no exceptions. He's not a distant protector; He's right there, ready to shield you, no matter the situation.

The incredible benefits of protection, health, deliverance, and a long, satisfying life come out of a real relationship with Him. It's not just about knowing *of* God; it's about *knowing* Him and making Him your dwelling place. When you set your love on Him, He becomes your refuge and friend, always standing by you!

And here's the truth you can declare daily: no evil has permission to touch you, and no sickness is allowed near your dwelling—your house *or* body! These promises are part of your spiritual inheritance. Walk in them confidently, claiming protection, peace, and health as your birthright.

You have nothing to fear or be in dread about. There is nothing you need to be worried over. You're loved, you're covered, and you're secure in Him. Let these truths be the foundation of your life and a constant reminder of His faithful presence with you.

*As you therefore have received Christ Jesus the Lord,
so walk in Him, rooted and built up in Him and
established in the faith, as you have been taught,
abounding in it with thanksgiving.*

Colossians 2:6-7

Faith is what brought us into relationship with Jesus, and faith is what carries us through each day. Sometimes we may feel like our footing is shaky, but remember that the same trust we had when we first received Him is what keeps us moving forward! Each step in faith is an invitation to lean in closer, to go deeper, to rely on Him more.

As we spend time with Jesus, building that relationship, we start to see our roots grow stronger. Think about the strength of a tree deeply rooted in rich soil. It withstands storms, stays grounded in high winds, and doesn't sway with every little shift around it. When we spend time in His presence, in His Word, in moments of prayer, in praise and worship, declaring truth over ourselves, we are growing roots. These roots are what ground us, providing stability no matter what comes our way.

A life that is rooted and built up in Jesus can't help but overflow with thanksgiving. Gratitude springs up naturally because we realize that every good thing comes from Him, that even the challenges we face—although not caused by God—are still turned around and used for our good! With a grounded relationship, we see God's work everywhere and in everything, and it causes us to overflow with thankfulness. A grateful heart isn't weighed down by worries; it's lifted up by the joy of knowing Jesus.

So today, let faith be your guide as you walk, let your roots grow deep in Him, and let thanksgiving overflow. The journey with Jesus is steady, unshakable, and filled with abundant gratitude.

March 8

Therefore humble yourselves under the mighty hand of God, that He may exalt you in due time, casting all your care upon Him, for He cares for you.

1 Peter 5:6-7

True humility isn't about feeling small or undervaluing who you are; it's simply agreeing with God! It's about recognizing His wisdom, timing, and instruction as higher than our own, even when our instincts want us to take control. Humbling yourself before Him means saying, "God, I trust You to lead me, and I believe what You say about me." It's choosing to respect His direction over our own desires or doubts, placing our confidence in His way rather than in our limited understanding.

Yet, how often do we hold on to our worries, keeping them close, as if somehow our own minds and hands are better equipped to handle life's burdens? Sometimes, without even realizing it, we're telling God, "I think I can handle this better than You." The truth is, our own striving can't solve every problem, and keeping our cares bottled up only adds to our stress. God's invitation is simple: let it go. Cast your cares onto Him because He truly cares for you. He's not waiting to catch you in weakness or remind you of what you "should" be able to handle on your own; He's waiting to relieve the weight you've been carrying.

Trusting in God with everything—even the little worries, the unspoken fears, the things we think we should "figure out ourselves"—opens the door for Him to work in extraordinary ways. When we allow Him to step in, He's able to lift us up at just the right time, not only for our own good but for a greater purpose. In His perfect timing, He brings promotion, blessing, and encouragement. So, today, lean into His wisdom, let go of what's weighing you down, and allow Him to lift you up!

March 9

But his delight is in the law of the Lord, and in His law he meditates day and night. He shall be like a tree planted by the rivers of water, that brings forth its fruit in its season, whose leaf also shall not wither; and whatever he does shall prosper.

Psalm 1:2-3

Imagine standing by a river, watching the water flow by. The trees lining the bank are healthy and vibrant, reaching toward the sky, deeply rooted into the soil where they constantly soak up nutrients and life-giving water. That's a picture of what God wants for you—to be like one of those trees, constantly thriving, always bearing fruit, and never running dry.

When you make time each day to soak in God's Word, it's like planting yourself right beside that river. God's Word refreshes you, giving you what you need to grow strong and stand tall. Meditating on it isn't just reading a verse and moving on; it's sitting with it, letting it sink into your soul—renewing your mind—and allowing it to shape the way you see the world and make choices. When His Word becomes the heartbeat of your life, you step into the abundant life Jesus promised, one filled with true joy, strength, and purpose.

As you grow in this practice, you'll find yourself becoming resilient. Hardships might come; storms might rage, but you won't be shaken! With roots anchored in His truth, you'll stay upright, thriving even in tough seasons. And in time, you'll see the fruit—evidence of God's work in your life—in both big and small ways. Prosperity and blessing won't be occasional, but an overflow of a life lived close to Him. Today, plant yourself by the rivers of His Word, and watch as He makes you flourish beyond what you could ever imagine!

Behold, I give you authority to trample on serpents and scorpions, and over all the power of the enemy, and nothing shall by any means hurt you.

Luke 10:19

J esus has given us authority as a gift—real, powerful, unshakable authority—over every scheme, trick, and snare the enemy might throw our way. The power we've been given through Him is unmatched, greater than any force we might face, no matter how intimidating it seems. When the enemy shows up in our lives, whether it's through fear, doubt, or physical circumstances, we can stand firm, knowing we aren't battling alone or from a place of weakness.

This promise from Jesus is bold: *"Nothing shall **by any means** hurt you."* It's easy to think, *Really? Nothing?* Yes! His Word is absolute truth, and when we place our faith in what He says, we're tapping into a supernatural power that's not limited by our circumstances. It's a statement meant to give us courage and build a confidence that doesn't come from our own strength but from a God who completely backs us up!

The enemy might try to throw you in the fire, but we have the authority to walk through it without even smelling of smoke. When doubts creep in or challenges loom large, we can remind ourselves of this promise and stand on it, confidently expecting His protection and strength.

Trusting in His Word means we don't just survive; we overcome! Every fear, every worry—none of it stands a chance when we're empowered by His authority. So, today, let's embrace that authority, face whatever comes with unwavering faith, and live in the assurance that we will not be defeated. His Word is the truth that protects us and gives us the victory!

March 11

So you shall serve the LORD your God,
and He will bless your bread and your water.
And I will take sickness away from the midst of you.
No one shall suffer miscarriage or be barren in your land;
I will fulfill the number of your days.

Exodus 23:25-26

This passage offers a promise packed with love, healing, and hope, making it a perfect scripture to pray over your meals. When God speaks of blessing our bread and water, He assures us He will provide for us in every way. As you sit down to eat, thank God for His promise to bless your bread and water. Praying this verse at mealtimes invites God's presence into your life, asking Him to nourish your body and protect you and your loved ones from sickness. Let each meal be an opportunity to declare His blessings and remind yourself of His faithfulness to fulfill every day with purpose and vitality.

This verse also carries special encouragement for women who have faced miscarriage, are fearful of it, or have struggled with infertility. God's words, "You will not suffer miscarriage, and you are not barren," are filled with His compassion, love, and desire to see your family increase! This is His invitation to trust in His ability to bring life where there has been loss, and to even heal broken or missing parts that are needed for you to bear children. God's design for your life is one of blessing and multiplication, as He Himself commanded us to "Be fruitful and multiply!"

Lastly, God promises us a long and fulfilling life. Life is meant to be lived fully and joyfully, and dying young is not part of God's blessing! Through Jesus, we are redeemed from the curse of a short life; He promises to fulfill the number of our days. You are meant to experience an abundant life brimming with purpose, health, and peace.

But Jesus looked at them and said,
"With men it is impossible, but not with God;
for with God all things are possible."

Mark 10:27

Have you or someone you loved been diagnosed with an "incurable" disease? Or are you on a fixed income, where it seems like there's no way for you to increase? Is it "impossible" to afford to buy a house in your current economy?

Many of us face situations that the world labels as "incurable" or "unfixable," whether it's a disease or a financial struggle. But God's power isn't limited by human minds or economic systems. What's impossible for us is precisely where God loves to show up in ways we might never have expected!

Think of the times Jesus healed the sick, even when there was no earthly solution. He wasn't limited by the lack of medical knowledge or technology; He healed because it's in His nature to bring life and wholeness. Just as He did then, He does now. There's no "incurable" in God's vocabulary!

Or maybe your struggle is financial, where the numbers don't seem to add up. Jesus multiplied a few loaves and fishes to feed thousands—what's stopping Him from multiplying your resources, even when you're on a fixed income? God's provision defies what seems possible because He isn't limited by what we see with our natural eyes.

Jesus loves taking what seems impossible and making it possible. When He moves in our lives in these ways, it's a testament to His greatness and love. Each "impossible" moment that turns into a miracle just points back to Him, giving Him glory and strengthening our faith. So, whether it's health, finances, or any other need, remember that God is more than able! Let faith rise, and trust that He's working, even if you can't yet see how.

March 13

All your children shall be taught by the Lord,
and great shall be the peace of your children.

Isaiah 54:13

It's easy to feel like we're missing something as parents, especially when it comes to guiding our children toward a relationship with God. We wonder if we're saying the right things, setting the best example, or if we even have the tools or knowledge we need to teach them well. But here's the beautiful truth: God didn't just give us our children—He's also equipped us to be their parents! He knows our strengths, and He's aware of our weaknesses. And He's more than ready to fill in every gap.

When you feel like your efforts are lacking, remember that God Himself is teaching your children. The Lord's guidance is constant, reliable, and uniquely suited to their hearts. As you trust Him to do what you cannot, you can rest in knowing that His hand is on their lives. You don't have to stress over every detail or wonder if you're falling short. You are supported by His wisdom—and so are they.

The promise is that your children will live in peace. Not a fragile, fleeting peace, but one that is whole and unshakable—nothing missing, nothing broken. God is working in their lives in ways you may not see immediately, but His presence brings completeness. So, trust that He is moving, guiding, and nurturing their spirits as only He can. Your job isn't to be perfect; it's to rely on the perfect One who loves them even more than you do! As you lean into that truth, you can rest assured that your children will know His peace and walk confidently in it.

March 14

But thanks be to God, who gives us the victory through our Lord Jesus Christ.

1 Corinthians 15:57

Victory isn't something you have to chase—it's something you already have in Christ! Life can throw some curveballs, and it's easy to feel overwhelmed by challenges. But no matter what situations you're facing, you can stand confidently, knowing that God has already provided the victory through Jesus. It's not a "maybe" or a "someday"—it's yours right now.

So often, we can get caught up in the struggle, thinking we have to earn or fight for success, healing, peace, or breakthrough. But here's the truth: the battle has already been won. When Jesus declared, *"It is finished,"* He wasn't leaving anything undone. Your job isn't to strive for victory but to walk in the victory that's already been given to you. This shift in perspective changes everything. You're not striving to overcome; you're standing in what's already been accomplished.

Think of it like this: imagine a champion passing their trophy and prize money to you. You didn't run the race or fight the fight—they did it all. But now, that victory is yours. It's a gift, not something you had to earn. That's exactly what Jesus has done for you. He fought the battle, defeated sin and death, and handed you the prize.

Take a moment to thank God today. Celebrate His goodness, knowing that you're not a victim of circumstances but a victor in Christ. When challenges come, remind yourself of this truth: you're battling from a place of victory, not for it. Walk in confidence, knowing that through Jesus, every battle you face has already been conquered. You're living on the winning side—so go ahead and live like it!

Looking unto Jesus, the author and finisher of our faith, who for the joy that was set before Him endured the cross, despising the shame, and has sat down at the right hand of the throne of God.

Hebrews 12:2

Sometimes the things we are facing cause us to struggle with doubt and unbelief. Challenges come, and suddenly we're scrambling to muster up enough faith to deal with them. It's easy to fall into the trap of thinking faith is something we have to conjure up on our own—like if we just try harder, think positively enough, or pray loudly enough, then maybe we'll have what it takes. But that's not how faith works. Jesus is the source of our faith, and we don't have to squeeze it out of thin air. He's already given us all the faith we need (Romans 12:3)!

Faith begins when we take our eyes off ourselves and our problems and fix them on Jesus. He's the author and finisher of our faith—the one who started it, grows it, and brings it to completion (Hebrews 12:2). Instead of wrestling to believe harder, simply focus on Him. Faith isn't about how much effort we put in but about how closely we stay connected to the One who gives it to us.

One of the best ways for you to keep your eyes on Jesus is to spend time in the Word. He is the Word, after all! When you meditate on Scripture, it shifts your focus off yourself and onto Him. It reminds you of who He is and what He's already done for you. Suddenly, the weight you felt to "make faith happen" begins to melt away, because you realize it's not about you.

Faith grows in His presence. Rest in the truth that He's already given you everything you need. Keep your eyes on Jesus, not on your circumstances, and trust that He's faithful to finish the work He's started in you.

Keep your heart with all diligence,
for out of it flows the issues of life.

Proverbs 4:23

Your heart is like a wellspring from which every part of your life flows—your thoughts, words, decisions, and the very direction of your life. The Hebrew word for "keep" in this verse paints the picture of someone on high alert, a guard standing watch. It's not casual or half-hearted; it's intentional and focused. Why? Because what flows out of your heart impacts everything about you.

In medieval times, castles had "keeps," strong, fortified towers where the most valuable treasures and people were protected. It was the last line of defense when the enemy came knocking. Your heart is your spiritual "keep," and it's meant to be guarded just as fiercely. What are you allowing past the gates? Are you letting in worry, bitterness, or unhealthy influences? Those things don't just come in quietly—they take root and pollute the wellspring of your life.

Your life flows from your heart like a spring, but the moment you open the gates to what's harmful, that water becomes murky. The words you speak, the choices you make, and the paths you follow all begin to reflect what you've allowed into your heart.

Guarding your heart doesn't mean shutting it off from the world; it means being wise about what you let in. Keep it fresh and pure by focusing on what's good, godly, and life-giving. Spend time in God's Word, choose uplifting relationships, and let go of anything that threatens to pollute the stream. When you guard your heart well, you're not just protecting your thoughts and actions—you're safeguarding the very source of your life. Let your heart flow with clarity and purpose, bringing life to you and those around you.

*My sheep hear My voice, and I know them,
and they follow Me.*

John 10:27

As a child of God, you've got something incredible going for you—you're hard-wired to hear His voice. Think about that! The Creator of the universe designed you to recognize and respond to Him. Sometimes, we overcomplicate things, doubting whether we can really hear from God. But Jesus made it clear that His sheep hear His voice. If you've said yes to Jesus, that means you!

The enemy loves to sow seeds of doubt, whispering that you're not good enough, spiritual enough, or "holy" enough to hear from God. Don't buy into those lies! God isn't playing hide-and-seek with you, nor is His voice reserved for some kind super-spiritual elites. He speaks to you because He loves you, and He knows exactly how to get your attention. Whether it's through His Word, a nudge in your spirit, or even the wisdom of others, you can trust that His voice is accessible to you.

And here's the best part: you don't have to be afraid of what He'll say! God's heart for you is always good. He knows your struggles, your strengths, and the deepest desires of your heart. His plans are for your joy, even when they stretch you. When He speaks, it's to guide you, encourage you, and lead you closer to Him. So, when you sense Him calling, you can follow with confidence, knowing His ways will always enrich your life.

God's voice isn't a mystery—it's a gift. When He speaks, it's to draw you closer, to reveal His goodness, and to remind you that you're never walking alone. So lean in. Expect to hear Him. Trust that He's speaking in a way you can understand. And when you do hear Him, follow boldly—because your Good Shepherd is leading you into life, hope, and so much more than you could ask for!

Yet they will by no means follow a stranger, but will flee form him, for they do not know the voice of strangers.

John 10:5

There's so much freedom in knowing that we don't have to live in fear of making the wrong choices. Life often throws us into moments of uncertainty—decisions to make, paths to choose, and voices all around trying to pull us in different directions. But as followers of Jesus, we have His promise to guide us. He's not leaving us to figure it all out alone, nor is He expecting perfection. He reassures us that His sheep—us—know His voice and won't be led astray by a stranger. That's a promise you can trust.

The enemy loves to whisper doubts and fears, planting seeds of anxiety about whether you're doing the right thing. But Jesus says otherwise. His word is clear: you belong to Him, and you are attuned to His leading. Even if it feels like you're standing in the middle of a noisy crowd, unsure of what to do next, His voice cuts through the chaos. When you focus on Him and lean into the peace that comes from trusting His Word, you'll find clarity and confidence.

And what about those times when we stumble or take a wrong turn? We're human—it's going to happen. But here's the good news: Jesus is bigger than any mistake you could ever make, and He's faithful to work all things together for your good. Even if you misstep, He'll gently redirect you, turning what feels like a setback into part of His greater plan for your life.

So, rest in this truth today: you're not walking alone, and you don't have to live in fear of missing the mark. Jesus is with you, guiding you every step of the way, always ready to lead you back into the fullness of His love and purpose.

What do you conspire against the LORD? He will make an utter end of it. Affliction will not rise up a second time.

Nahum 1:9

There's nothing more frustrating than experiencing God's healing in your life, only to have doubts or symptoms creep back in, whispering, *"Maybe it didn't really happen. Maybe you weren't actually healed."* Those thoughts can feel so real, especially when physical sensations seem to back them up. But here's the truth: those symptoms are nothing more than a lie—a conspiracy against the Lord and His promise to you!

When you gave your life to Jesus, your body became the temple of the Holy Spirit, a sacred dwelling place for God Himself. He doesn't dwell in broken-down temples! Sickness has no right to linger, let alone return. It's not just an attack on your health; it's an attempt to challenge the work of God in your life. Don't take the bait. When those symptoms try to knock on the door of your heart, stand firm and remind yourself—and the enemy—of what God has said: affliction will not rise up a second time!

God's Word is your weapon. Speak it out boldly! Declare, "This body belongs to the Lord! Healing is mine, and sickness has no place here." Don't be intimidated by temporary symptoms; they're powerless in the face of His eternal promise. The enemy may try to get you to agree with his lies, but you have the authority to shut him down every time.

Hold onto the truth: when God heals, He heals completely. Affliction doesn't get a second chance to take root. Whatever you're facing today, reject the lie, believe His Word, and stand in the victory He has already won for you. Let your faith rise, because His promise is unshakable—sickness and affliction are finished, once and for all.

Wherever He entered...they laid the sick in the marketplaces, and begged Him that they might just touch the hem of His garment. And as many as touched Him were made well.

Mark 6:56

In the hustle and bustle of life, it's easy to forget how accessible Jesus really is. In the time of His ministry, people would crowd around Him, hoping to catch just a glimpse of Him. But some came with a bold determination to receive, like the woman who pushed through the crowd, risking everything, just to touch His garment. Her faith was extraordinary—and it changed her life (Mark 5:27-29). That moment wasn't just her miracle; it became a revelation for others, inspiring them to believe they, too, could receive healing in the same way.

What's incredible is that this woman's faith wasn't based on a precedent. No one had ever been healed by touching the hem of His garment before. She didn't have a testimony to rely on, yet her faith created a path for herself and countless others. After her, the Bible records others being healed in the same way! They reached out in faith, and the Bible says as many as touched Him were healed. Her story wasn't just about healing; it was about the power of believing.

The best part? You can have the same confidence today. Jesus hasn't changed. The same healing power that flowed from Him then is available to you now. You don't have to beg or plead for it—He already provided it through His finished work. What He asks is that you simply believe and receive. Take that step of faith, no matter how unconventional it might feel. Just like the woman, you don't need a precedent to experience His goodness. Faith isn't about what's been done before; it's about knowing who He is and reaching out with expectation. He is ready to meet you, right where you are!

While we do not look at the things that are seen,
but at the things which are not seen.
For the things which are seen are temporary,
but the things which are not seen are eternal.

2 Corinthians 4:18

It's easy to get caught up in what we can see, hear, and feel around us. Pain, lack, stress—they scream for our attention and can seem overwhelming. But the truth is, these things are temporary. They don't define your reality; they're just passing through. What you see with your natural eyes isn't the full picture.

There's a greater reality, one that goes beyond what you can see or touch. In the spiritual realm, where God's promises reside, healing, provision, and peace are already yours. When you shift your focus from the chaos around you to the truth of what God says about you, you align yourself with what's eternal. This isn't denial—it's faith. Faith chooses to see what is unseen and calls it into being.

Think of it like this: the spiritual realm isn't some far-off, mystical place. It's the ultimate reality. Everything we experience in the physical came from the spiritual first. God spoke, and the world was created. His words shaped the seen from the unseen. That same creative power is available to you through faith. When you speak God's truth and hold onto His promises, you're pulling what's already real in the spiritual realm into the here and now.

So, don't be discouraged by temporary symptoms or circumstances. They don't have the final say. Instead, fix your eyes on what's eternal—on the promises of God. They are more real and more lasting than anything you can experience with your five senses. Stay focused on Him, and watch as the eternal breaks through into your everyday life!

As His divine power has given to us all things that pertain to life and godliness, through the knowledge of Him who called us by glory and virtue.

2 Peter 1:3

God's power is limitless, and He's already provided everything we need to live a life full of purpose, joy, and abundance. That's not just spiritual abundance but all things that pertain to life and godliness. Think about that—He's already done it! He's not holding back or waiting for us to earn it. Through His love and grace, it's all available right now. The question is, how do we access it?

The key is our knowledge of Him. Knowing God isn't just about head knowledge or memorizing scriptures (though those are valuable). It's about a personal, intimate relationship where we learn His heart, hear His voice, and understand His ways. The more we get to know Him, the more we recognize what He's provided and how to walk in it. It's like being given the keys to a treasure chest; knowing God helps us unlock it.

That's why time spent with Him is so important. Prayer, worship, and meditating on His Word are more than religious routines; they're opportunities to deepen our connection with the One who's already given us everything we need. The closer we grow to Him, the clearer we see His provision and power working in our lives.

Take a moment today to lean into that relationship. Whether it's a heartfelt prayer, a quiet moment of reflection, or simply thanking Him for His goodness, every step toward knowing Him more brings us closer to living the abundant life He's already provided. You don't have to strive for what He's freely given—just draw near, listen, and let His divine power work in and through you. That's where life and godliness flow.

March 23

*Finally, my brethren, be strong in the Lord
and in the power of His might.*

Ephesians 6:10

L ife often demands more from us than we feel capable of giving. There are times when our strength feels spent, energy gone, and it's hard to keep going. But here's the good news: we were never meant to rely on our human strength alone! God's plans for our lives are far greater than anything we could accomplish on our own. They require a power that goes beyond human ability—a power that only comes from Him.

True strength isn't found in grit or determination alone; it's found in surrender. When we shift our focus from our limitations to His limitless ability, we position ourselves to experience His strength working through us. God doesn't just top off our tank when we're running on empty; He is the source of our strength, renewing and empowering us for whatever we face.

This is why Philippians 4:13—which says we can do *all things* through Christ—resonates so deeply. It's not about what we can do, but what Christ can do *through* us. God told Paul, *"My grace is sufficient for you, for My strength is made perfect in weakness"* (2 Corinthians 12:9). So, His strength is perfect, even in our weakness! When we face challenges, instead of relying on our own effort, we can lean into Him and trust that His power will carry us through.

Today, let go of the pressure to do it all in your own strength. Instead, take a moment to rest in His power. Whether you're navigating a tough decision, pursuing a God-given dream, or simply managing the demands of everyday life, remember this: His strength is more than enough! As you trust in Him, you'll find that what once seemed impossible becomes possible—not because of you, but because of Him.

Call upon Me in the day of trouble;
I will deliver you, and you shall glorify Me.

Psalm 50:15

When life gets messy and trouble comes knocking, it's easy to pick up the phone and call a friend, a family member, a pastor, or even a professional advisor. We naturally want help from someone we trust, either because they know us or because they are an expert in what we are dealing with. But here's the thing: while people can offer support, they're not always equipped to deliver what we truly need. But God always is.

When challenges arise, the first response of our hearts should be to call on the Lord. He's not a backup plan or a last resort; He's the One who sees the whole picture and has the perfect solution. Sometimes we lean too heavily on human advice, forgetting that God's wisdom far surpasses anything man can offer. Asking for help isn't wrong, but our first call should always be to the One who never fails.

People, no matter how well-intentioned, can't always follow through. They may lack the resources, insight, or ability to meet our needs. God, however, is always faithful. He promises to deliver us—not just eventually, but right on time. His rescue comes in ways that remind us He's in control, ways that strengthen our faith.

And when He delivers, it's not just for *our* benefit! God's deliverance in our lives points others to Him. When we share how He brought us through, it glorifies Him. It tells the world that our God is trustworthy, powerful, and good.

So, the next time trouble shows up, take a deep breath and go straight to God. Call on Him first. Let His faithfulness shine through in your life, and you'll see how He turns every challenge into an opportunity to glorify His name.

March 25

Therefore they stayed there a long time,
speaking boldly in the Lord, who was bearing witness to
the word of His grace, granting signs and wonders
to be done by their hands.

Acts 14:3

The apostles didn't shy away from sharing the truth, even when opposition arose. Their boldness wasn't based on their own abilities or charm but on the assurance that God was with them, proving His Word through miraculous signs and wonders. When we step out in faith, God always backs us up!

The miraculous is more than just something extraordinary—it's evidence. It's the living proof that the message of Jesus is real and powerful. When God grants us the ability to operate in His power, He's not just putting on a show. He's confirming the truth of His Word and His love. This should give us great confidence. When we share the Gospel, it's not all up to us to convince people. God shows up, demonstrating His grace in tangible ways that no argument can refute.

Miracles also have a unique way of capturing attention. They're like a divine billboard, turning hearts toward God. For those who are lost, the miraculous becomes a signpost pointing them to Jesus. It's not about glorifying the person through whom the miracle comes—it's all about glorifying God and drawing people into relationship with Him.

So, don't hold back. Share boldly, love freely, and trust God to confirm His message. As you step out in obedience, He'll show Himself faithful, working in ways that only He can. And when He does, lives will be changed, hearts will be softened, and His name will be glorified. Miracles are God's way of showing the world His incredible love and grace!

For whatever is born of God overcomes the world. And this is the victory that has overcome the world—our faith. Who is he who overcomes the world, but he who believes that Jesus is the Son of God.

1 John 5:4-5

Being an overcomer isn't just a distant dream or an ideal for someone more "spiritual" than you. It's your identity as a child of God. If you believe that Jesus is the Son of God, you've been born of God—and that makes you a world overcomer. You aren't trying to become one, striving to earn that status. It's already who you are because of what Jesus has done.

But how do we live like overcomers? By faith! Faith isn't some abstract concept; it's a deep trust in God's promises, His character, taking Him at His Word. It's *choosing* to believe His Word is true, even when the circumstances scream otherwise. Faith is the key that unlocks the victory already promised to you. It enables you to rise above the struggles and challenges that life throws your way.

Let's be honest—sometimes it feels like the world is winning! The challenges can be overwhelming, the problems relentless. But here's the good news: when it feels like you're being overcome, that's not the end of the story. It's a temporary, physical condition, not your spiritual position! As you stay rooted in faith, trusting that God's power is greater than any obstacle, victory will come.

This isn't about ignoring the hard stuff or pretending everything is fine. It's about knowing that your faith connects you to a God who is bigger than the struggle. So, don't give up. Keep believing. Keep declaring the truth of God's Word over your life. You were born to overcome, and through faith, you will!

March 27

Jesus Christ is the same yesterday, today, and forever.

Hebrews 13:8

J esus is unchanging, constant, and steady. His love, His power, and His will are as consistent as the rising sun. The same Jesus who walked the earth healing the sick, raising the dead, and restoring broken lives is the same Jesus who works in your life today. He hasn't changed His heart toward you or His desire to see you whole and thriving. When you read about His miracles in the Gospels, remember that His compassion and willingness to heal remain just as strong today as they were then.

From the beginning, God never intended for you to struggle with sickness. When He created you, His design was perfect—health and vitality were part of the plan. Though sin introduced brokenness into the world, God's heart for your well-being hasn't wavered. His Word is full of promises about your health because He still wants you to live in the fullness of the life He created for you. His intention for you to live in health wasn't a one-time idea—it's His eternal will.

With God, there's no guessing game. His motives are pure, His plans are good, and His faithfulness is unshakable! You don't have to wonder where you stand with Him or question His intentions. His consistency makes trusting Him simple and secure. You can see the proof of His heart throughout the Bible!

So, no matter what circumstances you face, His unchanging nature provides a firm foundation. You can rest in the assurance that He is for you, that He loves you, and that He desires good things for your life. Trust in His faithfulness and lean into the truth that He is the same yesterday, today, and forever.

When evening had come, they brought to Him many
who were demon-possessed. And He cast out the spirits
with a word, and healed all who were sick,
that it might be fulfilled which was spoken by Isaiah the
prophet, saying: "He Himself took our infirmities
And bore our sicknesses."

Matthew 8:16-17

The evening air buzzed with expectation as crowds brought their loved ones to Jesus. What did He do? With a single word, He cast out demons and healed every sickness. Every. Single. One. No exceptions, no conditions. His compassion wasn't selective, and His power wasn't limited. He extended His heart toward everyone!

This wasn't just an act of kindness; it was fulfillment in action. Isaiah's prophecy declared the Messiah would take our infirmities and bear our sicknesses. On the cross, Jesus didn't just carry the weight of sin; He also carried sickness and disease. Healing isn't extra—it's included in everything Jesus came to do for you.

Throughout Jesus' ministry, a clear pattern emerges: He taught about the kingdom of God and then healed the sick. Luke 4:40 says that at sunset, people brought all who were sick, and He healed them. Luke 9:11 shows Him welcoming the crowds, teaching them, and healing their needs. Again and again, the Gospels reveal His heart—*Jesus healed them all.*

Here's the amazing part: there's not one instance in the New Testament where someone came to Jesus for healing and He turned them away. Not one! And His heart for healing hasn't changed. What He did then, He still does today. If you're carrying sickness or pain, remember this: Jesus has already borne it for you. He is willing. He is able. Healing is part of the abundant life He came to bring! Lean into His promises, because He hasn't left anyone out—including you.

I will bring the blind by a way they did not know; I will lead them in paths they have not known. I will make darkness light before them, and crooked places straight. These things I will do for them, and not forsake them.

Isaiah 42:16

Sometimes life feels like stumbling through a maze with no map. You've probably been there—unsure of your next move, uncertain about what's ahead. It's easy to feel lost in the dark, like you're groping for direction but coming up empty. But God promises that He doesn't leave us in the dark. He lights the way, even when the path ahead seems hidden. His light isn't just a vague idea; it's real, personal, and available for you today.

Picture this: you're blindfolded, but someone you trust grabs your hand and guides you step by step. You don't know what's ahead, but they do, and their touch reassures you. That's how God leads us. Even when we can't see the path—or don't even know a path exists—He's already paved the way. He's not just pointing you in the right direction; He's walking with you, leading you like a loving guide. He knows the terrain, and He's taking you somewhere good.

But here's the key: you have to trust Him enough to take His hand. It's tempting to pull away and try to figure things out ourselves, but His way is better. He's the one who turns darkness into light and makes crooked places straight. When we let Him lead, we find peace, even in uncertainty.

Today, if you're feeling unsure or overwhelmed, pause. Take a deep breath and remind yourself that God hasn't left you to figure it all out on your own. Grab hold of His hand through prayer and trust. Let Him guide you. He knows the way, and He's got good things in store for you.

*That which is born of the flesh is flesh, and
that which is born of the Spirit is spirit.*

John 3:6

L ife is a mixture of the seen and the unseen, the tangible and the intangible. You might wake up every day and feel your physical body reminding you it needs coffee, or notice your mind sorting through the to-do list. But beneath all of that—deeper than flesh and mind—there's your spirit, the part of you that connects directly to God.

We're all born into this world with a body and a soul. The body gives us a way to interact with the world around us, and the soul—our mind, will, and emotions—shapes how we experience it. But there's another dimension to who we are, one that can't be measured or observed with physical tools. Our spirit is where the true essence of life exists, and it's also the part of us that longs for something eternal.

That's why Jesus talked about being "born again." It's not just a nice idea or a fresh start; it's the moment we come alive spiritually. While our first birth introduces us to the physical world, the second birth opens the door to relationship with God. And here's the incredible part: this spiritual birth doesn't just happen for the sake of eternity—it transforms how we live here and now. It's where peace, power, and purpose flow from, and it's how we align with God's plans.

If you've ever felt that something is missing or that life is more than just the everyday grind, that's your spirit calling out for connection with its Creator. When you say yes to Jesus, that connection is restored, and your spirit comes alive in a way that nothing else can match. The best part? Once you've been reborn, you're equipped to live from that spiritual reality every single day.

*And my speech and my preaching were not with
persuasive words of human wisdom,
but in demonstration of the Spirit and of power,
that your faith should not be in the wisdom of men
but in the power of God.*

1 Corinthians 2:4-5

Have you ever been in a conversation where you felt like you had to have the perfect response, a flawless argument, or an encyclopedia of facts at your fingertips to make your point? It's easy to think that a well-worded explanation is what really changes hearts. But as powerful as words can be, they don't come close to the kind of impact God's power can have when it shows up in real life.

Paul didn't count on polished speeches or persuasive language to get the job done. Instead, he leaned on the Spirit of God to demonstrate powerfully what words alone could never accomplish. Miracles, healing, peace that passes understanding—these expressions of God's power cut through any debate and touch the heart in a way no logical argument ever could. They show, beyond doubt, that God is real, and He is working.

When someone experiences God's power for themselves, it forms a foundation that no human logic can shake. It's one thing to be convinced by a clever argument; it's another thing entirely to encounter the living God and have your life transformed. This kind of persuasion isn't just impactful—it's eternal. Faith built on human wisdom will waver when circumstances change. But faith rooted in God's power stands firm through every storm.

So, the next time you're tempted to rely on fancy words or a well-rehearsed response, remember that the most effective witness isn't in what you say but in how God shows up. Let Him demonstrate His power through you and watch how hearts are transformed in ways you could never achieve on your own.

By which have been given to us exceedingly great and precious promises, that through these you may be partakers of the divine nature, having escaped the corruption that is in the world through lust.

2 Peter 1:4

God's promises are not just good—they're exceedingly great and precious. They aren't flimsy hopes or empty assurances but the foundation of a powerful, abundant life. Every word He speaks carries the full weight of His nature: faithful, unchanging, and overwhelmingly generous. These promises aren't just for encouragement; they are your access to a divine partnership with Him. When you grab hold of what He's said, you're not just surviving—you're thriving in the fullness of His provision, healing, and peace.

God's promises open the door for you to partake of His divine nature. Think about that for a moment. You're not stuck living by the world's standards or limited by its brokenness. The divine nature is your inheritance—it's your right as a child of God to walk in His strength, wisdom, and victory. When the world shouts chaos, you can live in calm assurance. When lack seems certain, you can declare abundance. His nature infuses your spirit, giving you what you need to rise above every challenge!

The corruption of the world doesn't get the final say in your life. Greed, fear, sickness, and strife—these are not your inheritance. God's promises pull you out of the grip of this broken system and plant you firmly in His kingdom. Through His Spirit, you have access to everything you need to live above the noise and negativity. You've been set apart to experience His goodness daily, not just occasionally. So, lean into those exceedingly great promises today. Declare them over your life, believe in their power, and watch as His divine nature transforms your everyday life!

April 2

Then Amaziah said to the man of God, "But what shall we do about the 100 talents which I have given to the troops of Israel?" And the man of God answered, "The Lord is able to give you much more than this."

2 Chronicles 25:9

Mistakes. We've all made them—some small, some big, and some that hit our wallets so hard we feel the sting for weeks, months, or even years. Amaziah knew what that felt like. He shelled out a fortune to hire troops, only to realize it was a terrible decision. Imagine the sinking feeling when the man of God told him to cut his losses and send them packing. That money was gone. But instead of leaving him in despair, the prophet offered a powerful truth: God is able to give you *much more* than this!

We're not perfect. Amaziah hadn't sought God's guidance in the first place, and that lack of wisdom cost him. Maybe you've been there, too—making financial decisions that seemed smart at the time, only to realize later they were anything but! While God doesn't give us a free pass to be careless, He also doesn't leave us stuck in regret. His grace is bigger than our mistakes, even the expensive ones.

God's ability to restore isn't limited by the size of our failures. He doesn't look at your financial blunder and think, *Well, that's too much for Me to handle*. No, He's already factored your imperfections into His plan. That's why we needed a Savior in the first place! Jesus stepped in because we couldn't do it perfectly, and God's answer to every mess is His unshakable grace.

So, if you're staring at a financial misstep and wondering how you'll recover, take a breath. Surrender it to the One who isn't surprised by your situation and trust Him to provide—not just enough to make up the loss, but much more than you could have imagined!

And these signs will follow those who believe: In My name they will cast out demons; they will speak with new tongues; they will take up serpents, and if they drink anything deadly, it will by no means hurt them; they will lay hands on the sick, and they will recover.

Mark 16:17-18

As believers, we're called to live a life where the supernatural becomes natural—where miracles, healings, and divine protection are the norm. Jesus made it clear that these signs are meant to follow us, not just pastors or evangelists, but anyone who believes. They're like a heavenly trail we leave behind, evidence of God working in and through us.

To step into this reality, saturate your heart and mind with the Word of God. Think about how Jesus ministered—His compassion, authority, and confidence in the Father's power. Picture the apostles boldly laying hands on the sick, speaking life, and seeing transformation. The more you meditate on these accounts, the more you'll see yourself in that role. Imagine praying for someone and watching their pain dissolve or boldly declaring freedom over someone bound by fear.

And remember, Jesus promised we would do even greater works than He did (John 14:12). Let that sink in—greater works! Not because we're more qualified, but because His Spirit empowers us. There's no limit to what God can do through a believing heart. So, dream bigger, step out in faith, and expect to see God show up in powerful ways.

Today, let this truth embolden you. You're not called to just survive life; you're called to live it with power and purpose. Signs and wonders aren't just for someone else—they're for you! Believe, step out, and watch what God will do.

Most assuredly, I say to you, he who believes in me, the works that I do he will do also; and greater works than these he will do, because I go to My Father.

John 14:12

I t's easy to read a verse like this and feel overwhelmed. Greater works? Us? How is that even possible? But Jesus meant what He said. When we truly believe in Him, we're not only invited into His miraculous works but empowered to exceed them. That's not about one-upping Jesus—it's about stepping into the fullness of what He's provided.

The key lies in what Jesus did after His resurrection. He didn't just ascend to heaven and leave us to figure things out on our own. He sent the Holy Spirit to live in us, equipping us with the same power that raised Him from the dead. Think about that for a moment. The same Spirit that hovered over the waters at creation, that empowered Jesus to heal the sick, raise the dead, and calm storms, now lives in you!

This isn't about striving or trying to muster up faith in your own strength. It's about partnership. The Holy Spirit isn't a distant force; He's your ever-present helper. When you believe in Jesus and lean into the Holy Spirit's leading, His power works through you. Suddenly, the impossible becomes possible—lives are transformed, the sick are healed, and miracles flow, not because of you, but because of Him.

So, don't let doubt hold you back. Jesus promised this. Step out in faith, trust the Holy Spirit within you, and watch as He works through your hands, your words, and your life. The "greater works" aren't just for pastors or missionaries—they're for *every* believer. That includes you. God has placed His Spirit in you for a reason, and the world is waiting to see Him move through you.

April 5

For we walk by faith, and not by sight.

2 Corinthians 5:7

Faith is meant to guide us, not what we see or feel in the moment. Living by faith means trusting in what God has said, even when circumstances around us seem to shout otherwise. It's easy to let the natural world influence our decisions—what we can see, hear, and touch feels tangible and real. But God calls us to something higher. He calls us to trust Him, to let His Word direct our steps instead of what we perceive in the here and now.

Sometimes, God's instructions may not make sense. His ways often defy human logic and worldly wisdom. That's because His perspective is eternal, far beyond what we can grasp in our limited understanding. The world might call it foolish to forgive someone who's wronged you deeply, or to give generously when you're already stretched thin. But walking in the Spirit means aligning our lives with His wisdom, not our fleshly instincts or the opinions of others.

To live this way, we need to change how we see things! Instead of focusing on the obstacles in front of us or the storms we're facing, we can begin to see with spiritual eyes. What does God see? What is His plan in this situation? Faith invites us to step back and view life from His perspective—a perspective filled with hope, promise, and victory!

As you walk through today, practice tuning out the noise of circumstances and focusing on what God is saying. Trust His Word, follow His leading, and watch how He shapes your steps with purpose and power. Faith may not always feel easy, but it will always lead you into the abundant life He has promised.

April 6

The Lord is not slack concerning His promise,
as some count slackness, but is longsuffering toward us,
not willing that any should perish but that
all should come to repentance.

2 Peter 3:9

It's easy to feel like God's timeline is taking forever. When we look at the world and all its chaos, we might find ourselves thinking, *Lord, are You coming back soon, or what?* Apparently, we're not the first ones to feel this way. Even in Peter's day, people were questioning why Jesus hadn't returned yet.

Peter had a great explanation for the delay. It's not that God is slow or has forgotten His promise. No, it's the opposite. His timing reflects His incredible love and patience. He's holding back because He's giving every person every possible chance to turn to Him.

God's heart is for everyone. He's not sitting back, crossing His arms, and waiting for people to figure things out on their own. His desire is for all of humanity—every single soul—to come into relationship with Him. He's not just offering a chance to escape judgment; He's offering eternal life, a vibrant relationship, and an eternity spent with Him. He's not slow because He's uncaring. He's patient because He cares that much.

This perspective shifts how we see delays, doesn't it? What might feel like slowness to us is really an extension of God's grace. He's working, loving, and waiting, not wanting anyone to miss out on what He's offering. And while He waits, He's inviting us to join Him in sharing that same love and message with the people around us. After all, His delay isn't just for the world out there—it's for someone close to you, too. Let's make the most of this time He's giving us!

He also brought them out with silver and gold,
and there was none feeble among His tribes.

Psalm 105:37

When God led the Israelites out of Egypt, it wasn't just freedom from slavery—it was an overwhelming victory! They didn't sneak away with nothing but their freedom; they marched out with silver and gold, the riches of the nation that had oppressed them for generations. Imagine the astonishment as they left, arms full of treasure, heads held high. God didn't just set them free; He made sure they were abundantly provided for!

But that's not all. Among over a million people, not a single one was weak or feeble. Picture the elderly walking steadily, their steps firm and sure. Every child, strong and vibrant, ready for the journey ahead. No one lagging behind. No one left out. This wasn't just a coincidence or a stroke of luck—it was God's supernatural provision, restoring what slavery had taken from them. Every body made whole, every spirit revived. What a powerful testimony to His goodness!

The same God who delivered the Israelites promises us prosperity and health through Jesus, the perfect Lamb of God. His sacrifice opened the door for us to live abundantly, not just scraping by, but thriving in every area of life. Just as the Israelites experienced supernatural restoration, we too can walk in the fullness of His provision.

So today, take heart! You serve a God who brings freedom, healing, and abundance. He is the same yesterday, today, and forever. Whatever has been stolen from you—peace, strength, finances—God is more than able to restore it. Walk confidently in His promises, knowing that He has already made the way for your victory.

April 8

He did not waver at the promise of God through unbelief,
but was strengthened in faith, giving glory to God.

Romans 4:20

Faith isn't about waiting until everything in life is perfect—it's about standing firm when it isn't. Sometimes, the promises of God seem distant, overshadowed by the challenges we face. That's when unbelief tries to creep in. It's what happens when we let the weight of circumstances drown out the voice of God's promises. But here's the good news: you don't have to give unbelief a foothold!

Faith is the antidote. It's not passive or timid; it's active and bold. Faith isn't just believing that God can; it's being fully convinced that He will. And here's the secret: faith grows when we praise God, giving Him glory. Worship is like fuel for your faith—it shifts your focus off the problem and onto the Problem-Solver. When we declare who God is, we remind ourselves of His power, faithfulness, and love. That reminder strengthens our hearts to stand firm, no matter what.

The real test of faith isn't praising God *after* you see the breakthrough—it's praising Him *before*. Praising God in advance says, "Lord, I trust You completely. Your promise is as good as done." It's a declaration of confidence, a way of saying, "I know You're working, even if I can't see it yet." This kind of faith brings heaven to earth, positioning you to receive what God has promised.

Today, whatever you're believing for, take a moment to praise God. Speak out His promises. Thank Him as though it's already done, because it is! Let your praise stir your faith, pushing unbelief to the side. You'll find that as you lift your eyes to Him, His strength becomes your strength—and faith makes the impossible possible.

So Jesus answered and said to them,
"Have faith in God."

Mark 11:22

When it comes to facing the mountains in your life, it's tempting to overthink your role in the process. You might wonder, *Did I say the right thing? Am I believing hard enough? Did I pray the right way?* But here's the truth: it's not about how perfectly you perform. Your authority to speak to the mountain doesn't come from your flawless Christian behavior. It comes from the One in whom you place your faith.

Doubt creeps in when we focus on ourselves—our abilities, our shortcomings, our track record. But when your faith is in God, not yourself, doubt has no foothold. It's not about getting it all right; it's about trusting the One who never fails.

We're human, and we're going to mess up. It's inevitable. But God doesn't mess up. Ever. He's steady, unchanging, and perfectly reliable. That's why it's so important to place your faith solely in Him. Other people, no matter how well-intentioned, will let you down at some point. Systems and leaders, even the ones that seem trustworthy, can falter. But God never will. When you anchor your trust in Him, you're standing on unshakable ground.

So, whatever mountain you're speaking to today—whether it's a financial challenge, a health issue, a broken relationship, or an impossible decision—remember where your faith belongs. It's not in your ability to move that mountain; it's in God's power to do what He promised. Keep your eyes on Him, trust His faithfulness, and watch what happens when you simply believe.

April 10

I call heaven and earth as witnesses today against you,
that I have set before you life and death,
blessing and cursing; therefore choose life, that both you
and your descendants may live.

Deuteronomy 30:19

In life, we're faced with choices all the time, but some choices are bigger than others. There's one particular choice that stands above the rest, and it's a decision that affects not just you, but those around you and even future generations. The good news? God has made it crystal clear, and He's even given us the answer!

God has given us the freedom to choose—life or death, blessing or cursing—and He encourages us to choose life. Now, this isn't a test where you have to guess the right answer; He's already told you what to choose! But here's the catch: choosing life isn't something that just happens by accident. It's a decision we make daily, with our thoughts, our words, and our actions. Every time you speak life and think positively in alignment with God's Word, you're choosing life. When you focus on His promises and trust in His plan, you're choosing to walk in His blessing.

Abundant life is available to us, but it's up to us to embrace it! You can either dwell on negative situations and give in to despair, or you can choose to speak life over those challenges, trusting that God's Word will always lead you to victory. It's all about what you believe. If you believe God's promises, you'll begin to see them unfold in your life. You'll find the strength to overcome whatever comes your way, knowing that His promises are sure and He is faithful to bring them to pass.

So, today, make the choice to believe in God's Word, receive His promises, and choose life. It's the best decision you can ever make, not just for you, but for generations to come!

Submit yourselves therefore to God.
Resist the devil, and he will flee from you.

James 4:7

True submission to God is an act of trust, a way of saying, "God, You know better than I do." It means stepping off the throne of our own hearts and allowing Him to take His rightful place as Lord. When you submit to God, you're choosing to align yourself with what He says, rather than what your circumstances, emotions, or fears might be saying. It's saying, "God, I trust You. I agree with Your Word over everything else."

That kind of agreement is powerful. It means letting go of the need to have it all figured out and trusting that His truth is higher, stronger, and more stable than your own understanding. It's surrendering your plans not because you've failed, but because you believe His are better.

Humility plays a big role here. It's not thinking less of yourself—it's choosing to think rightly according to God's truth. When He says you're healed, whole, forgiven, and strong, agreeing with Him is an act of humility! It's strength under control, rooted in the unshakable foundation of His Word.

When you come into agreement with God and stand your ground against the enemy, the devil has to flee. Not because you yelled louder—but because you stood firm in truth. Agreement with God disarms the enemy every time!

So today, make the choice to submit—to agree with what God has already said about you and your situation. Resist the lies, the fear, and the pressure. And watch what happens when truth takes over. Peace follows. Victory comes! Because there's no safer, stronger place to stand than in full agreement with Him.

*And the Word became flesh and dwelt among us,
and we beheld His glory, the glory as of the only
begotten of the Father, full of grace and truth.*

John 1:14

God's Word isn't just a collection of stories or ancient texts—it's alive and powerful because it's directly tied to Jesus Himself. When John opens his Gospel, he takes us back to the very beginning, before time as we know it even existed. He reveals that Jesus, the Word, was there with God and was God. Everything we see, from the stars in the sky to the ground beneath our feet, was spoken into being through Him. That's the power of the Word.

But here's where it gets personal. The same Word that brought the universe into existence didn't stay distant or detached. Jesus, the Word, came down to live among us, taking on flesh and walking through the highs and lows of life. He didn't come just to observe or critique; He came to rescue, heal, and bring us into relationship with Him.

When you read the Bible, it's not just ink on paper—it's Jesus speaking directly to your heart. His words carry the same creative power that formed the world. Think about that. When you declare God's Word over your life, you're releasing that same life-giving, transformative power into your circumstances!

So, if you're facing challenges today, remember that the Word isn't just a concept or a book; it's Jesus, alive and active in your life. Speak His promises boldly. Just as the Word created the universe, it has the power to create hope, healing, and victory in your world. Let the truth of who He is fill your heart with confidence—Jesus, the Word, is with you, working in and through you, every step of the way.

*So shall My word be that goes forth from my My mouth;
it shall not return to me void, but it shall accomplish
what I please, and it shall prosper in the thing
for which I sent it.*

Isaiah 55:11

God's Word is powerful. When God speaks, His Word is alive and full of purpose. It never fizzles out or gets lost along the way—it always accomplishes what He intends. The Word of God never fails. Not sometimes. Not maybe. Not "hopefully, if all the stars align." It *never* fails! That's a bold promise, and God always keeps His Word.

When you declare His Word, it's like firing an arrow straight at a target. It doesn't take a detour or waste time—it goes exactly where it's sent and starts working immediately. Maybe you've been praying over a situation for what feels like forever, wondering if your words are just evaporating into thin air. Take heart: God's Word is busy doing its job, even if you can't see the results just yet!

Here's the best part: God's Word doesn't just barely scrape by to fulfill its mission. It prospers. Think about that! It thrives, flourishes, and brings abundance wherever it goes. Picture a seed growing into a thriving, fruit-filled tree—it's not just surviving; it's thriving. That's what God's Word does in your life when you plant it deep in your heart and speak it out in faith.

So, don't let doubt creep in or silence your voice. Speak His Word with boldness and confidence. Know that every promise He's spoken over you is working behind the scenes, producing life, healing, and victory. Trust that it's not only doing what it's meant to do but is flourishing beyond what you can imagine. His Word never fails, and neither will He! Keep speaking, keep believing, and watch His Word prosper in your life.

...For I am the Lord who heals you.

Exodus 15:26

God's nature is rich with love and compassion, and one of the most beautiful revelations of His character is that He is your Healer. When you think of Him, it's not just about what He can do; it's about who He is. Healing isn't just an action He takes; it's an extension of His very identity. That's a game-changer for how we see Him and relate to Him.

The Hebrew word *rapha* paints a vivid picture of what it means for God to be your Healer. It means so much more than a simple fix for what's broken. It's about being restored, repaired, and made whole in every sense—physically, emotionally, and spiritually. He's not merely applying a bandage to your wounds. Instead, He's working to bring complete restoration, like a skilled physician who sees beyond the symptoms to the root of the issue.

God doesn't bring sickness to teach you a lesson or test your faith. That's not His nature. He is Healer, not harm-bringer! He is a loving Father, not an abusive parent. No good father would bring harm to his children, even to try to teach them a lesson! God's desire is to see you thriving, whole, and walking in the fullness of life He's prepared for you. Every time you reach out to Him in faith, you're connecting with the One whose very essence is healing and restoration.

Today, let this truth sink deep into your heart: the One who created you knows how to make you whole again. He is your Healer—always has been, always will be. Trust Him with whatever needs repair in your life and expect His healing touch to bring you the restoration you need.

...Most assuredly, I say to you, whatever you ask the Father in My name He will give you. Until now you have asked nothing in My name. Ask, and you will receive, that your joy may be full.

John 16:23b-24

God delights in giving good gifts to His children. When Jesus said that the Father would give whatever we ask in His name, He wasn't making an empty promise. He was revealing the heart of a loving Father who is ready to respond to His kids. But here's the thing—before we can receive, we have to ask! Asking isn't about informing God of our needs as if He doesn't know them. It's about building trust, surrendering to His will, and recognizing Him as our source.

Asking requires faith. It's a step of confidence, saying, "God, I know You hear me, and I believe You'll answer." Sometimes we hesitate to ask, thinking we're bothering God or doubting that He'll come through. But Jesus invites us to be bold! He reassures us that when we come to the Father in His name, we have His authority backing us up. The Father loves to answer those prayers because they align with His heart for us.

And when we see His answers come to fruition it brings Him glory! Receiving from God doesn't just meet our needs—it fills us with gratitude and strengthens our relationship with Him. It's a reminder of His goodness and faithfulness. Every answered prayer becomes a testimony of His love and power, a beacon to others of just how wonderful He is.

So, what's on your heart today? What do you need? Don't hold back. Ask the Father boldly, trusting Him to respond. Then watch as He not only meets your needs but fills you with the joy that comes from seeing His hand at work in your life. And as you rejoice, remember: your joy brings Him glory.

*Meditate on these things; give yourself entirely to them,
that your progress may be evident to all.*

1 Timothy 4:15

The Word of God is like a seed—it holds incredible potential, but it needs to be planted to grow. When you take time to meditate on His Word, letting it sink deep into your heart, it begins to transform you from the inside out. This process may not be instant, but it is guaranteed. Just like a seed doesn't sprout overnight, the Word takes root and begins to grow, producing real and lasting change in your life.

This growth, though, doesn't happen by accident. You have to give yourself over to it. Make it a priority. Let God's Word take center stage in your day. Instead of squeezing it into the cracks of your schedule, let it *shape* your schedule. When you allow the Word to guide your decisions, conversations, and even your thoughts, you're giving it the space it needs to work in your life. It's not about perfection; it's about surrender. Let His truth replace the lies you've believed. Let His promises overshadow your doubts.

As you stay faithful to the Word, others will notice! The changes in your life will be undeniable. People will see the peace you walk in, the joy that radiates from you, and the strength that carries you through challenges. Your progress will be evident—not just in what you say, but in how you live.

It's not about drawing attention to yourself, but about reflecting the goodness and power of God. Stay faithful. Stay rooted. The transformation is already happening, and the evidence will speak for itself!

I shall not die, but live, and declare
the works of the Lord.

Psalm 118:17

There's amazing power in the words we speak—more than we often realize. Our words have the ability to shape our circumstances and even impact the course of our lives. God has given us the authority to speak life, and when we align our words with His promises, things begin to shift in the spiritual and physical realms.

No matter what challenges you're facing—sickness, fear, or any other obstacle—you can boldly declare, "I will live and not die!" This isn't just wishful thinking; it's a faith-filled proclamation of God's truth. He has promised you life, healing, and wholeness. When you speak those words, you're not only agreeing with God but also releasing His power into your situation. The same God who breathed life into Adam is the one who backs your words when they align with His Word.

Healing is more than just for your benefit—it's an opportunity to glorify God. When we experience His healing and restoration, it becomes a testimony of His goodness and faithfulness. Declaring His works doesn't have to be complicated or formal; it's as simple as telling someone, "God healed me. He showed up in my life." Your testimony can inspire hope and faith in others, showing them that what God has done for you, He can do for them too.

So today, let your words be filled with life. Speak healing, speak hope, and speak the promises of God over yourself and those around you. Let your testimony shine as evidence of a God who still works miracles and is faithful to His Word. You are living proof of His power—so declare it boldly!

April 18

Let us hold fast the confession of our hope without wavering, for He who promised is faithful.

Hebrews 10:23

God's faithfulness is the rock on which we stand. It's not about how strong our hope is or how determined we feel in the moment—it's about Him. He is steady when we are shaky. He is unwavering when we feel like crumbling. His promises are not based on our ability to receive them, but on His absolute commitment to fulfill them. That's why we can confidently declare what He has spoken, even when circumstances scream otherwise.

Think about it—God has never broken a promise. Every single word He has spoken is backed by His unchanging nature. If He said He would provide, He will. If He said He would heal, He will. If He said He would bring breakthrough, He will. There is no uncertainty with God. He doesn't change His mind, He doesn't forget, and He certainly doesn't fail!

That's why we don't quit. We hold fast. We keep speaking His Word, not because we're trying to convince Him to be faithful, but because we are reminding ourselves that He already is. The enemy wants nothing more than to get us to waver—to question, to doubt, to back off. But we stand firm. Even when we don't see the answer right away, even when it feels like nothing is happening, we refuse to be moved.

So don't give up. Keep declaring God's promises over your life. Keep believing. Keep standing. Not because of how strong you are, but because of how faithful He is. He who promised is faithful, and He will do it!

April 19

Fear not, for I am with you; be not dismayed, for I am your God. I will strengthen you, yes, I will help you, I will uphold you with My righteous right hand.

Isaiah 41:10

There's a reason the Bible tells us over and over again not to be afraid. Fear tries to creep in when we face uncertainty, challenges, or the unknown. But God makes it clear—fear has no place in the life of a believer! He is faithful to fulfill every promise He has spoken over you, so there is absolutely nothing to fear. His Word is more reliable than anything you can see, feel, or experience.

When God says He will help you, He means it. He's not just giving you a pat on the back and sending you on your way—He's right there, holding you up with His strength. Every single one of His promises is a resounding "Yes!" (2 Corinthians 1:20). You don't have to wonder if He'll come through for you; you can be confident that He already has. His help, His strength, and His power are already at work in your life.

Fear is not your inheritance. God didn't give you a spirit of fear—He gave you power, love, and a sound mind (2 Timothy 1:7)! That means you are not weak, abandoned, or alone. You are strong in Him. His perfect love drives out every trace of fear (1 John 4:18). The more you grasp how deeply He loves you, the less room fear has in your heart. It loses its grip when you truly know that God will never fail you, never leave you hanging, and never let you down.

So, take a deep breath. Stand firm. No matter what comes your way, you are not alone. The Almighty God is holding you up, strengthening you, and helping you every step of the way. Fear doesn't stand a chance against that kind of love!

These things I have spoken to you, that in Me you may have peace. In the world you will have tribulation; but be of good cheer, I have overcome the world.

John 16:33

J esus never promised we would avoid the storms of life, but He did make it clear that we could have peace in the middle of them. He has already overcome the world, and because of that, we can stand firm no matter what comes our way.

The disciples learned this lesson firsthand when they found themselves caught in a violent storm on the Sea of Galilee. Even though they had spent time with Jesus, watched Him perform miracles, and heard His teachings, fear still gripped them. They panicked, thinking they were going to drown. Meanwhile, Jesus—completely unshaken—was asleep! When they woke Him in terror, He calmed the storm with a word. Then, He turned to them, questioning their faith. They had forgotten two critical things: Who was in the boat with them and the authority they had been given.

Jesus knew the storm was coming, yet He had already declared, "Let us cross over to the other side." His word was enough to guarantee their safe passage. The same is true for you. If God has spoken a promise over your life, no storm can stop it from coming to pass. Challenges may arise, but they don't have power to win, unless you allow them to.

Jesus has already given you authority to overcome. You don't have to beg Him to calm the storm; He has given *you* the ability to speak to it yourself! When difficulties come, don't panic. Stand in faith, knowing that God is in your boat, His promises are sure, and victory is already yours. Storms will come, but they don't get to define you. You are an overcomer!

For to be carnally minded is death, but to be spiritually minded is life and peace.

Romans 8:6

It's easy to get caught up in what's right in front of us. Bills stack up, the doctor's report looks grim, relationships get messy, and emotions run high. When we focus all our attention on these things, it's like we're tuning in to a radio station that only plays fear, stress, and doubt on repeat. That's what it means to be carnally minded—letting the natural world dictate our thoughts, emotions, and decisions.

The problem is, the natural world is unstable. One moment, things look fine; the next, chaos breaks out. If we base our mindset on what our five senses tell us, we're in for a rollercoaster of uncertainty! But there's a better way.

Being spiritually minded doesn't mean ignoring reality; it means choosing to put more weight on God's truth than on our circumstances. The world says sickness is the final word, but God says He is our Healer. The bank account says "not enough," but God says He is more than enough. Feelings say, "You're alone," but God says, "I will never leave you."

Faith isn't about denying what's happening—it's about choosing what voice you'll believe. Spiritual-minded people lock their focus on the Word of God and His promises, regardless of what their eyes see or their emotions scream. They live from the inside out, letting God's truth shape their reality rather than letting reality shape their faith.

Peace and life aren't found in perfect circumstances. They're found in trusting the One who never changes. So today, make a decision. What's going to have the final say in your heart—your circumstances or God's Word? Choose life. Choose peace. Choose to be spiritually minded.

Rejoice in the Lord always. Again I will say, rejoice!

Philippians 4:4

L ife can be unpredictable, but one thing remains constant: we are called to rejoice. Not just when things are going well, but always. Jesus made it clear—cheer isn't a result of perfect circumstances; it's a choice we make in the middle of them. When He told His disciples they could be of good cheer, He wasn't ignoring the troubles they would face. He was giving them a powerful key to overcome.

God wouldn't command us to do something that was out of reach. If He says to rejoice always, then it must be possible! That means joy isn't dependent on what's happening around you—it's rooted in what's happening inside you. Joy is a supernatural force, anchored in the unshakable truth of who God is and what He's done for you. You can rejoice in the fact that He loves you, that He is faithful, and that He's already secured your victory.

Rejoicing isn't just a nice idea—it's a weapon! Nehemiah 8:10 says, *"The joy of the Lord is your strength."* That means joy isn't just a feeling; it's a source of power. It strengthens you, giving you the endurance to stand firm, the clarity to see God's perspective, and the confidence to move forward in faith.

The enemy knows that if he can steal your joy, he can steal your strength and weaken you. But when you choose to rejoice, even in the face of difficulty, you cut off his ability to influence your emotions, your decisions, and your life.

So, no matter what today brings, make the choice to rejoice. It's not about denying reality—it's about declaring a greater one: God is with you, He is for you, and His joy is your strength!

April 23

*For the word of God is living and powerful, and sharper
than any two-edged sword, piercing even to the division
of soul and spirit, and of joints and marrow, and is a
discerner of the thoughts and intents of the heart.*

Hebrews 4:12

There's something incredible about those moments when a scripture suddenly jumps off the page and straight into your heart. It's a feeling similar to being stabbed—but in a good way! You've probably experienced this—maybe in a church service, during your quiet time, or even in a random moment when a verse comes to mind and it hits you deep. That's because the heart—the core of who you are—isn't just your spirit or your soul; it's the unique connection of both. And the Word of God is sharp enough to cut right to the center of it.

The Bible isn't just ink on paper—it's alive. It carries power beyond human words because it is God-breathed, carrying His wisdom, His love, and His direction for our lives. That's why, when you hear a *rhema* word—a specific, timely word from God—it can shake you, change you, or confirm something you already sensed deep inside. It's not just a nice thought or an inspiring phrase; it's God Himself speaking directly to your situation.

God's Word is His tool for revealing truth. It doesn't just skim the surface—it cuts straight through to the deepest places, exposing what's really going on inside us. Maybe it encourages you, maybe it corrects you, maybe it gives you the clarity you've been needing. Either way, it's always working, always transforming, and always leading you closer to Him. So, lean in, listen, and let the living Word do its powerful work in your heart today.

April 24

Every good gift and every perfect gift is from above, and comes down from the Father of lights, with whom there is no variation or shadow of turning.

James 1:17

There's a lot of good in our lives that we take for granted. We celebrate when things go right, enjoy the blessings around us, and sometimes chalk it all up to hard work, good timing, or even just luck. In fact, there are likely countless times when God has provided for us or kept us safe without us even realizing it! But the truth is, every good thing—every blessing, every moment of favor, every bit of joy—is a gift straight from the hand of God. It's not just coincidence. It's Him.

Too often, we focus on what we lack rather than what we've been given. We pray for provision, for healing, for breakthrough, and when it happens, we're thrilled—but do we always stop to recognize where it truly came from? Giving God glory for the good things in our lives should be second nature, not an afterthought. When we shift our perspective to see His fingerprints on everything—from the roof over our heads to the relationships that uplift us—we cultivate gratitude and faith.

God has never changed, and He never will. He's not moody or unpredictable, handing out blessings one day and withholding them the next. He is consistently good, loving, and always generous toward His children. When we truly believe that, we stop questioning whether He'll come through for us. We stop wondering if He's holding out on us. Instead, we trust that His goodness is constant, that His heart is for us, and that His gifts—both big and small—are a reflection of who He is.

Take a moment today to recognize the good in your life and give credit where it's due. Whether it's the air in your lungs, a kind word from a friend, or a miracle breakthrough, every good and perfect gift is from Him!

Now this is the confidence that we have in Him, that if we ask anything according to His will, He hears us. And if we know He hears us, whatever we ask, we know that we have the petitions that we have asked of Him.

1 John 5:14-15

Prayer isn't a guessing game. It's not about crossing our fingers and hoping God hears us. When we pray according to His will, we can be absolutely sure—100% confident—that He is listening. This means we don't have to wonder if our words are reaching heaven or if God is paying attention. He is, and He cares deeply about what we bring before Him.

So how do we know we're praying His will? It's actually simple: pray His Word! The Bible isn't just a collection of ancient writings; it's God's will in written form. Every promise for healing, provision, restoration, and victory is a declaration of what He desires for us. When we take those promises and make them our prayers, we can be certain we are in perfect alignment with what God already wants to do in our lives. His Word is our foundation, and when we stand on it, we are unshakable.

And if He hears us—which He does—He always answers! There's no need to second-guess or wonder if He'll follow through. He is faithful to every promise He has made. The answer might not always come in the way we expect or on our timeline, but it will come. Our job isn't to figure out the "how" or "when"—it's simply to trust that God is who He says He is and will do what He said He would do.

Pray boldly. Pray confidently. Pray in the Spirit, too! Speak His promises over your life, knowing that He hears you and is already at work bringing them to pass.

*For You will light my lamp; the Lord my God
will enlighten my darkness.*

Psalm 18:28

There are times in life when everything feels dim—like you're fumbling around, trying to find your way but coming up empty. Maybe it's the weight of uncertainty, the sting of disappointment, or just an overwhelming sense of not knowing what to do next. That feeling of being in the dark can seem real, but the good news is, you're not left there! God is your light. Not just a flickering candle struggling to stay lit, but a steady, unwavering source of illumination that drives out every shadow.

When God says He will bring light to your situation, He means it. His light isn't dim; it's powerful! When it shows up, darkness has no choice but to disappear. Just like when you flip on a light switch in a dark room, the shadows don't argue or slowly fade away—they're gone instantly. That's what happens when God's truth, wisdom, and presence invade your life. Whatever confusion, despair, or fear has tried to cloud your mind *has* to go.

His light doesn't just expose what's wrong; it reveals what's hidden. He uncovers solutions, gives wisdom in decisions, and shines clarity on things that once seemed impossible to figure out. He's not leaving you to wander aimlessly. He lights your path, guiding each step, making sure you don't stumble.

If you're feeling stuck in the dark today, don't let it convince you that you have to stay there. God is faithful to His promise. Ask Him for light, and He will shine it exactly where you need it most. Darkness doesn't get the final say—His light does.

And you shall remember the Lord your God,
for it is He who gives you power to get wealth,
that He may establish His covenant which He swore
to your fathers, as it is this day.

Deuteronomy 8:18

God's plan for your prosperity isn't some last-minute idea—it's been part of His covenant since the beginning. When He promised to bless the Israelites, it wasn't just spiritual riches—He meant real, tangible increase. Their crops flourished, their livestock multiplied, and they lived in abundance because His blessing was on them.

But let's be real—He didn't drop bags of gold into their tents or make manna rain down every day forever. Instead, He gave them the power to create wealth—wisdom to manage resources, strength to work their fields, and divine strategies to increase. The same principle applies today. God doesn't randomly make money appear in your bank account, but He does give you insight, creativity, and the ability to generate increase.

Here's the best part: the covenant didn't end with the Israelites. When Jesus went to the cross, He secured an even *greater* covenant for you! God made a promise with His Son, and because of that, you are now part of an unbreakable agreement. His desire is to prosper you—not just for your own comfort, but as a testimony to the world. When you walk in divine increase, it's proof that God's Word is true, that His covenant is real, and that He is faithful to His promises.

So don't shrink back from believing for prosperity. God isn't trying to withhold from you—He's empowering you! Trust in His covenant, listen for His wisdom, and step into the blessing He's already made available. You have the power to get wealth, and that power comes straight from Him.

Trust in the Lord forever, for in Yah,
the Lord, is everlasting strength.

Isaiah 26:4

S trength is something everyone needs, yet so often, we look for it in the wrong places. Some rely on their own abilities, others on relationships, money, or status. But all of these things can fail. This verse reminds us that the only source of true, unfailing strength is God Himself.

The word *trust* here implies a firm confidence, a complete reliance on God's faithfulness. It's not a fleeting emotion but a deliberate choice to lean on Him in all circumstances. Proverbs 3:5-6 echoes this, saying, *"Trust in the Lord with all your heart, and lean not on your own understanding."* When we stop depending on our own strength and fully rely on Him, we step into a life of peace, security, and abundance. Trusting God is not just for emergencies; it's meant to be our daily posture.

The phrase *everlasting strength* comes from the Hebrew word *tzur*, which means *rock* or *fortress*. This paints a picture of God as our unshakable foundation. Unlike worldly sources of strength that fade, His strength never diminishes. Psalm 18:2 declares, *"The Lord is my rock and my fortress and my deliverer."* No matter what comes against you, He is your immovable source of power and protection. He is the tower you can run to when the enemy comes knocking.

Are you feeling weary? Do the pressures of life seem overwhelming? Shift your focus from your own ability to God's unlimited strength. He does not expect you to carry the weight of life alone. When you lean on Him, you will find endurance beyond your own capacity. Trust in Him—not just today, but forever. His strength is more than enough!

*You will show me the path of life; in your
presence is fullness of joy; at your right hand
are pleasures forevermore.*

Psalm 16:11

Knowing where you are seated changes everything. Jesus isn't standing, pacing, or stressing—He's seated at the right hand of the Father, in a position of authority and rest. And here's the incredible part: you're seated with Him! That means you have access to everything He has—peace, joy, power, and victory—right now.

Too often, we think of joy and fulfillment as things we have to wait for, something reserved for heaven. But the truth is, God's presence is here with us, and with Him comes fullness of joy—not partial, not occasional, but *fullness*. The world might tell you that joy is found in circumstances, in success, or in the approval of others, but real joy comes from knowing who you are in Christ and where you are seated.

Think about it—if you're seated with Jesus, then you have access to everything in His kingdom. That means "pleasures forevermore" aren't just for eternity; they're for today. Healing, peace, wisdom, provision—these aren't things you have to strive for; they're already yours in Him.

So, how do you experience this kind of life? The same way you receive every promise from God—by faith. You don't have to wait until you feel it or see it; you take hold of it now. Instead of hoping for joy one day, declare, "I have fullness of joy right now because I am in His presence." Instead of waiting for breakthrough, say, "I walk in His blessings today."

God has already shown you the path of life—it's in His presence, in His Word, and in His promises. Walk in it. Believe it. Live in the reality of His joy and pleasures today!

Oh, that men would give thanks to the LORD for His goodness, and for His wonderful works to the children of men!

Psalm 107:21

Gratitude is a powerful force. It shifts our focus from what we lack to what we have, from problems to promises. When you're believing God for something—whether it's healing, provision, or breakthrough—thank Him in advance! Thank Him for what He has already done, for what He is doing now, and for what He will do. It's amazing how thanksgiving can transform your perspective. Instead of dwelling on the problem, you start recognizing His goodness all around you. A great way to build this habit is by writing down at least one thing you're thankful for every day.

God's Word makes it clear that thanksgiving isn't just a nice idea; it's His will for us (1 Thessalonians 5:18)! He doesn't ask us to be thankful *for* every challenge we face, but to be thankful *in the midst of them*. Why? Because gratitude keeps our hearts open to receive. When we complain, we magnify our troubles. But when we thank God, we magnify Him! A thankful heart is a receiving heart—one that is positioned to experience His peace, His provision, and His power.

No matter what you're going through, there is always something to be grateful for. Maybe it's the beautiful weather, the love of a friend, or simply the promise of God's faithfulness. Choosing gratitude isn't denying reality; it's choosing to see God's hand at work even when things seem uncertain. But if negativity takes over, it can cloud your vision and make it harder to see His blessings. Shake off discouragement, lift your eyes to Jesus, and give thanks! As you do, you'll find your heart lightened, your faith strengthened, and your life enriched by the goodness of God.

Is anyone among you sick? Let him call for the elders of the church, and let them pray over him, anointing him with oil in the name of the Lord. And the prayer of faith will save the sick, and the Lord will raise him up. And if he has committed sins, he will be forgiven. Confess your trespasses to one another, and pray for one another, that you may be healed. The effective, fervent prayer of a righteous man avails much.

James 5:14-16

If you're battling sickness, you don't have to go through it alone. God designed the body of Christ to stand together, support, uplift, and agree in faith. When you invite like-minded believers to pray with you, you tap into supernatural power. Healing isn't just something we hope for—it's something Jesus paid for, and unity in prayer positions you to receive.

But healing isn't only physical. Sometimes, what's weighing us down is in our hearts. Unconfessed sin keeps us in bondage, making us feel distant from God. He's already forgiven you, but confessing it releases sin's grip. Hiding sin gives it power, but bringing it into the light breaks its hold.

When you confess your sin to others, it weakens its ability to keep you in bondage. It doesn't have to be to a priest, either! Even just sharing your struggle with a trusted friend will help. Letting go of shame and receiving God's grace opens the door to true healing—spirit, soul, and body.

And here's the best part: your prayers are powerful—not because you've earned it but because Jesus made you righteous! Your effectiveness in prayer isn't based on performance but on your position in Him. So, when you pray, do it boldly! Your words carry weight in the kingdom of God. Healing isn't for a select few—it's for *you*. Stand in faith, join with other believers, and watch God move in your life!

*You are of God, little children, and have overcome
them, because He who is in you is greater than
he who is in the world.*

1 John 4:4

L ife has a way of throwing challenges at us that feel bigger than we can handle. Whether it's a difficult relationship, financial pressure, a battle in our minds, or recurring physical symptoms, sometimes it seems like the enemy is gaining ground. But the truth is, no matter what comes against you, *you have already overcome*—not because of your own strength, but because of the One who lives in you.

1 John 4:4 reminds us that the power of God inside us is *greater* than anything we will ever face. The moment you made Jesus your Lord, you became part of God's family, and that means *His* victory became *your* victory. The enemy may try to convince you otherwise—whispering lies that you're not strong enough, not worthy enough, or that you'll never get past your struggles. But he is already defeated, and you don't have to fight *for* victory. You fight *from* victory!

The key to walking in that victory is recognizing who you are in Christ. You are *of God*—born of Him, empowered by Him, and filled with His Spirit. That means you're not striving to overcome; you *have already* overcome. The pressure isn't on you to be strong enough because the Greater One is inside you. His strength, wisdom, peace, and provision are already working!

So today, shift your focus. Instead of magnifying the problem, magnify God's power within you. Instead of agreeing with fear, agree with His Word. When you stand in the confidence of who He is in you, the challenges of this world shrink in comparison. Whatever you're facing, remind yourself: *Greater is He who is in me than he who is in the world!* Victory isn't a distant hope—it's your present reality.

May 3

*Now to Him who is able to do exceedingly
abundantly above all that we ask or think, according
to the power that works in us.*

Ephesians 3:20

Have you ever asked God for something and thought, *I
don't want to ask for too much?* Maybe you've limited your prayers to what seems reasonable or
possible. But God doesn't have limits. He's not just capable of
meeting your expectations; He can exceed them!

God can do *"exceedingly abundantly above"* all that we ask
or even imagine. That means if you can dream it, God can do
more. If you can ask for it, He can go beyond it. And He's not
doing it from some far-off place—His power is actually working
in you!

Think about the times you've seen God work in ways you
didn't expect. Maybe you were believing for a job, and He gave
you an opportunity better than you hoped for. Maybe you were
praying for healing, and He restored not just your body, but
your peace and joy, too. That's *exceedingly abundantly above*
in action!

But notice the last part of the verse—this isn't just about what
God *can* do. It's about what He's doing *through* you. His power
is alive in you, actively working. The same Spirit that raised Jesus from the dead *lives* in you (Romans 8:11)! God's supernatural power is operating in and through you, equipping you to
believe for more, step out in faith, and walk in victory. When
you partner with Him, you are a vessel for His miracles to flow
through.

Dream big. Ask boldly. Believe beyond what makes sense.
Because God isn't limited by circumstances, and He's certainly
not limited by your imagination. He's already preparing something *greater* than you can even begin to comprehend.

I will both lie down in peace, and sleep;
for You alone, O Lord, make me dwell in safety.

Psalm 4:8

A good night's sleep is something many people struggle to find. Worry, stress, and fear can keep the mind racing long after the body is exhausted. But this verse is a reminder that true rest doesn't come from perfect circumstances—it comes from trusting in God.

David, the writer of this psalm, faced many dangers. As a king and a warrior, he had enemies seeking to destroy him. Yet he didn't say, "I will sleep because my army is strong" or "I will rest because my problems are solved." He declared that his peace came from God alone.

Many people seek security in things like finances, relationships, or personal achievements. But real peace isn't found in what we control—it's found in who we trust. When we know that God is watching over us, providing for us, and surrounding us with His presence, we can release anxiety and enter into rest.

Jesus echoed this promise in John 14:27 when He said, *"Peace I leave with you, My peace I give to you; not as the world gives do I give to you. Let not your heart be troubled, neither let it be afraid."* The world's peace depends on external conditions, but God's peace remains unshaken, even in the midst of chaos.

If you've been struggling with fear, anxiety, or sleepless nights, let this verse be a declaration over your life. God alone is your refuge. His presence is your safety. You don't have to figure everything out before you can rest—He is already holding you securely. Lie down in peace tonight, knowing that He is watching over you.

And the Lord will deliver me from every evil work
and preserve me for His heavenly kingdom.
To Him be glory forever and ever. Amen!

2 Timothy 4:18

C hallenges in life are inevitable, but God's deliverance is real and active—right here, right now. Paul had faced intense opposition, betrayal, and prison walls, yet he still declared with confidence that the Lord would deliver him. This was a man who had experienced God's hand time and time again, even in the face of being stoned to death. His trust wasn't wishful thinking—it was built on lived experience.

The word *deliver* in Greek is *rhyomai*, meaning to draw to oneself, to rescue, or to snatch from danger. This isn't just a passive escape—it's God actively pulling us into His protection. It's the same word used in the Lord's Prayer when Jesus said, *"Deliver us from the evil one"* (Matthew 6:13). No matter what attack the enemy tries to launch, God's power is greater, and He is faithful to bring us through.

But notice that Paul doesn't say he'll never face trouble. He had already been through beatings, shipwrecks, and imprisonment for the gospel. This promise isn't about avoiding hardship—it's about God's faithfulness to sustain and preserve us through it. Even when life feels uncertain, He is securing our future, both here on earth and for eternity. His protection isn't just for the physical battles we see, but also for the unseen spiritual battles He fights on our behalf.

The same God who delivered Paul is still delivering His people! He is not distant or unaware—He is actively working on your behalf. His power, love, and presence surround you, and He will never leave you defenseless. Trust Him to rescue you, strengthen you, and bring you safely through every trial. He is faithful, and He will never fail you.

We are hard-pressed on every side, yet not crushed; we are perplexed, but not in despair; persecuted, but not forsaken; struck down, but not destroyed.

2 Corinthians 4:8-9

Difficult seasons can feel overwhelming, but this passage reminds us that no matter how intense the pressure, we are never without hope. Paul, who wrote these words, endured imprisonment, beatings, and rejection, yet he refused to be defeated. He understood that the power of God within him was greater than any opposition around him.

Being *hard-pressed* means experiencing pressure from all directions, yet Paul says we are *not crushed*. The weight of challenges may feel heavy, but they do not have the power to break us. Being *perplexed* means facing uncertainty, but we are *not in despair* because God is still leading us. Being *persecuted* means opposition may come, but we are *not forsaken* because God never abandons His children and He is always for us, never against us. Being *struck down* may feel like defeat, but we are *not destroyed* because God's resurrection power sustains us.

Jesus told His followers, *"In the world you will have tribulation; but be of good cheer, I have overcome the world"* (John 16:33). Victory is not about avoiding hardship—it's about overcoming through faith! Life's difficulties may shake us, but they cannot win against us.

If you're feeling pressure today, remember that God is holding you together. You may be in a battle, but you are not alone. His strength is greater than the weight of any struggle, and He will see you through to victory! What may seem like a setback is just another setup for His glory to shine in your life.

You shall tread upon the lion and the cobra, the young lion and the serpent you shall trample underfoot.

Psalm 91:13

Spiritual attacks are real, but so is the authority God has given His people! This verse is a declaration of victory over the enemy, showing that through faith in God, we have power over any of the forces of darkness that try to rise against us.

In Scripture, both lions and serpents are symbolic of spiritual opposition. *"The devil walks about like a roaring lion, seeking whom he may devour"* (1 Peter 5:8), and in the garden, Satan took the form of a serpent to deceive Adam and Eve. Yet here, God promises that these threats will not have the final say—we will tread upon them, meaning they will be beneath our feet, powerless to harm us when we stand firm in faith.

Jesus reinforced this truth when He told His disciples, *"Behold, I give you the authority to trample on serpents and scorpions, and over all the power of the enemy, and nothing shall by any means hurt you"* (Luke 10:19). In Him, we are not victims but victors. No attack of the enemy—whether in the form of fear, sickness, temptation, or oppression—has the right to overpower a child of God who stands in faith and walks in spiritual authority.

If you feel like the enemy has been coming against you, remember your position in Christ. You are not under attack— you are *above* it! Walk in the confidence that God has given you authority over every scheme of the enemy. Whatever has tried to hold you back or intimidate you must bow to the power of Jesus within you. You are not fighting for victory—you are fighting *from* victory, and the enemy is already defeated!

A man will be as a hiding place from the wind, and a cover from the tempest, as rivers of water in a dry place, as the shadow of a great rock in a weary land.

Isaiah 32:2

Unpredictable storms come in life, but God has provided a refuge. This verse paints a picture of security, provision, and refreshment for those who put their trust in Him.

Biblically, wind and tempests often represent trials, uncertainty, or opposition. When the winds of life try to shake you—whether through hardship, stress, or fear—God is your hiding place. He is not a distant observer but a present refuge, covering and protecting you from harm. Psalm 46:1 declares, *"God is our refuge and strength, a very present help in trouble."* He is not just available—He is near, shielding you from what would otherwise overwhelm you.

The imagery continues with rivers of water in a dry place. Just as water brings life to barren land, God sustains His people in difficult seasons. His presence refreshes, His Word revives, and His Spirit strengthens us when we feel drained. Jesus echoed this promise when He said, *"If anyone thirsts, let him come to Me and drink"* (John 7:37). No matter how weary you feel, He is your source of life, energy, and refreshing!

Lastly, the shadow of a great rock speaks of rest and protection. In the scorching heat of the desert, shade provides relief. Likewise, God is a covering from the pressures of life. You don't have to endure trials in your own strength—He offers rest, restoration, and peace.

If you are facing storms today, take refuge in Him. He is your shelter, your source, and your security. No matter what comes, you are covered!

But to him who does not work but believes on Him who justifies the ungodly, his faith is accounted for righteousness.

Romans 4:5

For many, the idea of being made right with God without earning it feels too good to be true. Religion often teaches that righteousness comes through effort, good deeds, or moral perfection. But this verse makes it clear—righteousness is not something we achieve; it is something we receive through faith.

Paul uses the example of Abraham earlier in this chapter, explaining that he was counted as righteous *before* he did anything to earn it. *"Abraham believed God, and it was accounted to him for righteousness"* (Romans 4:3). His right standing with God wasn't based on works but on faith. The same is true for us today.

The phrase *"does not work but believes"* doesn't mean we shouldn't live righteously—it means our righteousness isn't the result of our efforts. It is a gift given by God to those who put their trust in Jesus. No amount of striving, rule-following, or self-improvement could ever make us worthy before Him. But the good news is, we don't have to earn it. Jesus already did the work on our behalf!

This is the beauty of grace. God justifies the ungodly—not because they clean themselves up first, but because they believe. If you've ever felt like you're not "good enough" for God's blessing or love, remember this verse. Righteousness is not a reward for good behavior—it is a gift given freely to those who believe. Rest in that truth today, knowing that your standing before God is secure, not because of what you do, but because of what Jesus has done.

May 10

Many are the afflictions of the righteous,
but the Lord delivers him out of them all.

Psalm 34:19

Trouble is not a sign that God has abandoned you. This verse doesn't promise a life free from challenges—it promises that no matter how many trials come, God will bring deliverance.

The word *afflictions* refers to hardships, pressures, and distress. Being righteous does not exempt us from difficulty. In fact, Jesus told His followers, *"In the world you will have tribulation; but be of good cheer, I have overcome the world"* (John 16:33). The difference for believers is not the absence of trouble, but the presence of a Deliverer!

God's deliverance doesn't always mean immediate removal from a situation. Sometimes He rescues us by strengthening us through the trial, giving us wisdom, or providing supernatural peace. Other times, He leads us out of the difficulty entirely. Either way, His promise stands—He will not leave you stuck in affliction.

David, the writer of this psalm, experienced many hardships, from being hunted by King Saul, to experiencing emotional distress and depression, to facing personal failures. Yet he declared with confidence that the Lord delivers His people *out of them all*. Not some, not most—*all*. Whatever you are facing today, this promise is for you!

No trouble is too big, no situation too complicated, and no opposition too strong for God to handle. Stand in faith, knowing that His deliverance is not a matter of *if*—it's a matter of *when*. He is faithful, and He will bring you through.

But you, beloved, building yourselves up on your most holy faith, praying in the Holy Spirit.

Jude 1:20

Spiritual strength isn't automatic—it must be built. Just as muscles grow through exercise, faith grows through intentional action. This verse encourages us to actively strengthen our faith, with one key way being prayer in the Holy Spirit.

To *build up* means to strengthen, reinforce, or establish something firmly. Faith isn't meant to be stagnant; it is designed to grow. Romans 10:17 tells us, *"So then faith comes by hearing, and hearing by the word of God."* Feeding on Scripture strengthens our trust in God, and praying in the Spirit activates that faith in our daily lives!

Praying in the Holy Spirit refers to Spirit-led prayer, which includes praying in tongues and also to allowing the Holy Spirit to guide our prayers. Paul emphasized this in Ephesians 6:18, saying, *"Praying always with all prayer and supplication in the Spirit."* When we pray beyond our understanding, we tap into God's wisdom, power, and strength. It is so incredibly powerful!

If you feel spiritually drained, this verse offers the solution: build yourself up. Time in God's Word and prayer in the Spirit are not just religious habits; they are the fuel that keeps your faith strong. No matter what challenges arise, you can remain steadfast because your strength comes from Him.

Make it a priority to build yourself up daily. When you invest in your faith, you will be equipped to stand firm, walk in victory, and overflow with God's power in every area of life!

Be strong and of good courage, do not fear nor be afraid of them; for the Lord your God, He is the One who goes with you. He will not leave you nor forsake you.

Deuteronomy 31:6

Fear is one of the enemy's most often used weapons, but God's presence is the ultimate defense. As Moses spoke these words to Israel, they were on the edge of entering the Promised Land—a place full of both blessings and battles. The instruction was clear: they were not to fear, because God Himself would go with them.

Strength and courage are not about personality or willpower; they come from knowing who is with you. God's promise in this verse is deeply personal. *He* is the One who goes with you. You are not facing challenges alone. Whether you are stepping into something new, facing a difficult situation, or walking through uncertainty, God is already ahead of you, leading, strengthening, and equipping you.

The phrase *"He will not leave you nor forsake you"* is repeated multiple times throughout Scripture, showing us just how committed God is to His people. Jesus echoed this same promise when He said, *"I am with you always, even to the end of the age"* (Matthew 28:20). The enemy wants you to feel alone, but the truth is that God never abandons His kids. His presence is not conditional—it is a guarantee.

If you're feeling overwhelmed or unsure about what's ahead, let this promise settle your heart. God doesn't just encourage you to be brave—He tells you not to fear! You're not expected to muster courage on your own; your strength comes from knowing He's with you. The One who goes before you and stands beside you will never leave you to face things alone. So take the next step, not in fear, but in faith—because He's right there with you, and He's never failed.

For You, O Lord, will bless the righteous;
with favor You will surround him as with a shield.

Psalm 5:12

Blessing and favor are not just things God gives—they are part of who He is. When we walk in relationship with Him, His favor surrounds us like a protective shield, guarding, guiding, and opening doors that no one else can.

The word *favor* in Hebrew is *ratson,* meaning goodwill, acceptance, and divine pleasure. It is God's supernatural grace that causes people to bless you, opportunities to find you, and circumstances to align for your good. Proverbs 3:4 says, *"And so find favor and high esteem in the sight of God and man."* His favor doesn't just impact your relationship with Him—it influences how *others* see and respond to you.

The imagery of a shield is powerful. While we often picture a shield as guarding just one side, the Hebrew word used here paints a fuller picture—God's favor *surrounds* you. It's not limited to one area of your life or one direction of protection. His blessing covers every angle—front, back, and sides—watching over you even when you don't see it.

Favor doesn't mean life will be challenge-free, but it does mean God is working on your behalf. Consider Joseph: he was falsely accused and imprisoned, yet still favored. Even then, God was with him, showing mercy and positioning him for greater things (Genesis 39:21).

If you've ever felt overlooked or like things aren't going your way, remind yourself of this promise. You are not just getting by—you are surrounded by God's favor! Expect His blessing, walk in confidence, and trust that He is positioning you for great things.

I will make you a great nation; I will bless you and make your name great, and you shall be a blessing.

Genesis 12:2

God's blessings are never meant to stop with us—they are meant to flow through us. When God called Abraham, He made a powerful promise: not only would He bless him, but Abraham himself would become a source of blessing to others.

The Hebrew word for *bless* in this passage is *barak*, which means to prosper, to empower, and to extend divine favor. God wasn't just promising Abraham wealth or success—He was giving him a purpose. The blessing on Abraham's life would impact generations to come, ultimately leading to the greatest blessing of all: Jesus Christ. Galatians 3:14 says, *"That the blessing of Abraham might come upon the Gentiles in Christ Jesus, that we might receive the promise of the Spirit through faith."* Through Jesus, this same blessing now belongs to us!

It's easy to focus on receiving God's blessings, but this verse challenges us to think beyond ourselves. How can we use what God has given us—our time, talents, and resources—to be a blessing to others? Whether it's speaking encouragement, giving generously, or sharing the gospel, we are called to live with open hands. Proverbs 11:25 says, *"The generous soul will be made rich, and he who waters will also be watered himself."* God's blessings multiply when we use them to serve others.

If you've been asking God to bless you, remember why—so that His goodness can overflow from your life to those around you. When you align your heart with His purpose, you'll see His favor increase, not just for your benefit, but for the impact He wants to make through you. True prosperity isn't just about what you receive—it's about what you give.

*Who does great things, and unsearchable,
marvelous things without number.*

Job 5:9

Have you ever stopped to think about how much God is doing at any given moment? Right now, your heart is beating, your lungs are filling with air, and your body is functioning in ways you don't even have to think about. And that's just what's happening inside you! Beyond that, the sun is hanging in the sky, the earth is spinning at just the right speed, and oceans know exactly where to stop on the shore.

God is always at work, doing incredible things—too many for us to count or even understand. Sometimes, we only recognize His hand when we see something dramatic—a sudden healing, an unexpected financial breakthrough, or a situation that turns around in an instant. And while those are definitely His marvelous works, they're just a small glimpse of what He's doing all the time.

Consider that there may be situations where God protected you and you didn't even realize it. Or opportunities He placed in your path you didn't realize came from Him. The times He brought the right people into your life at the perfect moment. His wonders are not only constant, but they often go unnoticed—simply because we're not looking for them.

If you've ever doubted whether God is working in your life, take a moment to reflect. Look back at where He's brought you from. Look around at the ways He's sustaining you now. And remember—if He's done countless marvelous things before, He's certainly not stopping now!

God is moving in your life in ways beyond what you can see. Keep your eyes open, because He's got even greater wonders ahead!

*For by grace you have been saved through faith,
and that not of yourselves; it is the gift of God,
not of works, lest anyone should boast.*

Ephesians 2:8-9

Salvation is not something we can earn—it is a gift freely given by God. Many people struggle with the idea that righteousness isn't based on their performance. Human nature wants to measure our worth by our achievements, but this verse reminds us that we are saved *purely* by God's grace.

The word *grace* in Greek is *charis*, meaning unmerited (undeserved) favor. It is God's goodness poured out on us, completely independent of anything we have done. If salvation depended on our efforts, we could take credit for it, but God made sure it was something no one could boast about. Romans 11:6 says, *"And if by grace, then it is no longer of works; otherwise grace is no longer grace."* Grace and works cannot coexist as the basis for salvation—it is either one or the other.

This doesn't mean that works don't matter. James 2:17 reminds us, *"Faith by itself, if it does not have works, is dead."* Good works are the fruit of salvation, not the cause of it. They are the evidence of a transformed life, but they are never the *requirement* for receiving God's love. Titus 3:5 affirms this truth, saying, *"Not by works of righteousness which we have done, but according to His mercy He saved us."* Salvation is God's mercy in action, not a reward for human effort.

If you've ever felt like you had to work harder to earn God's approval, please let these verses set you free! You don't have to strive for what Jesus has already provided. Your salvation is secure, not because of what you do, but because of what He has done. Rest in that truth, knowing that grace is enough—and let your good works be the result of His grace working through you.

*Blessed is the man who trusts in the Lord,
and whose hope is the Lord. For he shall be like a tree
planted by the waters, which spreads out its roots by
the river, and will not fear when heat comes; but its leaf
will be green, and will not be anxious in the year
of drought, nor will cease from yielding fruit.*

Jeremiah 17:7-8

Think about the strongest tree you've ever seen—one with deep roots, thick branches, and vibrant green leaves. No matter how hot the sun gets or how long the dry season lasts, it doesn't shrivel up. Why? Because it's planted by a steady source of water. While other trees might struggle, this one thrives because its roots are tapped into something deeper.

That's exactly how God wants you to live. When you put your trust in Him, you're not dependent on the conditions around you. You're not at the mercy of the economy, your circumstances, your government, or what's happening in the world. Your strength, your provision, your ability to keep going—it all comes from the Lord.

And notice this verse doesn't say that heat and drought *might* come. They *will* come. Challenges will show up. Pressures will try to drain you. But you don't have to live in fear or anxiety. When your hope is in God, you can be stable and unshaken, no matter what's going on around you.

Even in tough seasons, your life can still produce good fruit! You can still walk in peace, still experience joy, still see God's provision at work. When others are barely hanging on, you can keep thriving. That's the blessing of being planted in Him.

May 18

*Blessed are those who hunger and thirst
for righteousness, for they shall be filled.*

Matthew 5:6

Hunger is a powerful thing. It pushes us forward, keeps us restless, and won't let up until we find something that fills the emptiness. Think about how you feel when you're really hungry—your stomach growls, your energy dips, and all you can think about is food. You start looking for something—anything—that will satisfy that craving.

Jesus says that kind of hunger is a good thing—when it's for righteousness. He's talking about a deep, relentless craving for God's presence, His ways, and His truth. It's not a casual interest or a Sunday-morning-only appetite. This hunger keeps us coming back for more, pressing in, growing, and refusing to settle for anything less than God's best.

The promise here is amazing: if you stay hungry for righteousness, you *will* be filled! God is not stingy with His goodness. He's not holding back His presence, wisdom, or blessings. He's ready and willing to satisfy those who come to Him truly hungry for what He has for them.

But just like in the natural, what we feed on matters. If we try to satisfy our spiritual hunger with empty distractions, quick fixes, or even good things that aren't *God*, we'll stay spiritually malnourished. Real satisfaction comes from pursuing Him— through His Word, time in His presence, and aligning our lives with His truth.

So, stay hungry. Keep pressing in. Don't settle for a life of just getting by spiritually when God has invited you into something so much deeper, richer, and more fulfilling. He's ready to fill you—more than you can imagine.

*I sought the Lord, and He heard me,
and delivered me from all my fears.*

Psalm 34:4

F ear is something everyone faces at some point, but it should never be able to control us. This verse is a powerful reminder that when we turn to God, He not only listens—He delivers. David, who wrote this psalm, knew what it was like to be surrounded by danger. Yet instead of letting fear consume him, he turned to the One who had the power to set him free.

To *seek the Lord* means to pursue Him, come before Him in prayer, and trust in His presence. Jeremiah 29:13 says, *"And you will seek Me and find Me, when you search for Me with all your heart."* God is not distant or indifferent. When we seek Him, He responds. He is always near, ready to replace our fear with peace.

Fear often grips our hearts when we focus on circumstances instead of God's promises, like when the disciples feared in the middle of a storm while Jesus slept on a pillow! But Isaiah 41:10 reminds us, *"Fear not, for I am with you; be not dismayed, for I am your God. I will strengthen you, yes, I will help you, I will uphold you with My righteous right hand."* Deliverance from fear doesn't necessarily mean the situation changes instantly, but it does mean that we can walk through it with confidence, in peace, because we know He is with us and on our side.

The enemy wants fear to hold you back, but God's presence empowers you to move forward. 2 Timothy 1:7 assures us, *"For God has not given us a spirit of fear, but of power and of love and of a sound mind."* When fear rises, turn to Him. He hears you, He cares for you, and He will always be faithful to deliver you into peace and victory.

He who has a slack hand becomes poor,
but the hand of the diligent makes rich.

Proverbs 10:4

God's blessings often flow through the work of our hands. This proverb highlights a key principle of prosperity: diligence leads to increase, while laziness results in lack. While God is our ultimate provider, He calls us to partner with Him by being faithful in what we do!

The word *diligent* in Hebrew is *charuts*, meaning sharp, decisive, and industrious. It describes someone who works with purpose and persistence. Diligence is not about striving in our own strength—it's about being faithful with what God has entrusted to us. Colossians 3:23 reminds us, *"And whatever you do, do it heartily, as to the Lord and not to men."* When we commit our work to God, He blesses and multiplies our efforts.

This principle goes beyond finances—it applies to how you pursue God, invest in people, and steward what He's placed in your hands. Proverbs 13:4 reinforces this truth: *"The soul of a lazy man desires, and has nothing; but the soul of the diligent shall be made rich."* Those who consistently pursue God's wisdom, work with integrity, and steward their time well will see the fruit of their labor.

Laziness, on the other hand, doesn't just refer to avoiding work—it can also mean procrastination, inconsistency, or neglecting the things God has called us to do. When we fail to act, we limit the opportunities God has prepared for us.

If you've been feeling stuck or discouraged, ask God to strengthen your hands for the work ahead. He has placed gifts, ideas, and opportunities in your life! As you step forward with diligence, trust that He will bring increase, favor, and blessing to all you do.

*I will go before you and make the crooked places straight;
I will break in pieces the gates of bronze and cut the bars
of iron. I will give you the treasures of darkness and hidden
riches of secret places, that you may know that I, the Lord,
who call you by your name, am the God of Israel.*

Isaiah 45:2-3

When God calls you to something, He clears the path ahead. These verses were originally spoken to Cyrus, a Persian king God would use to fulfill His purposes. Yet the principles remain true for all who trust in Him—God goes before us, removing obstacles and providing unexpected blessings.

Life's journey can feel uncertain, with obstacles and detours, but God promises to straighten the path. Proverbs 3:6 declares, *"In all your ways acknowledge Him, and He shall direct your paths."* Some versions say, *"make your paths straight."* When we trust Him, He clears the way, leading us into His promises.

The imagery of *gates of bronze* and *bars of iron* represents barriers—things that seem impossible to break through. Yet God declares that He will shatter them! What seems unmovable in the natural must yield to His power.

Beyond breaking obstacles, God promises *treasures of darkness and hidden riches of secret places.* This refers to provision we don't see coming—unexpected opportunities, divine connections, and favor that only He can strategize. His resources are limitless, and He knows where every blessing is stored and how to get them into our hands.

If you're facing uncertainty, trust that God is already ahead of you. He is clearing the path, breaking barriers, and unlocking hidden blessings. Walk forward in faith, knowing that He is leading you to greater things!

Commit your works to the Lord,
and your thoughts will be established.

Proverbs 16:3

Success in life isn't just about working hard—it's about working *with God*. This verse reminds us that when we commit our plans to Him, He brings clarity, direction, wisdom, and success to our efforts.

The word *commit* in Hebrew is *galal*, which means to roll away or transfer. It paints the picture of rolling a heavy burden off our shoulders and onto God's. Instead of carrying the weight of making everything work out on our own, we release it to Him. Psalm 37:5 echoes this truth: *"Commit your way to the Lord, trust also in Him, and He shall bring it to pass."* True success isn't found in striving—it's found in surrendering all of our burdens to Him.

When we commit our works to the Lord, He aligns our thoughts with His plans. He brings stability, wisdom, and divine strategy to our thoughts. Rather than second-guessing or feeling uncertain, we gain confidence in knowing that we are walking in His will.

James 1:5 assures us, *"If any of you lacks wisdom, let him ask of God, who gives to all liberally and without reproach, and it will be given to him."* Sometimes we just need to ask for His wisdom and guidance! He is always ready to direct us when we seek Him.

If you've been feeling overwhelmed by decisions, take this verse to heart. Don't carry the pressure alone—roll it onto God. When you surrender your plans to Him, He will establish your thoughts, guide your steps, and lead you into success. His way is always better, and when you trust Him, you will see His hand move in ways you never expected.

May 23

The Lord is my light and my salvation;
whom shall I fear? The Lord is the strength of my life;
of whom shall I be afraid?

Psalm 27:1

Fear starts to lose its grip when you remember who's standing with you. This verse isn't just poetic—it's a powerful declaration of confidence in God's presence. David had been through it all: enemies, betrayal, danger at every turn. But instead of letting fear take over, he reminded himself who his God was—his protector, his light, his strength, and the one who had never let him down.

When everything feels dark or uncertain, God is the one who brings clarity. His Word lights up the path ahead and gives you the wisdom to move forward. You don't have to stumble around in fear when His truth is guiding you. His light reveals what's real and silences the lies fear tries to whisper.

And He's not just your guide—He's your salvation. The Hebrew word for *salvation* here is *yeshuah*, the same root as the name Jesus. So this verse isn't just about rescue in the moment—it's a reminder that your life is secure in Him, now and forever. You're not just surviving—you're being kept, protected, and carried by grace.

David also called the Lord the strength of his life. That's not just poetic language—it's a reminder that your courage doesn't have to come from within. God is your strength. He's the one holding you up when everything around you feels shaky.

So, if fear's been trying to creep in, stop and speak this truth: *God is my light, my salvation, and my strength.* There's nothing bigger than Him and nothing will come that you'll face alone! Let His presence and His Word calm your heart and steady your steps today.

May 24

*For we are His workmanship, created in Christ Jesus
for good works, which God prepared beforehand
that we should walk in them.*

Ephesians 2:10

You are not an accident! God designed you with intentionality, crafting you for a unique purpose. This verse reminds us that we are His *workmanship*—His masterpiece, created to live out the good works He planned for us long before we were even born.

The Greek word for *workmanship* is *poiēma,* which means something skillfully crafted, like an artist's finest work. This means that God, the Creator of the universe, carefully designed you with precision and care. Psalm 139:14 echoes this truth: *"I will praise You, for I am fearfully and wonderfully made."* You are not random or insignificant—you are a masterpiece of God's hands.

But God didn't just create you to exist; He created you *for good works.* These aren't works that you do to earn His love or approval—rather, they are the natural result of your relationship with Him. True faith produces action (James 2:26). The good works God has prepared for you are part of what He has called you to do in this life, uniquely suited to the gifts and abilities He placed within you.

If you've ever wondered about your purpose, let this verse encourage you! You don't have to strive to find significance— God has already given it to you. Walk confidently in your God-given identity, knowing that you were created with intention and equipped for the good works He has planned. Step forward in faith, knowing that He is guiding you into the destiny He prepared just for you.

For with You is the fountain of life;
In Your light we see light.

Psalm 36:9

L ife at its fullest comes from God—it doesn't begin with us or anything we do. He is the source, the spring, the continual overflow of everything good and life-giving. David describes Him here as the *fountain of life*—not a trickle, not a stagnant pond, but a never-ending flow! In Hebrew, the word for *fountain* (*maqor*) refers to a spring that keeps bubbling up. That's who God is to us—an endless source of strength, joy, hope, and vitality.

When we're connected to Him, we don't have to rely on our own strength or hustle to keep going. He fills the dry places. He refreshes what feels weary. His presence doesn't just revive us—it sustains us. And it's not just for crisis moments. This fountain is flowing all the time, and you're invited to draw from it daily.

The second part of the verse is just as rich: *"In Your light we see light."* His light reveals truth, brings clarity, and exposes what we couldn't see before. Without Him, things stay dim. But when we walk with Him, suddenly the next step becomes clear, and hope replaces confusion. His light doesn't just shine around us—it awakens something within us.

If you've felt dry, overwhelmed, or unsure, you don't have to figure it out on your own. Come back to the source. Let Him refresh you. Let His light bring understanding. In Him, there is life that doesn't run out—and vision that doesn't fade.

You were never meant to run on empty. He is your fountain. Stay close, abide in Him, spend time with Him in prayer and in the Word, and you will always have life and light flowing from within and through you!

For every beast of the forest is Mine,
and the cattle on a thousand hills.

Psalm 50:10

God is not limited in resources—He owns everything. While we don't measure richness by how many head of cattle we own (although maybe some of us do!), this is simply a reminder that He is the ultimate provider, and nothing is beyond His ability to supply.

The phrase *"the cattle on a thousand hills"* symbolizes vast abundance. In biblical times, livestock was a primary measure of wealth. By declaring ownership over all the cattle and the entire forest, God is emphasizing that His provision is limitless. There is nothing we need that He cannot provide.

Sometimes, we struggle with a poverty mindset, worrying if we will have enough. But God is not a God of lack—He is a God of abundance! He is the God of more than enough, and He never runs out of supply. His riches are not just financial; they include peace, wisdom, opportunities, and every resource necessary to fulfill His purpose for our lives.

Trusting in God's provision doesn't mean sitting back and doing nothing. It means living with confidence that as you walk in obedience, He will take care of your needs. You still plan, work, and steward what's in your hands—but without the fear and striving that come from thinking it's all on you. When you rely on Him as your source, you live from a place of peace, not pressure!

If you're facing financial stress or uncertainty, remember who your source is. You are not limited by the economy, your job, or your circumstances—your provision comes from the One who owns it all. Trust Him, and watch Him supply in ways beyond what you could imagine.

For this reason we also, since the day we heard it, do not cease to pray for you, and to ask that you may be filled with the knowledge of His will in all wisdom and spiritual understanding; that you may walk worthy of the Lord, fully pleasing Him, being fruitful in every good work and increasing in the knowledge of God; strengthened with all might, according to His glorious power, for all patience and longsuffering with joy.

Colossians 1:9-11

Living the abundant life God intends for us is so much more than just having material blessings—it includes wisdom, strength, fruitfulness, creativity, spiritual growth, and any other blessing you can imagine! Paul prays here that believers would be filled with the knowledge of God's will so they can live lives that are pleasing to Him, fruitful, and strengthened by His power.

The abundant life isn't about striving in our own strength but about walking in divine wisdom and purpose. Proverbs 3:5-6 reminds us, *"Trust in the Lord with all your heart, and lean not on your own understanding; in all your ways acknowledge Him, and He shall direct your paths."* When we seek God's wisdom, we gain clarity, confidence, and direction.

Paul also prays for believers to be *strengthened with all might.* This is not just physical strength but spiritual endurance—empowerment to persevere through challenges with patience and joy. The abundant life doesn't mean an absence of trials, but it does mean having the power to overcome them!

God desires for you to live a life of purpose, strength, and fruitfulness. As you grow in the knowledge of Him and walk in His wisdom, you will experience His abundance in every area—spiritually, emotionally, and practically.

Honor the Lord with your possessions, and with the firstfruits of all your increase; so your barns will be filled with plenty, and your vats will overflow with new wine.

Proverbs 3:9-10

True financial security doesn't come from having vast amounts of wealth but from how we steward what God has already blessed us with. This verse reveals a powerful principle: when we honor God with our current resources, He ensures that we always have more than enough.

To honor the Lord with your possessions means recognizing Him as the source of every blessing. It's not just about tithing or giving—it's about a heart condition of trust and thankfulness. Deuteronomy 8:18 reminds us, *"And you shall remember the Lord your God, for it is He who gives you power to get wealth."* Acknowledging God in our finances invites His supernatural provision!

The firstfruits of all your increase refers to giving God the first and best, not what's left over. In biblical times, farmers and livestock herders brought the first portion of their harvest and flocks to God as an act of faith. Today, this principle applies to prioritizing God in our finances, time, and talents. When we worship Him with our material increase, everything else falls into place (Matthew 6:33).

God's response to our obedience is overflow. He promises that our barns will be *filled with plenty* and our vats will *overflow*. This isn't limited to material wealth—it includes peace, opportunities, fulfillment, and divine favor.

When you put God first, He takes care of the rest! Trust Him, give with a willing heart, and watch as His faithfulness unfolds in every area of your life.

But you are a chosen generation, a royal priesthood, a holy nation, His own special people, that you may proclaim the praises of Him who called you out of darkness into His marvelous light.

1 Peter 2:9

God never intended for His people to blend in! This verse declares that as believers, we are chosen, set apart, and called to reflect His glory. Our identity in Christ is not based on our background, achievements, or mistakes—it is rooted in His purpose for us.

God handpicked you for this time. You are *chosen!* You are not here by accident; He has placed you in this season for a purpose. Before you were even formed in your mother's womb, before you were ever born, you were set apart for a reason (Jeremiah 1:5). God has a specific calling for your life, one designed for your success and to bring Him glory!

Being a royal priesthood signifies both authority and access. In the Old Testament, priests had the privilege of entering God's presence, and royalty carried influence. Now, through Jesus, we have both. Hebrews 4:16 tells us, *"Let us therefore come boldly to the throne of grace."* You don't have to approach God timidly—He welcomes you with open arms.

God has *called you out of darkness into His marvelous light.* This means leaving behind fear, shame, and limitation to walk in the fullness of His promises. Your life is meant to be a testimony of His goodness. As you live in this truth, you'll not only experience His blessings, but you'll also shine as a beacon of hope to those around you.

You were created to stand out! Embrace your identity in Christ, walk in His purpose, and let His light shine through you.

*And the Spirit and the bride say, "Come!" And let him
who hears say, "Come!" And let him who thirsts come.
Whoever desires, let him take the water of life freely.*

Revelation 22:7

There's nothing quite like an ice-cold drink of water on a hot day, right? When you're parched, nothing else matters—you just need water. Your body craves it. And the moment you take that first sip, and that cold hits your stomach, relief floods through you.

God designed us to need water physically, but He also created us with a spiritual thirst. Deep down, every person is looking for something to satisfy that longing—something real, something lasting. The good news? God has already provided exactly what we need!

The invitation in Revelation 22:17 is wide open. The Spirit says, "Come." The Church—the bride of Christ—says, "Come." Those who have already tasted and seen God's goodness say, "Come." And the only requirement is being thirsty.

Jesus isn't rationing out the water of life. He's not making us earn it or prove we're worthy. He simply says, "If you're thirsty, come and drink." No charge. No conditions. Just come.

So why do so many people hesitate? Maybe they think they have to get their life together first. Maybe they've tried other things to satisfy their thirst—success, relationships, even religion—but nothing has truly quenched it. Maybe they don't realize how thirsty they really are.

But here's the truth: nothing in this world will satisfy like Jesus. He is the source of living water, the only one who can refresh and renew from the inside out. And He isn't holding back.

So, come. Drink deeply. Be satisfied. Because life—real, abundant, overflowing life—is found in Him.

May 31

*Give, and it will be given to you: good measure,
pressed down, shaken together, and running over will
be put into your bosom. For with the same measure that
you use, it will be measured back to you.*

Luke 6:38

Have you ever filled a container with something like flour or coffee beans? At first, it looks full, but when you shake it, the contents settle, making room for more. Then you press it down, and there's even more room! That's the kind of abundance Jesus is talking about here. When we give—whether it's finances, kindness, encouragement, or time—God doesn't just return it in equal measure. He goes above and beyond, making sure the return is overflowing.

But notice the key: *with the same measure that you use, it will be measured back to you.* Our generosity sets the standard for what we receive. If we give sparingly, we reap sparingly. If we give abundantly, we reap abundantly. It's not about convincing God to bless us; it's about stepping into the overflow He's already set in motion.

But listen, this isn't just about money! Some of the wealthiest people financially are the poorest in joy and relationships, true wealth that goes far beyond material riches. But when we give from a heart of faith, we see God's provision show up in every area—peace, strength, divine connections, and blessings beyond what we would even imagine.

God's system of giving is a cycle, not a one-time event. When we live open-handed, blessing others, we create a flow that keeps coming back to us. So today, what's in your hands? Whatever it is, sow it generously, knowing that God's return is always *more than enough*.

June 1

A faithful man will abound with blessings, but he who hastens to be rich will not go unpunished.

Proverbs 28:20

Success in God's kingdom is built on faithfulness, not shortcuts. This verse reminds us that true blessing comes from a life of integrity, consistency, diligence, and trust in God's timing and provision.

To be faithful means to be steadfast, reliable, and committed to what God has called you to do. Luke 16:10 reinforces this principle: *"He who is faithful in what is least is faithful also in much."* When we steward what we have well—our time, resources, relationships, and opportunities—God increases it. Faithfulness is the key to lasting success.

In contrast, chasing quick success without integrity will not bring good or godly results. The world promotes get-rich-quick schemes and shortcuts to prosperity, but God's way is different. Proverbs 13:11 warns, *"Wealth gained by dishonesty will be diminished, but he who gathers by labor will increase."* Rushing ahead often leads to compromise, frustration, or loss. God's blessings come in His perfect timing, and they add no sorrow with them (Proverbs 10:22)!

God desires for His people to experience increase, but He is more concerned with our character than our speed of success. When we remain faithful in small things, He entrusts us with greater things.

If you've been discouraged by slow progress, take heart. God sees your faithfulness, and He is preparing greater blessings for you. Stay committed, trust His process, and know that the reward for faithfulness is far greater than anything gained through shortcuts or temporary fixes that don't last.

*But to you who fear My name the Sun of Righteousness
shall arise with healing in His wings; and you shall
go out and grow fat like stall-fed calves.*

Malachi 4:2

G od's desire is not just for us to survive but to thrive.
This verse paints a picture of restoration, healing, and
overflowing life for those who honor Him.

The *Sun of Righteousness* is a prophetic reference to Jesus, the
Light of the world, who brings healing and renewal to all who
believe in Him. Just as the sun rises each day, dispelling
darkness, Christ's presence in our lives brings clarity, strength,
and wholeness. Psalm 84:11 reinforces this: *"For the Lord God
is a sun and shield; the Lord will give grace and glory; no good
thing will He withhold from those who walk uprightly."*

The phrase *healing in His wings* symbolizes complete restoration—physically, emotionally, and spiritually. When Jesus
walked the earth, He fulfilled this promise, healing the sick, restoring the broken, and bringing new life to those in need. He
healed anyone who came to Him, even to the point of raising
the dead! His power to heal has not changed. Whatever area of
life feels wounded, He is able to restore.

Cattle who are free-roaming get in their steps! So, they don't
get quite as fat as a calf who is just stuck in a stall all day. In
ancient times, well-fed calves were symbols of provision and
blessing. This represents the fullness of life God has in store for
His people—one marked by strength, peace, and overflowing
goodness.

If you've been weighed down by struggles, sickness, or
discouragement, take hold of this promise. Jesus has risen, and
His healing power is available to you. Step into His light,
receive His renewal, and walk forward in strength and joy!

June 3

But we have this treasure in earthen vessels, that the excellence of the power may be of God and not of us.

2 Corinthians 4:7

God has placed something extraordinary within you. As believers, we carry His power, His Spirit, and His life inside of us, even though in the natural we are just ordinary, fragile human beings. However, we aren't *only* human: we are one-third Holy Spirit! This verse reminds us that the abundant life we live is not by our strength, but by His power working through us.

The treasure Paul is referring to is the presence of God—the power of Jesus within us. No matter how weak, unqualified, or imperfect we may feel, God has chosen to dwell in us. His Spirit enables us to do what we could never accomplish on our own.

Calling us earthen vessels highlights our human frailty. In biblical times, clay pots were common, inexpensive, and easily broken—yet they were used to store valuable things. Likewise, though we may feel weak or unworthy, God sees us as worthy of carrying His presence. We are the temple of the Holy Spirit (1 Corinthians 6:19)! Isaiah 64:8 reminds us, *"But now, O Lord, You are our Father; we are the clay, and You our potter."* Just like a potter forms different pots for different uses, God shapes and strengthens us for His purpose.

Any success, strength, or impact we have in this world is by His grace, His ability within us moving through us. When we embrace our dependence on Him, we unlock the fullness of what He has placed inside us.

Don't underestimate what God can do through you. Though you may feel like an ordinary vessel, you carry divine treasure. Trust in His power, walk in His strength, and let His glory shine through your life.

*Now it shall come to pass, if you diligently
obey the voice of the Lord your God, to observe carefully
all His commandments which I command you today,
that the Lord your God will set you high above
all nations of the earth.*

Deuteronomy 28:1

For the next two weeks, we will dive into God's blessings outlined in Deuteronomy 28:1-14. These promises were originally given under the Old Covenant, where obedience to the law determined the blessing. But under the New Covenant, we receive God's blessings—not through our own obedience—but through faith in Jesus Christ.

It's important to understand this shift. Jesus said, *"Do not think that I came to destroy the Law or the Prophets. I did not come to destroy but to fulfill"* (Matthew 5:17). Jesus perfectly obeyed the law on our behalf, making us righteous by faith (Romans 3:22). Now, instead of striving to earn God's favor, we simply believe in the finished work of Christ.

When this passage speaks of obedience, don't feel pressure to "measure up." The obedience required has already been fulfilled by Jesus! Your role is to believe in Him, walk in the Spirit, and trust that His blessings are yours.

One of those blessings is promotion and influence. To be *"set high above all nations"* doesn't mean political rule—it means favor, leadership, and opportunities to be a light in the world. God elevates His people in their careers, businesses, ministries, and communities so they can reflect His goodness.

His promotion is not based on competition or human effort but on His supernatural favor. As you trust in Him, expect divine opportunities, honor, and influence to manifest in your life. Are you ready to embrace blessings by faith? In Christ, you are positioned to thrive!

And all these blessings shall come upon you and overtake you, because you obey the voice of the Lord your God.

Deuteronomy 28:2

I magine walking down the street and suddenly being chased down—not by trouble, but by blessings! This is the picture painted in Deuteronomy 28:2. God's blessings don't just trickle in; they pursue and overtake those who walk in obedience to Him.

The Hebrew word for *overtake* is *nasag*, meaning to catch, reach, or take hold of. This isn't about us striving to chase blessings—it's about blessings chasing us. Under the Old Covenant, obedience to God's law positioned people to receive. But under the New Covenant, we receive these blessings through faith in Jesus, whose perfect obedience has already secured every promise on our behalf (Romans 5:19).

How does this apply today? Many people exhaust themselves pursuing success, wealth, or influence, believing they must chase after opportunities to be blessed. But God's way is different. We are simply blessed because of our faith in Jesus and what He accomplished for us at the cross. Instead of striving to manufacture results, we focus on Him—and the benefits for being His children find us!

God's blessings manifest in many ways—peace in the midst of chaos, provision in times of need, divine opportunities, open doors, favor in relationships, and supernatural protection. They may not always come how we expect, but they always come when we trust in Him.

Are you tired of chasing success? Shift your focus. When you trust God's promises, His goodness runs after you. Expect blessings today—not because of your effort, but because of His faithfulness!

*Blessed shall you be in the city,
and blessed shall you be in the country.*

Deuteronomy 28:3

God's blessing isn't tied to a specific location. Whether you're in the heart of a busy city or out in the countryside, His favor is with you. In the Old Covenant, Israel's blessings depended on obeying the law, but under the New Covenant, we receive every blessing by faith in Jesus. Because we are in Him, His goodness and mercy follow us—no matter where we are.

At the same time, there are moments when God calls us to a specific place to receive His provision. When Elijah faced a drought, God told him to go to the Brook Cherith, saying, *"I have commanded the ravens to feed you there"* (1 Kings 17:4). Later, when the brook dried up, God led him to Zarephath, where a widow provided for him. Elijah's provision wasn't about striving—it was about following God's leading.

So, which is it? Are we blessed wherever we are, or is there a place where God wants us to be? The answer is *both*. His blessing isn't limited by geography, but when He gives us direction, we can trust that provision is already waiting for us "there."

If God is leading you somewhere new, don't be afraid—His favor is already ahead of you. But if He hasn't given you new instructions, don't stress. You're *already* in a place where He can bless you.

Your job is blessed whether you work downtown or remotely. Your home is blessed whether you live in a big city or a small town. Your ministry is blessed whether you're called to your local community or the nations.

God's blessing follows *you*. And when the time comes to move, He'll make sure His provision is waiting for you there, too.

June 7

Blessed shall be the fruit of your body, the produce of your ground and the increase of your herds, the increase of your cattle and the offspring of your flocks.

Deuteronomy 28:4

This verse speaks of abundance in every area of life. Under the Old Covenant, agricultural prosperity was a sign of God's blessing. Thriving crops and livestock meant security, provision, and the ability to bless future generations.

But what about today? Most of us don't rely on flocks or herds for our livelihood. Does this promise still apply? Absolutely! The heart of this blessing is increase, fruitfulness, and provision in every area that matters to you.

The fruit of your body represents children, family, and legacy. If you have kids, this is a promise that God's blessing is on them. If you desire children, it's a reminder that he is a God of life and abundance. But this also applies to spiritual children—the people you mentor, disciple, and pour into. Whether in a family setting, ministry, or friendships, God's blessing is on what you invest in others.

The produce of your ground speaks to the work of your hands. Maybe you're not a farmer, but God's blessing means you can expect productivity, favor, and supernatural provision in whatever it is that you do.

The increase of your herds and cattle refers to wealth and resources. In ancient times, livestock represented financial stability. Today, this translates to your income, investments, and financial well-being. When God's blessing is on your resources, He provides more than enough—not just to meet your needs, but to be a blessing to others.

God's will is not lack, but increase! Trust Him today to multiply the work of your hands, bless your family, and bring increase to every area of your life.

Blessed shall be your basket and your kneading bowl.

Deuteronomy 28:5

This may sound simple, but it carries a powerful promise: God's blessing is on both what you have now and what you will need in the future.

In biblical times, the basket was used to gather and store food, while the kneading bowl was used to prepare daily bread. One represented provision that had already come in, and the other represented what was still being worked on. This verse assures us that God's blessing is not just on what we already have, but also on what's still in process—what we're actively trusting Him to bring to completion.

For us today, this speaks to both our current resources and our ongoing supply. Maybe you're in a season where your basket feels full—your needs are met, and things are steady. Or maybe you're in a kneading bowl season, where you're actively trusting, preparing, and expecting God to show up with exactly what you need. The good news is, His blessing covers both!

God is not just the God of today—He is the God of tomorrow. He blesses the resources you've already received, and He also blesses the things that are still unfolding. Whether you're saving, investing, building a business, pursuing a dream, or simply trusting Him for your next step, know that His favor is on your efforts and His hand is in every detail.

You don't have to fear lack, because God is your provider. His blessing ensures that what you gather will be enough and that what you're working on will produce results. No matter what season you're in, trust Him to bless both your basket and your kneading bowl—and expect Him to do it faithfully, every single day!

June 9

Blessed shall you be when you come in,
and blessed shall you be when you go out.

Deuteronomy 28:6

W hat a powerful reminder that God's blessing isn't just for one area of life—it's with you everywhere, in every moment, and in every season of your life. No matter where you are, what age you are, what profession you are in, whether you are settled or in transition, you are blessed!

In ancient Israel, "coming in" and "going out" referred to daily activities—working, traveling, conducting business, and returning home. It was an all-encompassing phrase that meant no matter what they were doing, God's blessing was upon them.

For us today, this means that God's favor is with us in every part of life. When you leave your house in the morning, His blessing goes with you. When you return home at the end of the day, His peace and provision meet you there. When you start something new—a job, a business, a relationship—His hand is on it. When you close a chapter or walk through a season of change, He is guiding you into what's next.

Life is full of transitions, and sometimes they can feel uncertain. But this verse reminds us that whether we are stepping into something new or settling into a familiar place, we are never outside of God's blessing. Psalm 121:8 echoes this truth, saying, *"The Lord shall preserve your going out and your coming in from this time forth, and even forevermore."*

You don't have to fear what's ahead or regret what's behind. No matter where you go or what you do, God's blessing surrounds you. Step forward with confidence, knowing He is leading, providing, and protecting you every step of the way.

The Lord will cause your enemies who rise against you to be defeated before your face; they shall come out against you one way and flee before you seven ways.

Deuteronomy 28:7

Victory is a promise. This verse doesn't say that enemies won't come against you—it says that when they do, they won't succeed. God Himself guarantees that any opposition that rises up will be defeated.

In the Old Covenant, Israel's enemies were literal nations and armies that sought to destroy them. But under the New Covenant, our battles are often spiritual. Ephesians 6:12 reminds us that we don't wrestle against flesh and blood, but against spiritual forces of darkness. That means this promise isn't just about physical battles—it applies to any attack that comes against your life, whether it's fear, sickness, financial struggle, opposition at work, or any other challenge.

The phrase "flee before you seven ways" is significant. In Hebrew culture, seven represents completeness or totality. This means that when God defeats your enemies, it won't be a partial victory—it will be complete! The things that once tried to stop you will be scattered in every direction, powerless to hold you back.

So, what does this look like in daily life? It means that no matter what challenge you're facing, you don't have to fight alone. When you stand in faith, trusting in what Jesus has already done, the battle is the Lord's. The attacks of the enemy cannot prevail against a child of God who stands on His promises.

No matter what opposition comes your way, remember this: the victory has already been won through Jesus. Stand firm, knowing that the Lord fights for you, and the enemy has no choice but to flee!

*The Lord will command the blessing on you in
your storehouses and in all to which you set your hand,
and He will bless you in the land which the Lord
your God is giving you.*

Deuteronomy 28:8

G od is very intentional about how He blesses His people. He doesn't just allow blessings—He commands
them. That means *nothing* can stop them from coming
into your life when you walk in faith.

In biblical times, storehouses were where people kept their
harvest, savings, and resources. To have a blessed storehouse
meant having more than enough, not just for today, but for the
future. Today, this applies to our finances, businesses, investments, and any resources we manage. God's blessing isn't just
about meeting your immediate needs—it's about overflow. He
blesses you so that you can be a blessing to others!

But the promise doesn't stop there. God also blesses all to
which you set your hand. That means your work, your efforts,
your projects, and even your dreams are covered by His favor.
When you step out in faith, whether in your career, ministry, or
personal goals, His blessing is on what you do. It doesn't mean
there won't be challenges, but it does mean that what you put
your hand to will prosper under His guidance.

Finally, this verse reminds us that God blesses us in the land
He is giving us. That means His blessing is connected to where
He has placed you. Whether you're in a season of plenty or still
stepping into your promised land, you can trust that His
provision is already there.

God has commanded the blessing over you! Your resources
are blessed, your work is blessed, and your future is secure in
His hands. Walk in confidence today, knowing that He is the
source of your abundance.

June 12

*The Lord will establish you as a holy
people to Himself, just as He has sworn to you, if you
keep the commandments of the Lord your God
and walk in His ways.*

Deuteronomy 28:9

From the very beginning, God's desire has been to set His people apart—not just for blessing, but for a purpose. Under the Old Covenant, Israel's identity as a holy nation depended on their obedience to God's commandments. But under the New Covenant, Jesus has fulfilled the law on our behalf. Now, we are made holy, not by our own efforts, but through faith in Him.

The word *holy* in Hebrew is *qadosh*, meaning set apart, consecrated, or different from the rest. God's blessing isn't just about material provision—it's about being distinct in the way we live, think, and reflect His goodness. As believers, we don't blend in with the world. We are called to stand out, not in arrogance, but as a testimony of God's transforming power.

This also means that when God blesses you, it's not just for your benefit. His favor on your life is meant to be a light to others. The way you experience peace in uncertainty, joy in difficulty, and provision in need is a demonstration of His goodness. People should see something different in you that points them to Him.

Being established as God's holy people isn't about following rules—it's about walking with Him. As you trust Him daily, His Spirit leads you, shapes you, and empowers you to live in a way that reflects who you already are in Christ. You don't have to strive for holiness; you simply walk in the identity He has already given you.

God has set you apart, not just to be blessed, but to be a blessing. Live today knowing you are chosen, called, and established by Him.

Then all peoples of the earth shall see that you are called by the name of the Lord, and they shall be afraid of you.

Deuteronomy 28:10

God's blessing on your life isn't just for you—it's a testimony to the world. When He establishes His people, it is so evident that even those who don't know Him take notice. In the Old Covenant, nations feared Israel when they saw God's hand at work in their battles and victories. But under the New Covenant, this promise speaks to how God's presence in our lives sets us apart in a way that others cannot ignore.

To be "called by the name of the Lord" means belonging to Him. In ancient times, a person's name reflected their identity and authority. As believers, we bear the name of Jesus. We don't just follow Him—we represent Him. His nature, His power, and His Spirit dwell within us. That means when people see us, they should see something different. They should see peace when the world is in chaos, joy when circumstances say otherwise, and favor that cannot be explained.

The phrase "they shall be afraid of you" doesn't mean people will be terrified of Christians, but rather, they will be able to recognize that something greater is at work in their lives. Just as God's power caused nations to fear Israel, His favor on your life makes an undeniable impact and draws attention. It opens doors and makes others aware that something different, something powerful—something divine—is at work in your life.

You don't have to strive to make an impression—God's presence in you speaks for itself! Walk confidently today, knowing that you are called by His name. His blessing on your life is a light that draws others to Him.

And the Lord will grant you plenty of goods, in the fruit of your body, in the increase of your livestock, and in the produce of your ground, in the land of which the Lord swore to your fathers to give you.

Deuteronomy 28:11

God's nature is one of abundance. He is not a God of just enough—He is the God of more than enough! This verse reflects His desire to bless His people, not just spiritually, but in every area of life.

For Israel, this promise meant increase in their families, their livestock, and their harvests. These were the things that determined their wealth, security, and future. Today, the heart of this promise remains the same: God desires to bring increase and fruitfulness to the things that matter most to you. Whether it's in your family, your career, your business, or your ministry, His blessing brings supernatural provision.

Some struggle with the idea of abundance, thinking that prosperity is unspiritual, or even sinful. But throughout Scripture, God shows Himself as a provider who blesses His children so they can be a blessing to others. Abundance isn't about selfish gain—it's about having more than enough so that you can overflow into the lives of those around you!

Jesus confirmed this in John 10:10 when He said, *"I have come that they may have life, and that they may have it more abundantly."* This includes *every* area of life—peace in your home, joy in your heart, wisdom in your decisions, and provision for your needs.

Where do you need increase today? Trust that God is not withholding from you. His nature is to bless, and His desire is for you to thrive. As you walk in faith, expect His goodness to manifest in every part of your life.

June 15

The Lord will open to you His good treasure, the heavens, to give the rain to your land in its season, and to bless all the work of your hand. You shall lend to many nations, but you shall not borrow.

Deuteronomy 28:12

Opening the heavens points to God's unlimited supply. God is not a limited resource—He is the source of all things. When He promises to open His treasure, He is assuring us that what we need will come, and it will come at the right time.

In ancient Israel, rain was everything. It determined the success or failure of crops, which meant it directly affected provision, security, and stability. When God says He will send rain in its season, He is promising to provide exactly what is needed, exactly when it is needed. Whether it's financial provision, wisdom for a decision, or strength for the season you're in, He knows what you need and when you need it.

But notice that the rain comes in its season. A farmer doesn't expect a harvest the day after planting. Between the promise and the provision, there is always preparation. Sometimes we think God is delaying, but He is aligning circumstances, strengthening our faith, and preparing us to handle the blessing. For example: a huge harvest would be a problem, not a blessing, if you didn't have storehouses to keep it in. Instead of growing discouraged in the waiting, trust that He is working behind the scenes.

God's blessing positions us to be givers, not those barely getting by. His desire is that we would have enough resources to bless others, not just survive ourselves.

If you feel like you're in a dry season, don't be discouraged. The rain is coming! Trust in God's timing, prepare for the harvest, and expect His blessing to overflow in your life.

And the Lord will make you the head and not the tail;
you shall be above only, and not be beneath, if you heed
the commandments of the Lord your God, which I
command you today, and are careful to observe them.

Deuteronomy 28:13

R ising to the top isn't about striving—it's about walking in the blessing of God. This verse is a promise of promotion, leadership, and divine influence. Under the Old Covenant, this was tied to Israel's obedience to God's commandments. Under the New Covenant, Jesus has fulfilled the law, and through faith in Him, we now have access to every blessing He has provided for us.

Being the head and not the tail speaks of leadership and authority. A head makes decisions, sees clearly, and moves forward with direction. A tail simply follows wherever it's pulled. God's desire is that His people lead, create, and influence, not be dragged along by circumstances. This doesn't mean everyone will hold a leadership position in the traditional sense, but it does mean we are called to walk in wisdom, make an impact, and operate from victory rather than defeat.

Being above and not beneath means we don't live under oppression, fear, or lack. It doesn't mean challenges won't come, but it does mean that in Christ, we overcome them. The enemy wants believers to feel powerless—stuck in cycles of frustration—but God's promise is that we live from a place of authority, not victimhood.

If you've been feeling stuck, limited, or like life is pushing you around, remember who you are in Christ. You are called to lead, to rise, and to walk in the fullness of God's blessing. Step forward in faith, knowing that He has positioned you above, not beneath!

So you shall not turn aside from any of the words which I command you this day, to the right or the left, to go after other gods to serve them.

Deuteronomy 28:14

Life is full of distractions, and it's easy to get pulled in different directions. This verse reminds us of the importance of staying focused on God's truth, avoiding detours that lead us away from His best.

Under the Old Covenant, obedience to God's commands was required for blessing. Under the New Covenant, Jesus has fulfilled the law on our behalf, and we now walk in blessing through faith in Him. But this doesn't mean direction doesn't matter. Just like a traveler following a GPS, we have the choice to stay on the route God has laid out or to veer off onto side roads that slow us down.

Turning aside to the right or the left is usually less about outright rebellion and more about little distractions that pull you off course. It might look like entertainment that distracts and fills time but not your spirit, trying to please people instead of God, or letting fear call the shots. These things can seem harmless at first, but they slowly lead you away from the life God has for you—full of purpose, peace, and blessing.

The good news is that even if we've gotten off track, God is always ready to guide us back. His grace never runs out, and His Spirit continually leads us into truth. The safest, most fulfilling place to be is always in step with Him.

Stay focused on Jesus, trust His leading, and let His Word be your guide. Don't let the distractions of life pull you off course. When you keep your heart anchored in Him, you won't just avoid detours—you'll walk confidently in the direction of His best for you.

June 18

*By humility and the fear of the Lord are
riches and honor and life.*

Proverbs 22:4

God's path to true success looks different from the world's. This verse reveals a key to experiencing a life of blessing—humility and reverence for the Lord. When we walk in these qualities, we position ourselves to receive the rewards of riches, honor, and abundant life!

Humility is not weakness—it is a posture of the heart that recognizes our dependence on God. James 4:10 says, *"Humble yourselves in the sight of the Lord, and He will lift you up."* Those who trust in their own strength may rise temporarily, but those who submit to God's ways are established with lasting success.

The fear of the Lord is not about being afraid of God but having deep respect and reverence for Him. It means acknowledging His wisdom, obeying His Word, and seeking His direction in all things. Proverbs 9:10 affirms this: *"The fear of the Lord is the beginning of wisdom."* When we honor God first, He leads us into the best path for our lives.

The blessings of "riches and honor and life" go beyond financial prosperity—they include favor, influence, peace, and a meaningful relationship with God. These are the kinds of rewards that follow a humble heart. Jesus affirmed this in Matthew 23:12, saying, *"Whoever exalts himself will be humbled, and he who humbles himself will be exalted."* God's way to increase is through surrender, not striving!

If you desire to experience the fullness of God's blessing, choose humility and honor Him in all you do. As you walk in reverence and trust, He will bring increase, favor, and a life filled with purpose and abundance.

Therefore take up the whole armor of God, that you may be able to withstand in the evil day, and having done all, to stand. Stand therefore, having girded your waist with truth, having put on the breastplate of righteousness, and having shod your feet with the preparation of the gospel of peace; above all, taking the shield of faith with which you will be able to quench all the fiery darts of the wicked one. And take the helmet of salvation, and the sword of the Spirit, which is the word of God.

Ephesians 6:13-17

Living in the fullness of God's promises doesn't mean we won't face challenges. But He has given us everything we need to stand firm and walk in victory! This passage describes the armor of God—spiritual tools that equip us to overcome every attack of the enemy.

Just as a soldier wouldn't go into battle unprepared, we must clothe ourselves daily with God's protection and power! The belt of truth keeps us grounded in God's Word, protecting us from deception. The breastplate of righteousness guards our hearts, reminding us that we are made right with God through Christ. The shoes of the gospel of peace give us stability, allowing us to stand firm and share His message. The shield of faith blocks the enemy's attacks, extinguishing fear, doubt, and lies. The helmet of salvation secures our minds, keeping our thoughts aligned with God's promises. The sword of the Spirit—the Word of God—is our weapon against the enemy, giving us authority to stand in truth.

Victory isn't about our own strength; it's about being fully equipped in what God has already provided. When we put on His armor and stand firm in faith, we walk in the overcoming power He intended for us. No matter what comes against us, we are not defenseless—God has given us everything we need to live in triumph.

Return to your rest, O my soul,
for the Lord has dealt bountifully with you.

Psalm 116:7

Life has a way of pulling us into stress, worry, and exhaustion. But this verse is a reminder that we don't have to live overwhelmed—God calls us to rest in Him. The psalmist speaks to his own soul, telling it to return to a place of peace, not because circumstances have changed, but because God has already been faithful.

True rest isn't just physical—it's a state of trust in God's provision and care. Jesus invites us into this kind of peace in Matthew 11:28: *"Come to Me, all you who labor and are heavy laden, and I will give you rest."* The abundant life God desires for us isn't one of striving and struggling, but of confidence in His goodness. When we focus on His faithfulness instead of our fears, we step into the rest that He provides.

The phrase *"the Lord has dealt bountifully with you"* speaks of God's generous provision. He is not a God of scarcity but of abundance. Psalm 23:1 declares, *"The Lord is my shepherd; I shall not want."* This means we lack nothing in Him—whether it be strength, wisdom, provision, or peace. Looking back on the ways He has provided strengthens our faith for the future!

Yet, resting in God is a choice. Just as the psalmist commands his soul to return to rest, we must also remind ourselves to let go of anxiety and lean into His presence. When we bring everything to Him in prayer, His peace guards our hearts and minds (Philippians 4:6-7).

If worry has been weighing you down, remind your soul to return to rest. God has been faithful before, and He will be faithful again! Trust in His goodness, release your burdens, and let His peace fill your heart.

*Peace I leave with you, My peace I give to you;
not as the world gives do I give to you. Let not your
heart be troubled, neither let it be afraid.*

John 14:27

Unshakable peace is not found in perfect circumstances—it is found in Jesus. As He prepared His disciples for His departure, He reassured them that His peace would remain with them. This wasn't an ordinary peace, subject to change based on external factors, but a supernatural, lasting peace that would sustain them through every trial.

The world offers temporary peace—peace that depends on success, stability, or the absence of trouble. But the moment challenges arise, that kind of peace disappears. In contrast, Jesus gives us peace that remains, even in the midst of uncertainty. Philippians 4:7 describes it as *"the peace of God, which surpasses all understanding, will guard your hearts and minds through Christ Jesus."* This peace isn't logical—it's supernatural.

Jesus also commands us, *"Let not your heart be troubled, neither let it be afraid."* This means we have a choice. Fear and anxiety will try to take hold, but we don't have to accept them. Isaiah 26:3 assures us, *"You will keep him in perfect peace, whose mind is stayed on You, because he trusts in You."* Keeping our focus on Jesus allows us to walk in the peace He has already given us.

No matter what you're facing, His peace is yours. It's not something you have to earn—it's a gift! Receive it, rest in it, and refuse to let fear take its place. The peace Jesus offers is greater than any storm, and it will guard your heart every step of the way.

Arise, shine; for your light has come!
And the glory of the Lord is risen upon you.

Isaiah 60:1

God's glory is not distant or unreachable—it is upon you. This verse is not just an encouragement; it is a declaration that His presence, power, and favor have already been made available to His people. To live the abundant life means walking in that reality, fully embracing all that He has placed upon you.

The glory of the Lord represents His divine presence, goodness, and power. Throughout Scripture, God's glory is revealed in miraculous ways—leading Israel in a pillar of fire, filling the temple, and resting upon Jesus at His transfiguration. Now, that same glory is upon those of us who believe in Him. 2 Corinthians 3:18 tells us that His glory is not just around us—it is transforming us.

To arise means to step out of complacency, fear, or limitations and into the life God has designed for you. So many people live below their potential, weighed down by insecurity, past failures, or the everyday concerns of life. But when God's glory rises upon you, He empowers you to rise with it. Romans 8:11 reminds us that the same Spirit who raised Jesus from the dead lives on the inside of you! His power within you gives strength, wisdom, and the ability to shine.

Shining is not about striving—it is about reflecting. Just as the moon does not create light but reflects the sun, we are called to reflect the light of Christ (Matthew 5:16). His presence in you is meant to be seen, drawing others to Him.

You don't have to wait for something more—His glory has already risen upon you. Step into it, walk in confidence, and let the world see His light shining through your life.

I am the vine, you are the branches.
He who abides in Me, and I in him, bears much fruit;
for without Me you can do nothing.

John 15:5

True abundance isn't found in working—it's found in abiding. Have you ever seen a tree grunting in effort to try to pop out fruit? Of course not. Fruit happens naturally when the branch stays connected to the vine. That's the picture Jesus gives us here—a life that's fruitful not because we're working harder, but because we're abiding in Him.

To abide simply means to stay close, to remain. Just like a branch draws everything it needs from the vine, we draw strength, wisdom, peace, and provision from Jesus. When we stay connected, fruit shows up—without the pressure. Galatians 5:22–23 lists the kind of fruit we're talking about: love, joy, peace, patience, kindness, goodness, faithfulness, gentleness, and self-control. That kind of fruit doesn't come from effort—it comes from staying rooted in Him.

Jesus didn't say, "Without Me you can do less." He said, *"Without Me, you can do nothing."* We can fill our days, check off to-do lists, even achieve big things—but if it's not flowing from our connection with Him, it won't last. Psalm 127:1 puts it this way: *"Unless the Lord builds the house, they labor in vain who build it."*

So, if you've been feeling worn out from all the doing, maybe it's time to shift your focus. Don't try harder—abide deeper. Spend time in the Word, in prayer, in praise and worship with thanksgiving. As you lean into Him, fruitfulness will follow. Not forced. Not faked. Just the natural result of life in the Vine.

June 24

So I say to you, ask, and it will be given to you; seek, and you will find; knock, and it will be opened to you. For everyone who asks receives, and he who seeks finds, and to him who knocks it will be opened.

Luke 11:9-10

God desires an active relationship with His children—one where we confidently come to Him, knowing that He hears and responds. In this passage, Jesus encourages persistence in prayer, assuring us that when we ask, seek, and knock, we will receive, find, and see doors open before us.

The verbs in this verse—ask, seek, and knock—are not one-time actions but ongoing ones. Jesus is teaching us to be persistent, not because God is reluctant to bless us, but because our faith grows stronger as we continue to pursue Him. James 1:6 reminds us that when we ask, we must do so in faith, without doubting. Trusting God's timing is just as important as making our requests known.

Each step in this passage builds upon the last. Asking involves bringing our needs before God, seeking means actively pursuing His will, and knocking implies determination to walk through the doors He opens. Matthew 7:11 reassures us that if earthly parents give good gifts to their children, *"how much more will your Father who is in heaven give good things to those who ask Him!"*

If you've been waiting on an answer, don't give up! Keep asking, seeking, and knocking, knowing that God is faithful. The abundant life He has for you is not hidden—it is available to those who pursue Him in faith, with unwavering trust that He always fulfills His Word.

And have made us kings and priests to our God;
and we shall reign on the earth.

Revelation 5:10

God's plan for His people has always been one of authority, purpose, and dominion. This verse declares that through Christ, we have been made kings and priests—positions of both spiritual leadership and divine access. We are not meant to live powerless or defeated lives but to walk in the victory and authority that Jesus has secured for us.

As kings, we are called to rule, not in arrogance, but with wisdom and stewardship over what God has entrusted to us. Romans 5:17 says, *"For if by the one man's offense death reigned through the one, much more those who receive abundance of grace and of the gift of righteousness will reign in life through the One, Jesus Christ."* We reign by His grace, not our own strength, exercising faith, authority, and influence in the world around us.

As priests, we have direct access to God, no longer needing an earthly mediator. In the Old Testament, priests stood between God and the people, offering sacrifices on their behalf. But through Jesus, we have been brought into full, unrestricted relationship with the Father. Hebrews 4:16 encourages us to *"come boldly to the throne of grace, that we may obtain mercy and find grace to help in time of need."* This means we can approach God with confidence, anytime, knowing that He hears us.

Reigning in life doesn't mean living without challenges, but it does mean walking in the abundant life Christ has given—one marked by victory, purpose, and divine authority. You are not just getting by; you have been positioned to reign! Step into that identity and walk confidently in all He has called you to be.

A wholesome tongue is a tree of life,
but perverseness in it breaks the spirit.

Proverbs 15:4

Y our words carry power. This verse reveals that what you speak can either bring life and strength or cause harm and discouragement. The abundant life God desires for you isn't just about what you receive—it's also about what you release through your words.

A *wholesome tongue* refers to speech that is life-giving, uplifting, and full of wisdom. Proverbs 18:21 reinforces this truth: *"Death and life are in the power of the tongue, and those who love it will eat its fruit."* What we consistently speak shapes our reality. Encouraging words bring healing, while negative speech tears down, both in our own lives and in the lives of others.

On the other hand, *perverseness* in speech—words filled with negativity, deception, or criticism—can break the spirit. Harsh words don't just wound for a moment; they can leave lasting effects. James 3:6 compares the tongue to a fire, warning of its potential to bring destruction if not controlled.

Speaking life doesn't mean ignoring challenges or pretending difficulties don't exist, but it does mean choosing to align our words with God's promises instead of fear or doubt. For example, instead of saying, "I know the Bible says I'm healed, but my back really hurts," you can say, "Maybe my back *does* hurt, but the Bible says that by Jesus' stripes, I'm healed!" Sometimes to speak life you just have to change where you put your "but!"

If you want to see greater joy, peace, and victory in your life, start with what you speak. Choose words that are life-giving, encouraging, optimistic, and declare God's promises.

Dominion and fear belong to Him;
He makes peace in His high places.

Job 25:2

God is in charge of everything—and that's good news. His rule isn't harsh or distant; it's full of wisdom, power, and peace. This verse reminds us that He holds ultimate authority. That means no matter what's going on around you, He still has the final say.

Life can feel chaotic. Things shift, plans fall apart, and uncertainty creeps in. But when you know that God is in control, it changes how you respond. You don't have to panic or figure it all out—you can lean on the One who already sees the big picture. Psalm 103:19 says, *"The Lord has established His throne in heaven, and His kingdom rules over all."* That includes your situation.

What's amazing is that God's authority isn't cold or rigid—it brings peace. *"He makes peace in His high places"* means that wherever God reigns, peace follows. And because His Spirit lives in you, that peace isn't just in heaven—it's available in your heart, your home, and your daily life. In fact, the Word says we are seated with Him in heavenly places (Ephesians 2:6); there's no higher place than that!

So, if life feels chaotic or uncertain, take a breath and remember who's really in charge. You're not stuck, and you're definitely not powerless. You've been seated with Christ in heavenly places—that means you're not beneath the chaos, you're above it in Him! God's peace isn't just something you hope for; it's something you carry. So lean into His rule, rest in His presence, and let that deep-down confidence settle your heart today.

There is therefore now no condemnation to those who are in Christ Jesus, who do not walk according to the flesh, but according to the Spirit.

Romans 8:1

S hame and guilt were never meant to define your life. In Christ, you are completely free from condemnation. This verse declares the powerful truth that once you belong to Jesus, you are no longer judged by your past mistakes—you are covered by His grace and righteousness!

Condemnation is the weight of guilt, the feeling of being unworthy or disqualified. The enemy loves to remind believers of their failures, but God sees you through the finished work of Jesus. 2 Corinthians 5:21 affirms this: *"For He made Him who knew no sin to be sin for us, that we might become the righteousness of God in Him."* Your identity is no longer defined by sin but by the righteousness of Christ. God isn't angry with you. When He looks at you, He sees Jesus!

Walking *"according to the Spirit"* means living in the new life Jesus purchased for you. It's not about perfection but about surrender—allowing the Holy Spirit to lead you instead of being controlled by your flesh. Galatians 5:16 says, *"Walk in the Spirit, and you shall not fulfill the lust of the flesh."* The more you focus on who you are in Christ, the less power sin and condemnation have over you. It doesn't guarantee your perfection—you *will* make mistakes—but it enables you to stay in peace in spite of your failures.

The abundant life isn't one of striving for God's approval—it's resting in what Jesus has already done. If condemnation has been weighing you down, let this verse be your freedom. In Christ, you are forgiven, loved, and empowered to walk in His grace.

Do not sorrow, for the joy of the Lord is your strength.

Nehemiah 8:10

J oy is more than just a feeling—it is a powerful source of strength. The enemy knows this, which is why he works so hard to steal your joy. If he can take your joy, he can weaken your strength, leaving you discouraged, weary, and ineffective.

When Nehemiah spoke these words, the Israelites had just heard the law of God read aloud and were overwhelmed with sorrow. But Nehemiah reminded them that this was not a time for mourning—it was a time for rejoicing in God's goodness! Their strength would not come from dwelling on past failures but from focusing on the Lord. The same is true for us. If we fixate on our struggles, regrets, or disappointments, we open the door for the enemy to drain us spiritually. But when we choose joy, we walk in the strength God provides.

The joy of the Lord is not based on circumstances. Joy is actually a fruit of the spirit. Just like a tree doesn't stress or strain to produce fruit, joy is always present within you. You simply need to access it by faith!

Jesus said in John 16:22, *"Your joy no one will take from you."* That means the enemy cannot steal your joy unless you allow him to. The moment you start to feel weak, take a step back and ask yourself—*have I let go of my joy?*

Strength comes from maintaining your joy in the midst of life's battles. If you hold on to your joy, you will hold on to your strength. No matter what comes against you, refuse to let the enemy rob you. Rejoice in the Lord, and let His joy empower you to live in victory.

*For the eyes of the Lord run to and fro throughout
the whole earth, to show Himself strong on behalf
of those whose heart is loyal to Him.*

2 Chronicles 16:9

God is always looking for those who will trust Him completely. This verse reveals His desire to strengthen, support, and empower those whose hearts are fully committed to Him. He is not distant or indifferent—He is actively seeking opportunities to pour out His strength in the lives of His people.

To be loyal to God means to have a heart that is fully devoted, trusting Him above all else. It's not about being perfect, but about relying on Him instead of leaning on our own understanding. Proverbs 3:5-6 says, *"Trust in the Lord with all your heart, and lean not on your own understanding; in all your ways acknowledge Him, and He shall direct your paths."* When we stay devoted to Him, we position ourselves to receive His strength.

The enemy wants to convince you that you are alone, that you have to handle things on your own, but this verse reminds us that God is actively searching for those who will trust Him so He can step in and show His power. Psalm 46:1 declares, *"God is our refuge and strength, a very present help in trouble."* He is not passive—He is ready to act on behalf of those who call on Him.

If you've been feeling weak or uncertain, remember that God is looking to strengthen you. Keep your heart turned toward Him, trust in His faithfulness, and allow Him to show Himself strong in your life. He is not just watching—He is working on your behalf.

July 1

The Lord will fight for you, and you shall hold your peace.

Exodus 14:14

W hen the Israelites stood at the edge of the Red Sea with the Egyptian army closing in, fear threatened to overwhelm them. But Moses reminded them of a powerful truth—this battle was not theirs to fight! God Himself would deliver them, and their role was to trust and remain at peace.

How often do we find ourselves striving to fix our problems, worrying over solutions, or battling in our own strength? Yet God's promise remains the same: *He* is the one who fights for us. Our job is to stand firm in faith. 2 Chronicles 20:17 echoes this powerful promise: *"You will not need to fight in this battle. Position yourselves, stand still and see the salvation of the Lord."* The greatest victories come when we surrender control and let God move on our behalf.

Holding your peace doesn't mean doing nothing—it means refusing to give in to fear, anxiety, or doubt. Isaiah 26:3 says, *"You will keep him in perfect peace, whose mind is stayed on You, because he trusts in You."* When we trust in God's faithfulness, we can rest, knowing that He is working even when we can't see it.

The abundant life is not about struggling through every battle—it's about walking in the victory that God has already won for you! If you are facing a situation that feels impossible, take a step back and remember: the Lord is fighting for you. Stand in faith, hold your peace, and watch Him make a way where there seems to be none.

Blessed be the God and Father of our Lord Jesus Christ, who has blessed us with every spiritual blessing in the heavenly places in Christ.

Ephesians 1:3

God's blessings are not just occasional or conditional—they are already yours in Christ. This verse reveals that as believers, we have been given every spiritual blessing in the heavenly realm. We are not waiting to be blessed; we are already blessed through our relationship with Jesus.

Many people live as though they are still trying to earn God's favor, believing that blessings are something to be achieved. But this verse tells us that God has already poured out everything we need—His love, grace, healing, authority, provision, and peace—through Christ. 2 Peter 1:3 confirms this truth: *"His divine power has given to us all things that pertain to life and godliness."* The abundant life doesn't come from striving—it comes from receiving what has already been given.

These spiritual blessings are not just for eternity; they affect our lives now. Healing, wisdom, strength, joy, and the power of the Holy Spirit are all part of the inheritance we have in Christ. Jesus secured these blessings for us through His finished work, and as heirs of His kingdom, we have full access to them. Romans 8:17 says, *"If children, then heirs—heirs of God and joint heirs with Christ."*

If you have ever felt like you are lacking, remember that God has already given you everything you need. You don't have to strive to be blessed—you simply need to walk in the truth of what is already yours. Receive His blessings, live with confidence, and step fully into the abundant life He has provided for you.

July 3

Thus says the Lord, your Redeemer, the Holy One of Israel: "I am the Lord your God, who teaches you to profit, who leads you by the way you should go."

Isaiah 48:17

God is not only our Redeemer—He is our Teacher and Guide. He desires for us to walk in wisdom, to prosper in every area of life, and to follow the path He has laid out for us. True abundance is not found in trying to succeed in our own wisdom and knowledge but in being led by Him.

The word *profit* in this verse doesn't just refer to financial gain. It means to advance, to succeed, and to flourish according to God's design. His wisdom teaches us how to live in a way that brings true fulfillment, not just temporary success. Joshua 1:8 echoes this truth: *"For then you will make your way prosperous, and then you will have good success."* If there is "good success," then there can be "bad" success as well! Success God's way is always good, but when we try to do things our own way, the results aren't always as beneficial.

Beyond teaching, He also leads us in the way we should go. Many people struggle with uncertainty, wondering if they are making the right decisions. But God is not silent—He actively directs our steps. Psalm 32:8 assures us, *"I will instruct you and teach you in the way you should go; I will guide you with My eye."* His leading is personal, intentional, and always for our good.

If you've been feeling lost or unsure about your next step, take comfort in this promise. God does not leave His children to figure things out alone—He is the one who teaches and leads. Trust His wisdom, follow His guidance, and allow Him to bring you into the abundant life He has prepared for you.

Therefore if the Son makes you free,
you shall be free indeed.

John 8:36

Freedom is not about escaping hardship—it is about being released from bondage. Throughout history, people have longed for freedom from oppression, servitude, and the weight of sin. Jesus came to provide a freedom greater than any political or earthly liberation—He came to free us from the power of sin, the demands of the law, and the fear of separation from God.

Many people live as though they are still in chains, even after receiving Christ. They struggle under the pressure to earn God's approval, as if their salvation depends on their performance. But this verse reminds us that when Jesus sets us free, we are no longer slaves to sin or bound by the impossible standard of trying to be "good enough." Romans 8:2 confirms this: *"For the law of the Spirit of life in Christ Jesus has made me free from the law of sin and death."*

This freedom is not just about what we are freed *from*—it's also about what we are freed *into*. In Christ, we are free to live in His grace, free to walk in righteousness without fear of condemnation, and free to experience a relationship with God that is not based on our works but on His love. Galatians 5:1 urges us, *"Stand fast therefore in the liberty by which Christ has made us free, and do not be entangled again with a yoke of bondage."* We should be slaves of grace, not of the law!

If you've been weighed down by guilt, striving, or the fear that you will never be enough, let this truth settle in your heart: Jesus has already secured your freedom. You are not a slave to sin, to fear, or to religious performance. Walk in the fullness of His grace, knowing that the freedom He gives is absolute. You are free indeed!

*But the Lord is faithful, who will establish you
and guard you from the evil one.*

2 Thessalonians 3:3

God's faithfulness is unwavering. No matter what challenges arise, He remains steadfast in His commitment to protect, strengthen, and uphold His children. This verse is a powerful reminder that we are not left to fend for ourselves—God is actively guarding us and securing our steps.

To be established means to be firmly set, strengthened, and made unshakable. When we build our lives on God's truth, He establishes us in His will, ensuring that we stand strong no matter what comes against us. Psalm 37:23-24 assures us, *"The steps of a good man are ordered by the Lord, and He delights in his way. Though he fall, he shall not be utterly cast down; for the Lord upholds him with His hand."* Even in times of uncertainty, God is positioning us for victory!

Beyond establishing us, He also guards us. The enemy may try to attack, but he can't win against those who are protected by the Lord. Isaiah 54:17 declares, *"No weapon formed against you shall prosper."* This does not mean that difficulties won't come, but it does mean that they will not succeed. Whether it is an attack against your health, finances, relationships, or any other part of your life, the enemy simply can't have a victory that has already been promised to you!

If you've been feeling vulnerable or uncertain, let this verse encourage you. You are not alone in the battle—God is both your foundation and your shield. Trust in His faithfulness, stand firm in His promises, and walk with confidence, knowing that He is protecting and establishing you every step of the way.

July 6

*Though your beginning was small, yet your latter end
would increase abundantly.*

Job 8:7

E very great work starts with a single step. No matter how
small things may seem now, God's plan is always for
increase, growth, and abundance. This verse reassures
us that where we are today is not where we will stay—God is
faithful to bring increase to those who trust Him.

The world often measures success by immediate results, but
God values faithfulness in the process. Zechariah 4:10 reminds
us, *"For who has despised the day of small things?"* Small
beginnings are never insignificant when God is involved. Jesus
echoed this truth in Luke 16:10: *"He who is faithful in what is
least is faithful also in much."* What may seem like a small start
today can become something far greater than you imagined.
One small seed planted may take time to produce fruit, but
when it does, it is multiplied many times over! Even when
progress feels slow, God is working behind the scenes,
positioning you for increase.

This promise also speaks to those who have faced loss or
hardship. Job endured unimaginable suffering, yet God restored
him beyond what he had before. Job 42:12 says, *"Now the Lord
blessed the latter days of Job more than his beginning."* If you
feel like you're in a season of smallness or struggle, remember
that God's story for you is not finished. His plan is always for
increase, provision, and purpose. His nature is to multiply,
restore, and bless beyond what we can see in the moment.

No matter where you start, trust that greater things are ahead.
Stay faithful, keep believing, and watch as He leads you into
the abundant life He has prepared for you. The best is yet to
come!

July 7

Lord, You will establish peace for us,
for You have also done all our works in us.

Isaiah 26:12

Rest is found in trusting God. This verse is a powerful reminder that peace is not something we manufacture—it is something God establishes in our lives as we surrender to Him. True abundance is not just about what we achieve, but about walking in the peace that comes from knowing God is the One working in and through us.

The phrase *"You will establish peace for us"* shows that lasting peace is not based on circumstances but on God's faithfulness. The world offers temporary relief through accomplishments, success, or comfort, but none of these things create true, lasting peace. Jesus said in John 14:27, *"Peace I leave with you, My peace I give to you; not as the world gives do I give to you."* The peace of God is unshakable and anchored in His presence rather than in our circumstances.

The second part of this verse, *"for You have also done all our works in us,"* shifts the focus from our own efforts to God's power working through us. Philippians 2:13 affirms this: *"For it is God who works in you both to will and to do for His good pleasure."* Instead of striving to accomplish everything in our own strength, we can trust that He is actively working within us, changing and equipping us for what He has called us to do.

If you've been feeling pressure to figure everything out or make things happen, step into the peace God has already established for you. He is the One guiding your steps, working in your life, and fulfilling His promises. Let go of striving, trust His process, and rest in the truth that He is the One accomplishing His good work in you.

And he showed me a pure river of water of life, clear as crystal, proceeding from the throne of God and of the Lamb. In the middle of its street, and on either side of the river, was the tree of life, which bore twelve fruits, each tree yielding its fruit every month. The leaves of the tree were for the healing of the nations.

Revelation 22:1-2

The kingdom of God is full of life, healing, and continual provision. This passage gives a glimpse of eternity, where God's abundance flows freely, yet it also reflects His heart for us today. The same river of life that flows from His throne is available to refresh and sustain us now.

This river represents the Holy Spirit, lives within each believer today. Jesus spoke of this in John 7:38, saying, *"He who believes in Me...out of his heart will flow rivers of living water."* God's abundance represented by this river is something we can experience every day through our connection with Him in our spirits.

The tree of life symbolizes unending provision. It bears fruit every month, a picture of continuous supply. No season is ever barren in God's kingdom. Psalm 1:3 describes the righteous as *"a tree planted by the rivers of water, that brings forth its fruit in its season."* Those who remain in Him will always bear fruit!

The leaves of the tree bring healing, not just individually, but to nations. God's plan is complete restoration—spiritually, physically, and in every broken area. His abundant life brings wholeness to all who come to Him.

If you feel weary or in need of renewal, step into the flow of His river. His life is abundant, His provision unending, and His healing available. Stay connected to Him and let His refreshing presence renew you daily.

July 9

For the gifts and the calling of God are irrevocable.

Romans 11:29

God's gifts and calling on your life are permanent. He does not change His mind about you, nor does He withdraw His purpose because of mistakes, delays, or detours. When He calls you, He equips you, and His plan remains in place no matter what.

The word *irrevocable* means that His gifts cannot be taken back. Unlike human promises, which can be broken, God's word is unchanging. Numbers 23:19 confirms this: *"God is not a man, that He should lie, nor a son of man, that He should repent. Has He said, and will He not do?"* If He has given you a calling, He has not abandoned it. Even if you have walked away, He has not changed His mind and wants you to step back into it.

Many struggle with the idea that their past disqualifies them. But God knew every weakness, failure, and detour before He called you. Moses doubted his ability to lead, David made terrible mistakes, and Peter denied Jesus—yet God still fulfilled His plans in each of their lives. God's plan is greater than any mistake, and His grace is always enough to bring you back on course. When He starts something, He finishes it, and that includes the work He is doing in you (Philippians 1:6).

His calling is not based on your perfection but on His faithfulness. Even when you feel unworthy, God sees the potential He placed within you. No failure can cancel His purpose. If you've been holding back because of fear or doubt, it's time to move forward. Trust Him, embrace your calling, and walk in the gifts He has given you—because they are yours forever.

*A man will be satisfied with good by the fruit
of his mouth, and the recompense of a man's
hands will be rendered to him.*

Proverbs 12:14

What you speak and what you do both play a role in the life you experience. This verse highlights two key principles: the power of words and the blessing of diligent work. When we align both with God's wisdom, we set ourselves up to walk in the abundance He has for us.

Our words have an incredible impact. Proverbs 18:21 says, *"Death and life are in the power of the tongue, and those who love it will eat its fruit."* Our words shape our future, influencing our faith, relationships, and even our outlook on life. Speaking God's promises releases faith, brings encouragement, and positions us to receive His best. Negative words, however, can have the opposite effect!

The second half of this verse means that the work we do produces results. God designed work to be a source of satisfaction and provision, not toil and frustration. Adam was given a job almost immediately after he was created! Work is a good thing, not a curse. When we work with integrity and diligence, trusting God as our source, He blesses the labor of our hands.

Both our words and our actions matter. If we speak life and work faithfully, we will see the rewards. If you want to experience the abundant life in ever increasing ways, start by speaking God's truth and being faithful in what He has given you to do. His promises are sure, and when we align with His ways, we will enjoy the abundant life He has prepared for us.

The Lord shall preserve you from all evil;
He shall preserve your soul. The Lord shall preserve
your going out and your coming in from this
time forth, and even forevermore.

Psalm 121:7-8

God is not just a temporary protector—He is our eternal guardian. This passage reassures us that His protection is comprehensive, covering every part of our lives. From the moment we wake up to the time we rest, He is watching over us.

The phrase *"The Lord shall preserve you from all evil"* does not mean we will never face difficulties, but that God shields us from harm that would destroy us. Isaiah 54:17 confirms this: *"No weapon formed against you shall prosper."* Challenges may come, but His protection ensures they will not overtake us. He is our refuge, our defender, and our safe place.

"He shall preserve your soul" speaks of more than physical safety—it is a promise of spiritual security. God's care extends beyond outward circumstances to the deepest parts of who we are. Jesus said in John 10:28, *"And I give them eternal life, and they shall never perish; neither shall anyone snatch them out of My hand."* No force of darkness can separate us from His love.

"The Lord shall preserve your going out and your coming in" signifies His constant presence in our daily lives. Whether we are stepping into something new, facing the unknown, or simply going about our routine, He is with us.

If you've been feeling vulnerable or uncertain, hold onto this truth—God is your keeper. His protection is not limited to a season; it is everlasting. Trust Him, walk in His peace, and rest in the assurance that He is watching over you now and forevermore.

For whoever finds me finds life,
and obtains favor from the Lord.

Proverbs 8:35

True life and favor are found in seeking wisdom—God's wisdom. This verse is wisdom itself speaking, and she reveals that when we embrace God's instruction and guidance, we step into the fullness of life He intended for us.

This says that when you find wisdom, you find life. God's wisdom leads us into a life rich in peace, joy, and purpose. It protects us from destruction, aligns us with His will, and keeps us on a path of righteousness. Proverbs 3:18 describes wisdom as a tree of life to those who hold onto it. Without wisdom, people make impulsive, harmful decisions, but when we walk in God's wisdom, we live in the fullness of His blessings. His wisdom brings clarity in confusion and steadiness in seasons of uncertainty.

This verse also speaks of obtaining favor from the Lord. Favor is God's supernatural grace that opens doors, provides opportunities, and brings blessings beyond what we could achieve on our own. Psalm 5:12 says, *"For You, O Lord, will bless the righteous; with favor You will surround him as with a shield."* Walking in wisdom brings favor because we make decisions that align with God's will. His favor positions us for opportunities we could never create for ourselves and gives us influence that no human effort could accomplish! It surrounds your life with God's goodness in ways that even others can't help but notice.

If you want to experience more of God's favor and the fullness of life, pursue His wisdom above all else. Seek Him in His Word, listen to His guidance, and trust His ways. When you do, you will find yourself walking in the abundant life He has prepared for you, surrounded by His unshakable favor.

July 13

But you shall receive power when the Holy Spirit has come upon you; and you shall be witnesses to Me in Jerusalem, and in all Judea and Samaria, and to the end of the earth.

Acts 1:8

The abundant life God has for you is not meant to be lived in weakness or fear—it is a life of power, purpose, and impact. Jesus spoke these words to His disciples just before ascending into heaven, promising that they would receive supernatural power through the Holy Spirit. This same power is available to every believer today.

The word *power* in this verse comes from the Greek word *dunamis*, which means miraculous strength, ability, and force. It is not a natural power but a divine empowerment to live boldly, overcome obstacles, and fulfill God's calling. This power enables us to do what we could never accomplish on our own. Ephesians 3:20 confirms this: *"Now to Him who is able to do exceedingly abundantly above all that we ask or think, according to the power that works in us."*

But this power isn't just for personal benefit—it's given so we can be *witnesses* of Jesus. God's plan is for His message to spread, starting in our own communities and reaching the ends of the earth. When the Holy Spirit empowers us, we become living testimonies of His goodness, grace, and truth. Our words, actions, and lives reflect His transforming power to those around us.

If you've ever felt inadequate or unqualified, remember that God has already provided everything you need. You don't have to rely on your own strength—the Holy Spirit equips you. Step out in faith, embrace His power, and be a light that points others to Jesus. You are called, empowered, and sent to make a difference!

The righteous shall flourish like a palm tree, he shall grow like a cedar in Lebanon. Those who are planted in the house of the Lord shall flourish in the courts of our God. They shall still bear fruit in old age; they shall be fresh and flourishing, to declare that the Lord is upright; He is my rock, and there is no unrighteousness in Him.

Psalm 92:12-15

A life rooted in God is a life that flourishes. This passage paints a beautiful picture of the abundant life God intends for His people—one of strength, growth, fruitfulness, and endurance. When we stay connected to Him, we don't just survive—we thrive.

The palm tree and the cedar of Lebanon are symbols of resilience and strength. Palm trees bend but do not break in storms, while cedars grow tall and sturdy, representing endurance. Likewise, those who trust in the Lord will not be easily shaken by life's trials. Jeremiah 17:7-8 echoes this truth: *"Blessed is the man who trusts in the Lord…He shall be like a tree planted by the waters…he will not be anxious in the year of drought, nor will he cease from yielding fruit."*

Fruitfulness is not limited to a particular season of life. *"They shall still bear fruit in old age"* means that God's purpose for us never expires. No matter our age, we can remain spiritually fresh and flourishing. When we stay planted in His presence, He continually renews and strengthens us.

Flourishing isn't just about personal blessing—it's about declaring God's goodness. Our lives become testimonies of His faithfulness. If you want to live strong, grow deep, and remain fruitful, stay planted in Him. His presence is the source of unshakable strength and lasting abundance.

July 15

*Whatever your hand finds to do, do it with your might;
for there is no work or device or knowledge or wisdom
in the grave where you are going.*

Ecclesiastes 9:10

Go od created you with intention and purpose. That means your life—your work, your relationships, your gifts—matter deeply to Him. This verse encourages you to lean into life with passion and wholehearted effort. Whether you're tackling a major assignment or doing something as simple as folding laundry, God delights in your faithfulness.

Doing your work with all your might isn't about striving in your own strength—it's about showing up with excellence and purpose, knowing that God is in it with you. Colossians 3:23 puts it beautifully: *"And whatever you do, do it heartily, as to the Lord and not to men."* When we approach our daily tasks with that perspective, even the mundane becomes meaningful. Your effort becomes worship. It becomes a way to reflect God's character and carry His light into the world. And when you give your best, not only are you honoring Him, but you're also positioning yourself for growth and blessing.

There's also a gentle urgency in this wisdom. We're only here for a limited time, and one day, the chance to make an earthly impact will come to an end. But today? You have breath in your lungs, strength in your body, and opportunities in your path.

So don't hold back. Pour yourself into the calling in front of you—big or small. Whether you're raising children, running a business, serving in ministry, or learning something new, let your efforts reflect the God you serve. He's cheering you on, and He'll make your faithfulness count—both now and for eternity.

The eternal God is your refuge, and underneath are the everlasting arms; He will thrust out the enemy from before you, and will say, "Destroy!"

Deuteronomy 33:27

N o matter what you face, you are never alone. This verse is a powerful reminder that God is both our refuge and our strength. His presence surrounds us, His arms uphold us, and His power goes before us to drive out every obstacle that stands in the way of His plan for our lives.

When this verse refers to "eternal God," it is referring to His unchanging nature. Unlike natural, temporary sources of security, His protection is everlasting. Psalm 46:1 affirms this: *"God is our refuge and strength, a very present help in trouble."* He is always present to provide refuge, strength, and help! No matter how uncertain life becomes, we can rest knowing He remains constant.

Just as a parent holds their natural child securely, God holds us in His care. Isaiah 41:10 reminds us, *"Fear not, for I am with you; be not dismayed, for I am your God. I will strengthen you, yes, I will help you, I will uphold you with My righteous right hand."* His arms never fail, never weaken, and never let go.

The final part of the verse declares that God fights for us. He doesn't just shield us—He actively removes the enemy's plans from our path. When we trust in Him, we don't have to battle alone; He is the one who gives victory!

If you've been feeling weak or overwhelmed, take comfort in knowing that you are held, protected, and defended by the everlasting arms of God. His strength is greater than any challenge, and He will never let you fall.

"Bring all the tithes into the storehouse, that there may be food in My house, and try Me now in this," says the Lord of hosts, "if I will not open for you the windows of heaven and pour out for you such blessing that there will not be room enough to receive it."

Malachi 3:10

God's heart is to bless His people abundantly, but He also calls us to trust Him in the area of giving. This verse is one of the only places in Scripture where God invites us to *test* Him—to see for ourselves how faithful He is when we obey Him in tithing.

The phrase *"open for you the windows of heaven"* paints a picture of unlimited provision. Throughout the Bible, God consistently proves Himself as the provider of His people. In Philippians 4:19, Paul writes, *"And my God shall supply all your need according to His riches in glory by Christ Jesus,"* specifically to those who had faithfully given to his ministry. When we honor God with our resources, we are positioning ourselves to receive from the abundance of His kingdom.

God's blessings aren't just financial. While provision is part of it, His blessings also include favor, opportunities, wisdom, and divine connections. Even more exciting, God's provision exceeds what we can even contain! Luke 6:38 affirms this principle: *"Give, and it will be given to you: good measure, pressed down, shaken together, and running over."*

Tithing isn't about losing—it's about trusting. It's an act of faith that acknowledges God as our source. When we give, we align ourselves with His supernatural provision. If you've been holding back out of fear, take God at His word. Trust Him, release what's in your hand, and watch as He pours out blessings beyond measure.

Instead of your shame you shall have double honor, and instead of confusion they shall rejoice in their portion. Therefore in their land they shall possess double; everlasting joy shall be theirs.

Isaiah 61:7

God is a God of restoration. This verse is a powerful promise that He does not just replace what was lost—He restores and multiplies. Where there has been shame, He brings honor. Where there has been confusion, He gives clarity and joy. And where there has been loss, He promises *double* in return.

The concept of double restoration is seen throughout Scripture. In Job 42:10, after Job's season of intense suffering, God *"restored Job's losses when he prayed for his friends. Indeed, the Lord gave Job twice as much as he had before."* God's heart is not just to bring us back to where we were but to bless us beyond what we had before. He does not restore to the level of survival—He restores to the level of abundance.

This verse also speaks to everlasting joy. When God restores, He doesn't just give temporary relief—He gives lasting peace and rejoicing. Psalm 30:11 says, *"You have turned for me my mourning into dancing; You have put off my sackcloth and clothed me with gladness."* His restoration reaches deep, replacing sorrow with joy and lack with overflowing provision.

If you have experienced setbacks, disappointments, or loss, take heart. God is in the business of turning sorrow into joy and lack into abundance! He will not only restore what was taken, but He will multiply His blessings in your life. Trust in His faithfulness, expect His goodness, and receive His promise of double restoration. The best is yet to come!

July 19

For you are all sons of God through faith in Christ Jesus.

Galatians 3:26

Belonging to God's family is not something we earn—it is something we receive by faith. This verse is a reminder that our identity as His children is not based on performance, background, or our actions, but solely on our faith in Jesus.

Through Christ, we are no longer outsiders, but members of God's household. *"But as many as received Him, to them He gave the right to become children of God, to those who believe in His name"* (John 1:12). When we accept Jesus, we step into the fullness of this new identity. We are no longer defined by our past mistakes, our family history, or the world's opinions—we are defined by our relationship with Him.

Being a child of God also comes with privileges. Just as earthly parents care for their children, God provides, protects, and leads us. Romans 8:17 tells us, *"And if children, then heirs—heirs of God and joint heirs with Christ."* This means we are not just children—we are heirs of His promises. Everything that belongs to Jesus now belongs to us! He has given us access to His wisdom, strength, authority, and blessings so that we can live victoriously.

This identity also changes how we approach life. When we understand that we are children of the King, we stop living with a sense of lack, rejection, or unworthiness. Instead, we walk with confidence, knowing that we are fully accepted, deeply loved, and forever part of His family.

If you've ever struggled with feelings of insecurity or doubt, let this verse be your foundation. You are not an orphan—you belong to God. He has chosen you, redeemed you, and given you full access to His love and provision. Walk boldly as His child today!

July 20

The Lord is on my side; I will not fear.
What can man do to me?

Psalm 118:6

C onfidence and security are found in knowing that God is with you. This verse is a declaration of trust—no matter what opposition arises, fear has no power when the Lord is on your side.

Fear is a tool the enemy uses to keep believers from walking in their full potential. But Scripture repeatedly reminds us that we do not have to live in fear! Romans 8:31 asks, *"If God is for us, who can be against us?"* The truth that the very Creator of the universe is on our side is greater than any challenge, threat, or obstacle we may face. When we truly believe that He is with us, fear loses its grip.

The psalmist's bold statement, *"What can man do to me?"* is not a denial of hardships but a declaration that no earthly opposition can override God's plan. Jesus reinforced this in Matthew 10:28: *"And do not fear those who kill the body but cannot kill the soul. But rather fear Him who is able to destroy both soul and body in hell."* The opinions of others, the threats of the enemy, or the uncertainties of life do not have the final say—God does!

Living in the fullness of God's promises requires rejecting fear and embracing faith. Fear paralyzes, but faith propels us forward. 2 Timothy 1:7 reminds us, *"For God has not given us a spirit of fear, but of power and of love and of a sound mind."*

If fear has been holding you back, let this verse be your battle cry. God is on your side! He fights for you, defends you, and walks with you through every trial. Stand in confidence, knowing that nothing and no one can take you out of His hands.

So he answered and said to me: "This is the word of the Lord to Zerubbabel: Not by might nor by power, but by My Spirit," says the Lord of hosts.

Zechariah 4:6

S uccess in God's kingdom does not come through human effort alone—it comes by His Spirit. This verse was spoken to Zerubbabel, the governor of Judah, who faced the overwhelming task of rebuilding the temple after Israel's exile. God's message to him was clear: the work would not be accomplished through human strength, strategy, or resources, but by the power of the Holy Spirit.

How often do we try to force things to happen in our own strength? Many people rely on their skills, connections, or sheer determination to succeed, only to find themselves exhausted and frustrated. But God's way is different. Psalm 127:1 reminds us, *"Unless the Lord builds the house, they labor in vain who build it."* The abundant life is not about striving—it is about surrendering to the Spirit's power.

This truth applies to every challenge we face. Whether it's fulfilling our calling, overcoming obstacles, or walking in victory, the answer is not in human effort but in divine empowerment. Acts 1:8 declares, *"But you shall receive power when the Holy Spirit has come upon you."* The strength we need comes from Him, not from ourselves!

If you have been relying on your own abilities, shift your focus. God is not asking you to accomplish everything in your own power—He is asking you to trust His Spirit. The victory you seek, the breakthrough you need, and the calling you are meant to fulfill will come, not by might nor by power, but by His Spirit.

And we know that all things work together for good to those who love God, to those who are the called according to His purpose.

Romans 8:28

Life is filled with highs and lows, victories and challenges. But for those who belong to God, there is an unshakable promise—everything, even the difficulties, is working together for good. This doesn't mean that God *causes* bad things to happen, but rather that He can *use* every situation—good or bad—for His greater purpose.

The key phrase in this verse is *"all things."* Not some things, not just the good things—*all* things. Even the trials, failures, and disappointments in life are not wasted in God's hands. Joseph's story in Genesis is a powerful example. Though he was betrayed, enslaved, and imprisoned, God used every painful moment to position him for his destiny! In the end, Joseph declared to his brothers in Genesis 50:20, *"But as for you, you meant evil against me; but God meant it for good."* The harm done to him was not God's doing, but He redeemed it for a greater purpose.

This promise is for those who love God—those who trust Him and walk in His purpose. When we submit our lives to Him, He takes even the hardest situations and weaves them into something meaningful. Proverbs 3:5-6 encourages us, *"Trust in the Lord with all your heart, and lean not on your own understanding; in all your ways acknowledge Him, and He shall direct your paths."*

If you're facing challenges, take heart. God is not the author of pain, but He is the master of redemption! He can turn any situation around for your good and His glory. Trust Him, keep loving Him, and watch as He brings beauty from even the most difficult circumstances.

Blessed be the God and Father of our Lord Jesus Christ, who according to His abundant mercy has begotten us again to a living hope through the resurrection of Jesus Christ from the dead.

1 Peter 1:3

Hope is more than just wishful thinking—it is a confident expectation of God's goodness. This verse reminds us that through Jesus, we have been given a *living hope*, one that is secure, unshakable, and eternal. This hope is not based on circumstances but on the resurrection power of Christ!

When Peter wrote, *"begotten us again,"* refers to being born again into a new life. Through faith in Jesus, we are no longer bound by our past or defined by our failures. We have been made new, brought into God's family, and given access to His abundant promises. 2 Corinthians 5:17 declares, *"Therefore, if anyone is in Christ, he is a new creation; old things have passed away; behold, all things have become new."*

The living hope we have is rooted in Jesus' resurrection. Because He conquered death, we can live with the assurance that His victory is our victory. Unlike worldly hope, which fades with disappointment, our hope is alive because Christ is alive. Romans 15:13 reinforces this truth: *"Now may the God of hope fill you with all joy and peace in believing, that you may abound in hope by the power of the Holy Spirit."* This is a hope, powered by the Holy Spirit, that strengthens, sustains, and carries us through every trial.

No matter what you're facing, you have a hope that cannot be shaken! Jesus has already secured your future, and His promises are sure. Hold on to this living hope, knowing that He is faithful, His mercy is abundant, and His plans for you are good.

You did not choose Me, but I chose you and appointed you that you should go and bear fruit, and that your fruit should remain, that whatever you ask the Father in My name He may give you.

John 15:16

Y our life is not an accident. Before you ever sought God, He had already chosen you. This verse is a powerful reminder that God's calling is intentional—He has appointed you to live a fruitful life and to walk in His divine purpose.

The phrase *"You did not choose Me, but I chose you"* reveals the heart of God. His love and grace reached out to us first. Ephesians 1:4 says, *"He chose us in Him before the foundation of the world."* Before the world was even *created*, God chose you and designed you for a purpose!

Jesus didn't just choose us to exist—He *appointed* us to *bear fruit*. This means our lives are meant to make an impact. Galatians 5:22-23 describes the fruit of the Spirit—love, joy, peace, patience, kindness, goodness, faithfulness, gentleness, and self-control. But fruitfulness also includes influencing others for God's kingdom, living out our purpose, and making a difference in the lives of those around us.

The promise continues: *"That whatever you ask the Father in My name He may give you."* Wow, what a promise! *Whatever* we ask! When we align with God's calling, our prayers become powerful. We are not left to fulfill His purpose alone—He provides everything we need to walk in it.

If you've ever doubted your worth or purpose, let this verse remind you: You are chosen, appointed, and equipped. Walk boldly in your calling, knowing that your life is meant to bear fruit that lasts!

July 25

I know your works. See, I have set before you an open door, and no one can shut it; for you have a little strength, have kept My word, and have not denied My name.

Revelation 3:8

When God opens a door, no force in heaven or on earth can close it. This verse is a powerful declaration that God is the one who makes a way, positioning His people for opportunities, blessings, and advancement that no one can take away.

The phrase *"I have set before you an open door"* indicates supernatural access. God is the one who promotes, provides, and leads His people into new seasons of growth and purpose. Isaiah 22:22 echoes this truth: *"The key of the house of David I will lay on His shoulder; so He shall open, and no one shall shut."* When God opens a door for you, no opposition, rejection, or limitation can stop His plan.

This promise is given to those who remain faithful. Jesus commended the church in Philadelphia for keeping His word, even when they had *"a little strength."* This shows that God is not looking for perfect strength—He is looking for endurance and faithfulness. 2 Corinthians 12:9 reminds us, *"My grace is sufficient for you, for My strength is made perfect in weakness."* Even when we feel inadequate, He is the one who empowers us to walk through the doors He opens.

If you feel stuck or uncertain about the future, trust that God is the one leading you. His open doors cannot be shut by circumstances, people, or even your own limitations. Keep your eyes on Him, focus on His Word, stand firm in faith, and step boldly into what He has prepared for you. The way is open— walk through it!

*For as many as are led by the Spirit of God,
these are sons of God.*

Romans 8:14

L iving the abundant life means being led, not by emotions, opinions, or circumstances, but by the Spirit of God. This verse reveals an incredible truth—those who are guided by the Holy Spirit are not just followers; they are sons and daughters of God. Our identity is directly tied to our willingness to be led by Him.

To be led by the Spirit means walking in close relationship with God, allowing Him to direct our steps. The more you focus on listening to His direction and following His voice, the easier it will become. He is always speaking, constantly leading. We just need to learn to tune in to His frequency. You do hear His voice (John 10:27)! As you learn to listen and follow, instead of striving to figure everything out, you can rely on His wisdom, knowing that He sees what you can't.

Being a son of God is about more than just salvation—it's about inheritance and intimacy. Galatians 4:7 says, *"Therefore you are no longer a slave but a son, and if a son, then an heir of God through Christ."* As His children, we have access to His wisdom, His provision, and His guidance in every area of life. When we are led by the Spirit, we step into the fullness of His purpose for us.

If you've been struggling with uncertainty, ask the Holy Spirit to lead you. He speaks through His Word, through peace in your heart, and through His still, small voice. You don't have to navigate life on your own—God has already provided His Spirit to guide you every step of the way. Trust Him, follow His lead, and walk confidently as His beloved child.

July 27

*The blessing of the Lord makes one rich,
and He adds no sorrow with it.*

Proverbs 10:22

God's blessings bring increase without any kind of burden. Unlike the world's version of success, which often comes with stress, worry, and exhaustion, God's prosperity is accompanied by peace and fulfillment. When He blesses, it is complete—lacking nothing and free from regret.

The phrase *"makes one rich"* doesn't refer only to financial wealth but to a life that's enriched in every way. True abundance includes joy, health, strong relationships, purpose, and provision—all flowing from His goodness. His blessing touches every part of your life, bringing wholeness and victory. And when you receive His promises through faith in Jesus, it not only transforms your present—it impacts future generations. His blessing becomes part of the legacy you leave behind.

The world offers a counterfeit version of success—one that often comes at the cost of health, peace, or integrity. Many chase after riches only to end up worn out, anxious, or spiritually dry. But God's way is different. When you follow His wisdom and trust Him as your source, His blessings don't come with strings attached. You receive what you need—without the weight of striving or regret.

God's blessings are sustainable because they come from His hand, not from human effort alone. That doesn't mean you won't work hard, but it does mean your prosperity isn't rooted in pressure. When you walk in His ways, He provides in ways beyond what you could make happen yourself. So, if you've been striving, let this verse remind you: God's blessings don't drain you—they fill you! Trust Him as your provider and walk in the abundance He's already prepared for you. His way is always the best way.

If you are willing and obedient,
you shall eat the good of the land.

Isaiah 1:19

G od's promises of abundance are available to those who align their hearts with Him. This verse highlights two key conditions for receiving His best: willingness and obedience. But true obedience is not about striving—it flows naturally from a heart that trusts in Him.

To be *willing* means to have a surrendered heart, one that desires God's ways over our own. Many people see obedience as a burden, but when we walk in faith, it becomes effortless. Jesus said in Matthew 11:30, *"For My yoke is easy and My burden is light."* When we trust that His ways lead to life, we don't obey out of fear or obligation—we obey because we believe He is good.

Faith always leads to obedience. James 2:26 reminds us, *"Faith without works is dead."* When we truly believe God's Word, our actions follow naturally. Abraham didn't struggle to obey God when asked to leave his homeland—he trusted in God's promise, and his obedience was a response to that faith (Hebrews 11:8).

God's blessings—the good of the land—flow where there is trust. When we believe in His faithfulness, we naturally follow His lead, and He provides what we need. Deuteronomy 28:2 affirms, *"And all these blessings shall come upon you and overtake you, because you obey the voice of the Lord your God."*

If obedience has felt like striving, shift your focus. Rather than trying to "obey harder," lean into faith! Believe that God is working in you to do His will (Philippians 2:13). Trust Him completely and watch how obedience becomes the natural response of a heart confident in His goodness.

July 29

Why are you cast down, O my soul? And why are you disquieted within me? Hope in God; for I shall yet praise Him, the help of my countenance and my God.

Psalm 42:11

There are moments in life when discouragement tries to take hold. The psalmist here is speaking directly to his own soul, challenging feelings of despair and reminding himself where true hope is found. This verse teaches us that even when emotions pull us down, we can choose to put our trust in God.

The phrase *"Why are you cast down, O my soul?"* shows that even strong believers face seasons of struggle. David, a man after God's own heart, often wrestled with sorrow and fear. But instead of letting those feelings define him, he redirected his focus. He didn't deny his emotions, but he also didn't let them rule over him. 2 Corinthians 5:7 reminds us, *"For we walk by faith, not by sight."* Emotions can feel oppressing at times, but even in the depths of despair, turning our eyes to Jesus will help us cling to hope in Him.

Biblical hope is not wishful thinking—it is a confident expectation in God's goodness and faithfulness. Lamentations 3:21-23 declares, *"This I recall to my mind, therefore I have hope. Through the Lord's mercies we are not consumed, because His compassions fail not. They are new every morning."* He never fails! When we shift our eyes from our circumstances to His promises, our hearts are encouraged.

If you've been battling discouragement, follow the psalmist's example. Speak truth over your soul. Remind yourself that God is your help, your source, and your joy. Even in the hardest moments, *yet* you will praise Him. His faithfulness never fails, and your hope in Him will never be in vain.

*I have been crucified with Christ; it is no longer I
who live, but Christ lives in me; and the life which I now
live in the flesh I live by faith in the Son of God,
who loved me and gave Himself for me.*

Galatians 2:20

Your old life is gone. In Christ, you are not simply improved—you are completely transformed! This verse refers to the core of the abundant life: living by faith, fully surrendered to the reality that Jesus now lives in you.

When you received Jesus, your old self—your sin, guilt, and striving—was put to death with Him. You are no longer bound by your past, nor do you have to earn righteousness through your own effort. Romans 6:6 says, *"Our old man was crucified with Him, that the body of sin might be done away with."* The power of sin no longer defines you because Jesus has already overcome it.

"It is no longer I who live, but Christ lives in me" is the ultimate truth of the believer's new identity. You are not just *trying* to imitate Christ—you are empowered by His very life within you! His Spirit leads, strengthens, and transforms you from the inside out. You are a brand-new creation, with a renewed spirit, truly alive in Him (2 Corinthians 5:17).

This transformed life is walked out daily through trust in Him. You don't have to figure it all out—your job is to believe and let His life flow through you. His love made this possible, and His grace sustains you.

If you've been struggling to live the Christian life in your own strength, let this truth set you free: You are no longer striving to be good enough—Christ in you *is* enough! Rest in Him, trust in Him, and live fully through faith in Him.

July 31

Fight the good fight of faith, lay hold on eternal life, to which you were also called and have confessed the good confession in the presence of many witnesses.

1 Timothy 6:12

Faith takes grit. It's not passive or automatic—it's something you engage in, especially when life pushes back. Living in the fullness of what God has promised often requires spiritual persistence. There are days when doubts creep in, distractions pull your focus, and challenges try to wear you down. But faith isn't about how you feel—it's about what you choose to believe and continue standing on.

This kind of faith holds on, even when circumstances don't line up. It refuses to let go of what God has spoken, no matter how long it takes to see the results. And it's not just about enduring hardship—it's about taking hold of the life God intended for you: one filled with purpose, peace, and power. That life isn't just a far-off hope for eternity—it's something you begin to experience here and now as you walk with Him.

One key to staying strong in your faith is what you say. Your words matter. When you speak what God says—especially when it's hard—you're reinforcing your trust in Him. Confessing truth out loud doesn't change God, but it changes you. It strengthens your heart and pushes back against fear and doubt.

If you're feeling worn down, take a breath and refocus. You weren't meant to fight in your own strength. God's already equipped you, and He's walking with you every step of the way. Keep believing. Keep speaking truth. Keep moving forward. What He's promised is worth holding onto—and He'll give you what you need to stand strong until you see it come to pass.

The Lord will give strength to His people;
the Lord will bless His people with peace.

Psalm 29:11

Strength and peace—two things every person needs—are both found in God. This verse reminds us that He is the source of supernatural strength and the giver of unshakable peace. No matter what challenges arise, His provision is more than enough.

The phrase *"The Lord will give strength to His people"* reveals that we are not meant to rely on our own abilities. Human strength has limits, but God's strength is endless. Isaiah 40:31 assures us, *"But those who wait on the Lord shall renew their strength; they shall mount up with wings like eagles."* When we lean on Him, He empowers us to keep going, even when we feel weak. His strength enables us to endure, to overcome, and to stand firm in faith.

"The Lord will bless His people with peace" is a promise that goes beyond the mere absence of conflict. The Hebrew word for *peace, shalom,* means completeness, wholeness, and well-being. This is the kind of peace Jesus offers in John 14:27: *"Peace I leave with you, My peace I give to you; not as the world gives do I give to you."* The world's peace depends on circumstances, but God's peace is constant, guarding our hearts and minds no matter what we face.

If you are feeling weak or overwhelmed, take hold of this promise today. God has given you His strength to endure and His peace to sustain you. You don't have to strive—simply receive what He has already made available. In Him, you are strong, secure, and at rest.

August 2

He who gets wisdom loves his own soul;
he who keeps understanding will find good.

Proverbs 19:8

Seeking wisdom is one of the greatest investments you can make in your life. This verse reveals that gaining wisdom is not just about knowledge—it is about valuing and enriching your own soul. Those who pursue and hold onto wisdom set themselves up for a life of blessing and success.

Wisdom is not just an external pursuit—it affects our very being. To love your soul means to desire what is truly best for your life, beyond temporary satisfaction. Proverbs 4:7 tells us, *"Wisdom is the principal thing; therefore get wisdom. And in all your getting, get understanding."* True wisdom comes from God, and when we embrace it, we position ourselves for growth, protection, and fulfillment. It keeps us on the right path, turning us away from making decisions that will cause us harm and instead leading us into blessing.

The second half of the verse emphasizes that wisdom is not just something we look for once. Keeping understanding means to seek it consistently and guard it once you have it! Many hear wisdom but fail to apply it consistently. James 1:22 warns, *"But be doers of the word, and not hearers only, deceiving yourselves."* When we apply God's wisdom in our daily lives, we experience the good He has promised—whether in relationships, finances, decision-making, or spiritual growth.

If you desire to see God's best in your life, prioritize wisdom. Spend time in His Word, seek His guidance, and walk in understanding. The more you hold onto wisdom, the more you will see His goodness unfold in every area of your life. Loving wisdom is loving yourself, and those who embrace it will never regret the choice.

So then faith comes by hearing,
and hearing by the word of God.

Romans 10:17

F aith is not something we struggle to drum up on our own—it comes as a result of hearing God's Word. This verse reveals a simple but powerful truth: what we listen to shapes what we believe. If we want strong, unwavering faith, we must continually feed on the truth of Scripture.

Building up our faith is not a one-time experience but a continual process. Just as our bodies need daily nourishment, and building muscles needs repeat conditioning, our spirits need constant feeding on God's promises. Jesus said in Matthew 4:4, *"Man shall not live by bread alone, but by every word that proceeds from the mouth of God."* When we regularly hear and meditate on the Word, faith naturally grows.

The Word of God is the source of true, life-giving faith. The world is full of voices—fear, doubt, negativity—but only God's Word produces faith. Even simple things like the television shows we choose to watch, or the books we read, can affect our faith. What we hear repeatedly is what takes root in our hearts. Proverbs 4:20-22 instructs us, *"My son, give attention to my words; incline your ear to my sayings… for they are life to those who find them…."* If we allow God's truth to be our primary input, faith will be the automatic result.

If your faith feels weak, check what you've been hearing. Are you filling your heart with the promises of God or the worries of the world? Faith isn't something you have to force—it grows as you stay in His Word. Make time to hear, read, and meditate on Scripture, and watch as your faith strengthens and fuels the abundant life God has for you!

*You crown the year with Your goodness,
and Your paths drip with abundance.*

Psalm 65:11

God's goodness is not occasional—it is continuous. This verse paints a beautiful picture of how He surrounds and blesses our lives, not just at the beginning or the end, but all throughout. When we walk in His ways, we step into a life marked by His abundant provision.

The phrase *"You crown the year with Your goodness"* refers to divine favor encircling our lives. Just as a crown rests on the head, God's goodness is meant to cover and shape every season we walk through. His plans for us are filled with blessing, and He has already gone ahead to prepare good things. Jeremiah 29:11 confirms this: *"For I know the thoughts that I think toward you, says the Lord, thoughts of peace and not of evil, to give you a future and a hope."* Even when challenges arise, His goodness does not waver. He still has plans for our good, even on the other side of difficult circumstances.

Wherever God leads, provision follows. His paths aren't dry or uncertain—they're soaked with goodness. Think of walking through grass so drenched it soaks your shoes with every step. That's the kind of overflow this verse describes—blessings you can't help but step into. His abundance shows up as peace when life feels heavy, strength when you're worn out, and answers when you feel stuck. You don't have to chase provision—it's built into the path He's laid out for you.

If you've been worried about what lies ahead, take heart— God has already prepared a year crowned with His goodness. He is faithful to lead you, and His path always overflows with abundance. Trust Him, stay on His course, and watch as His provision meets your every need in every season.

Therefore do not cast away your confidence,
which has great reward. For you have need of endurance,
so that after you have done the will of God,
you may receive the promise.

Hebrews 10:35-36

F aith holds steady, even when things take longer than expected. This passage reminds us that God's promises aren't just handed out—they're received by those who keep showing up, keep believing, and keep trusting Him through the ups and downs. Staying confident in His goodness is a key part of walking in everything He's prepared for you.

Confidence isn't automatic. When things don't go the way we planned, it's easy to second-guess, to wonder if we missed it or if it's ever going to happen. But letting go of trust only delays what God is trying to bring into your life. When you stay anchored in His faithfulness, you position yourself to see the breakthrough!

It also takes endurance. Faith isn't just about a one-time belief—it's about holding your ground when pressure comes. Delays don't come from God; they often come from opposition, distractions, or spiritual resistance. But faith has the power to overcome every obstacle. When you stay rooted in truth and refuse to back down, those barriers begin to fall, and what God promised comes into view.

Hebrews 6:12 says that we inherit the promise through faith and *patience*. So if you're in a season of waiting, take this as encouragement: don't let go! Keep trusting, keep speaking His Word, and keep your eyes on what He's promised. The process may stretch you, but the reward is coming—and it will be worth every moment you held on in faith.

August 6

*Enlarge the place of your tent, and let them stretch out
the curtains of your dwellings; do not spare; lengthen
your cords, and strengthen your stakes.
For you shall expand to the right and to the left, and
your descendants will inherit the nations, and make
the desolate cities inhabited.*

Isaiah 54:2-3

God calls His people to think bigger, expect more, and prepare for increase. This passage was originally spoken to Israel, but it also reflects a powerful principle for every believer—God's plans are always greater than what we can see right now. He desires to bring expansion, blessing, and influence to those who trust Him.

The command to *"enlarge the place of your tent"* refers to making room for what God wants to do. Sometimes, people limit what God can do in their lives by small thinking or fear of change. But faith requires action. Just as Noah built the ark before the rain, we must prepare in expectation of what God is bringing. Ephesians 3:20 reminds us, *"Now to Him who is able to do exceedingly abundantly above all that we ask or think."*

The phrase *"do not spare"* means to remove hesitation and step fully into God's plan. He is not a God of lack—His supply is limitless. When we lengthen our cords and strengthen our stakes, we prepare for lasting, sustainable growth. Expanding faith often requires stretching beyond comfort zones, but the result is a life that reaches further than we ever imagined.

If you've been hesitant to believe for more, let this be your encouragement: God wants to enlarge your capacity to receive as well as to impact others. Step forward in faith, prepare for increase, and trust that He is leading you into a season of expansion and abundance!

You have made known to me the ways of life;
You will make me full of joy in Your presence.

Acts 2:28

Every step taken with God leads to life and joy. This verse, originally from Psalm 16:11 and later quoted by Peter at Pentecost, reminds us that God's presence is not only where we find guidance but also where we experience the fullness of joy.

God does not leave us to figure things out on our own. He actively reveals His wisdom and direction to us when we seek Him. The truth that He makes known to us "the ways of life" is an exciting promise! His guidance is not vague or hidden—He leads with clarity, speaking through His Word, His Spirit, and even through the circumstances of our lives. When we walk in obedience, we align ourselves with the abundant life He has prepared.

Joy from God is one that is deep, lasting, and independent of circumstances. The world offers fleeting happiness, but true joy is found in walking closely with God. Jesus said in John 15:11, *"These things I have spoken to you, that My joy may remain in you, and that your joy may be full."* His presence is the wellspring of joy that never runs dry. Even in difficult seasons, those who abide in Him find peace and strength that surpasses understanding.

If you've been searching for direction or longing for deeper joy, turn your heart fully toward Him. His presence brings clarity, comfort, and overflowing joy. Stay close to Him, follow His leading, and trust that His ways always lead to life. The more you dwell in His presence, the more His joy will sustain and strengthen you, no matter what comes your way.

*And whatever you do, do it heartily, as to the Lord
and not to men, knowing that from the Lord you
will receive the reward of the inheritance;
for you serve the Lord Christ.*

Colossians 3:23-24

Excellence in our work is not just about impressing people—it's about honoring God. This passage reminds us that everything we do should be done with a heart of dedication, knowing that our ultimate reward comes from Him. Whether big or small, seen or unseen, our work is an opportunity to serve the Lord.

The phrase *"whatever you do"* covers every area of life—our jobs, ministries, relationships, and responsibilities. God cares about the way we approach all tasks, not just the ones that seem spiritual. Even mundane work can be an act of worship when done with the right heart.

"Do it heartily, as to the Lord" reflects an attitude of enthusiasm and diligence. Half-hearted effort does not reflect God's excellence. When we work with a spirit of integrity and joy, we demonstrate His character. The world may only see our actions, but God sees our motives.

The promise in this verse is that *"from the Lord you will receive the reward."* Earthly rewards may come and go, but God never overlooks faithfulness. When we serve Him, whether in a job, a ministry, or daily life, He ensures that nothing is wasted.

If you've ever felt unnoticed or unappreciated, remember this truth: You are working for God, and He sees every effort. Keep giving your best, not for human approval but for His glory, knowing that He will reward you in ways beyond what you can imagine.

Do you not know that you are the temple of God and that the Spirit of God dwells in you?

1 Corinthians 3:16

U nderstanding who you are in Christ changes everything. This verse reminds us that as believers, we are not just ordinary people—we are the very dwelling place of God's Spirit. His presence is not found in a distant temple or a building made by human hands; He has chosen to make His home in us.

In the Old Testament, God's presence dwelled in the tabernacle and later in the temple, where only the high priest could enter the Holy of Holies. In fact, by entering this sacred place without being perfectly prepared, the priest could die! But through Christ, that separation has been removed and sin perfectly cleansed. At the moment of salvation, His Spirit takes up residence within us, making us living temples of His presence.

The truth that God's Spirit lives in us is a reality that should shape the way we live. The Holy Spirit is not a temporary visitor—He is a permanent resident. He leads, strengthens, convicts, and empowers us for every good work. Romans 8:11 declares, *"But if the Spirit of Him who raised Jesus from the dead dwells in you, He who raised Christ from the dead will also give life to your mortal bodies."* His power is actively working in us, renewing us from the inside out!

If you've ever felt distant from God, remember—He is not far away. He is within you, guiding, comforting, and empowering you. You are His temple, His dwelling place, and His Spirit is always with you. Live in the awareness of this truth, honoring His presence and walking in the abundant life He has provided.

*And what is the exceeding greatness of His power
toward us who believe, according to the working of His
mighty power which He worked in Christ when He
raised Him from the dead and seated Him at His right
hand in the heavenly places.*

Ephesians 1:19-20

The same power that raised Jesus from the dead is at work in you. This verse reveals the *exceeding greatness* of God's power toward those who believe—not a small measure, not just enough, but an overwhelming, limitless force. His power is not distant; it is active and available in your life right now.

Faith is the key to accessing this power. God's power is not just a concept—it is something He desires for us to walk in daily. Jesus said in Mark 9:23, *"If you can believe, all things are possible to him who believes."* When we truly believe in what God has made available, we begin to see His strength operating in and through us.

The power that raised Jesus from the dead is the same power that now works in every believer. It is a victorious, life-giving force that conquered death and is still transforming lives today. This means that His strength is not just for the future—it is for the present, empowering us to overcome obstacles, live victoriously, and fulfill His purpose.

If you've been feeling weak or inadequate, remember Who is living inside of you. The same power that raised Christ is alive in you today and is constantly giving life to your body (Romans 8:11). Walk boldly in that truth, knowing that His strength is always greater than your challenges.

Again I say to you that if two of you agree on earth concerning anything that they ask, it will be done for them by My Father in heaven.

Matthew 18:19

There is power in agreement. Jesus gives an incredible promise in this verse—when believers come together in faith and pray, Heaven responds! Prayer is not just an individual act; it is a powerful partnership that releases God's power into our lives.

This verse highlights the importance of unity among believers in faith. Agreement in prayer is more than just saying the same words—it means standing together, believing for the same outcome, and trusting that God will fulfill His Word. Amos 3:3 asks, *"Can two walk together, unless they are agreed?"* Unity in prayer strengthens faith and positions us to receive from God. Jesus Himself prayed for unity among believers, knowing that there is strength when we stand together.

When Jesus says, *"anything they ask,"* He's not limiting us to only what seems possible or practical—He's inviting us to come boldly, even with the small or seemingly impossible things. This kind of prayer is about hearts aligned with Him, praying in agreement and faith. When we're walking in relationship with God and with each other, our prayers naturally begin to reflect His heart. And in that space of unity and trust, nothing is off the table.

If you are facing a challenge, don't pray alone—find a faith-filled believer to stand with you. When two or more come together in faith, God moves. Unity is strength, and His power is released in ways that go beyond what we could accomplish on our own. Stand firm, believe together, and watch as He brings His will to pass in your life. His Word is true, and He is always faithful to fulfill His promises.

He gives power to the weak, and to those who have no might He increases strength. Even the youths shall faint and be weary, and the young men shall utterly fall, but those who wait on the Lord shall renew their strength; they shall mount up with wings like eagles, they shall run and not be weary, they shall walk and not faint.

Isaiah 40:29-31

L iving in this fallen world has a way of trying to wear us down and out, but God promises supernatural strength to those who trust in Him. This passage reminds us that even the strongest among us will grow tired, but the key to endurance is not found in our own ability—it is found in waiting on the Lord.

God has such a compassionate heart for those who feel overwhelmed. He doesn't expect us to rely on our own strength; instead, He pours His power into those who recognize their need for Him. 2 Corinthians 12:9 echoes this truth: *"My grace is sufficient for you, for My strength is made perfect in weakness."* True strength is found in receiving His ability, not striving in our own.

Waiting on the Lord is not passive—it is expectant faith, a confident hope that He will sustain and strengthen us. The imagery of mounting up with wings like eagles reminds us that God lifts us above life's challenges, empowering us to rise above obstacles rather than be weighed down by them.

If you are feeling weary, take heart—God has fresh strength for you. Don't rely on your own power. Wait on Him, trust in His promises, and let Him renew you. He will sustain you, strengthen you, and lift you higher than you ever thought possible.

*That He would grant you, according to the riches
of His glory, to be strengthened with might through
His Spirit in the inner man.*

Ephesians 3:16

True strength comes from within—not from willpower or human effort, but from the Spirit of God. This verse is part of Paul's prayer for believers, asking that they be empowered by God's Spirit according to the unlimited riches of His glory.

God does not give sparingly. His supply is limitless, and He strengthens us not based on our own merit, but according to His abundance. Whether you need strength for a trial, endurance for a calling, or peace in uncertainty, His provision is more than enough. He is willing and able to pour out anything you need from the *"riches of His glory."*

Again, this strength is not natural—it is supernatural empowerment. The word *might* in Greek (*dunamis*) refers to miraculous power, the same power that raised Jesus from the dead. It's the same root word from which we get the word *dynamite.* The strength we receive from relying on God's power is explosive in comparison to natural, human ability. God's strength is not momentary; it is a continual, life-giving force that sustains us from the inside out (Romans 8:11).

If you've been feeling weak, don't rely on your own ability—draw from His Spirit. He has already placed His power within you, strengthening you in your inner man. No matter what comes your way, His strength will uphold you, sustain you, and carry you through to victory!

*Blessed be the Lord, who daily loads us with benefits,
the God of our salvation! Selah.*

Psalm 68:19

God's blessings are not occasional—they are daily. This verse is a powerful reminder that He is constantly providing, sustaining, and pouring out His goodness upon us. He doesn't just give us enough to get by; He *loads* us with benefits, ensuring that we have everything we need to walk in His abundant life.

The phrase *"daily loads us with benefits"* reveals a continual outpouring. God's blessings are not limited to special occasions or seasons of success. Lamentations 3:22-23 reinforces this truth: *"Through the Lord's mercies we are not consumed, because His compassions fail not. They are new every morning."* Each day carries fresh mercies, new strength, and divine provision.

The benefits God provides go beyond material blessings. They include peace, provision, wisdom, protection, healing, and strength. James 1:17 reminds us, *"Every good gift and every perfect gift is from above, and comes down from the Father of lights."* When we recognize that His blessings surround us daily, we shift from a mindset of lack to one of gratitude and expectation.

Our redemption through Jesus Christ is the greatest of all benefits we receive from Him. Salvation is not just about eternity; it is about walking in the fullness of His grace and favor every single day.

If you've been feeling weighed down by life's challenges, shift your focus. Instead of seeing burdens, start recognizing His benefits. He has already provided everything you need for today. Trust Him, thank Him, and walk in the blessings He has abundantly supplied.

*So Jesus said to them, "Because of your unbelief;
for assuredly, I say to you, if you have faith as a mustard
seed, you will say to this mountain, 'Move from
here to there,' and it will move; and nothing will be
impossible for you."*

Matthew 17:20

E ven the smallest amount of faith has the power to produce incredible results! In this verse, Jesus wasn't saying we need enormous faith—He was emphasizing that even faith as tiny as a mustard seed can move mountains when placed in God. The power is not in the size of our faith but in the One we are trusting.

The mustard seed is one of the smallest seeds, yet it grows into a large tree. This illustrates that faith starts small but grows as we trust in God. Romans 10:17 tells us, *"So then faith comes by hearing, and hearing by the word of God."* The more we meditate on God's promises, the stronger our faith becomes.

"You will say to this mountain, 'Move from here to there,' and it will move" shows that faith is meant to be spoken. Jesus teaches that words aligned with faith have authority. Proverbs 18:21 declares, *"Death and life are in the power of the tongue."* When we speak in faith, believing in God's Word, we release His power into our circumstances.

If you've been facing a mountain—a challenge that seems immovable—don't focus on the size of the problem. Instead, focus on the faithfulness of God. Trust in Him, declare His promises, and take steps forward, knowing that with God, nothing is impossible. Even the smallest faith, when placed in Him, can bring supernatural breakthrough.

Brethren, I do not count myself to have apprehended; but one thing I do, forgetting those things which are behind and reaching forward to those things which are ahead, I press toward the goal for the prize of the upward call of God in Christ Jesus.

Philippians 3:13-14

L iving in the past can keep you from moving forward. In this verse, Paul encourages believers to let go of what is behind and focus on what is ahead. The abundant life God has for you is not found in dwelling on past mistakes, regrets, or even past successes—it is found in pressing forward toward His calling.

Forgetting the past doesn't mean erasing memories, but rather refusing to be controlled by them. Dwelling on failures can bring condemnation, while clinging to past achievements can create complacency. Isaiah 43:18-19 reminds us, *"Do not remember the former things, nor consider the things of old. Behold, I will do a new thing."* God is always calling us to something greater, and looking back hinders our ability to fully embrace it.

Reaching forward is an active pursuit of things that are coming. Walking in God's plan requires intentionality. Just as a runner stretches forward toward the finish line, we must focus on the *prize*—the fulfillment of God's purpose in our lives. Hebrews 12:1-2 urges us to *"lay aside every weight"* and fix our eyes on Jesus, the author and finisher of our faith.

If you've been stuck in the past, it's time to move forward. Let go of what was and embrace what God has ahead. Keep pressing on, knowing that the greatest prize is found in pursuing Him and His purpose for your life.

Wealth and riches will be in his house, and his righteousness endures forever.

Psalm 112:3

God's blessing extends to every area of life, including provision. This verse describes the life of a righteous person—one who fears the Lord and delights in His commandments (Psalm 112:1). For those who walk in His ways, wealth and riches are part of His provision, but even greater than material blessings is the enduring righteousness He gives.

This verse isn't symbolic—it's talking about actual provision. God has no issue with wealth; in fact, He's the one who provides it. This verse affirms that financial blessing is a real part of walking in His ways. It's not about greed or materialism—it's about receiving what you need and more, so you can live well and be a blessing. Biblical prosperity includes finances, but it also comes with peace, purpose, and the freedom to live generously. When God is your source, increase doesn't have to come through stress or striving—it flows from His hand.

Material possessions can fade, but the righteousness of those who trust in God has eternal value. Jesus taught in Matthew 6:19-20, *"Do not lay up for yourselves treasures on earth, where moth and rust destroy... but lay up for yourselves treasures in heaven."* So, even though God wants you rich, a life lived for Him leaves a lasting impact, far beyond earthly riches.

If you seek true abundance, focus first on righteousness. When God is your source, He provides more than enough—not just for yourself, but so you can be a blessing to others. Wealth that comes from Him is never just about accumulation; it's about stewardship. Walk in His ways, trust in His provision, and know that the greatest riches are found in Him.

Therefore be imitators of God as dear children.

Ephesians 5:1

A small child doesn't have to be told to imitate their parents—it comes naturally. They watch closely, mimic mannerisms, repeat phrases, and try to walk in their parents' footsteps, simply because they love and trust them. That's the kind of relationship God invites us into. We're not trying to earn His approval; we already have His love. He simply calls us to draw close and reflect who He is in the way we live.

Imitating God isn't about performing or pretending—it's about letting our closeness to Him shape us. When we spend time in His Word, listen to His voice, and stay aware of His presence, we begin to take on His nature. His love becomes our love. His grace softens our responses. His wisdom starts influencing our decisions. This isn't about striving—it's about becoming more like Him simply because we belong to Him.

That "dear children" part of the verse is important. It reminds us that we're not outsiders trying to measure up—we're sons and daughters learning from a good, faithful Father. Just like a child grows to reflect the values and heart of a loving parent, we grow into the likeness of our Heavenly Father the more we walk with Him.

If you want your life to reflect God's love and power, don't start with behavior—start with relationship. Spend time with your Father. Watch how He moves. Let His nature rub off on you. The more you know Him, the more you'll become like Him—and the world around you will notice.

Behold, I stand at the door and knock. If anyone hears My voice and opens the door, I will come in to him and dine with him, and he with Me.

Revelation 3:20

J esus extends a personal invitation to every believer to deeper fellowship, intimacy, and relationship with Him. This verse is often used in evangelism, but it was originally written to the church, reminding us that even as believers, we must continually welcome Him into every area of our lives.

The phrase *"I stand at the door and knock"* reveals God's desire for relationship. He does not force His way in; He patiently waits for us to invite Him into our hearts, our decisions, and our daily lives. Isaiah 30:18 confirms this: *"Therefore the Lord will wait, that He may be gracious to you."* His love is constant, but He longs for us to respond.

The decision to welcome Jesus is personal. He speaks to us through His Word, His Spirit, and even through the circumstances of life. But it is up to us to recognize His voice and respond in faith. John 10:27 reminds us, *"My sheep hear My voice, and I know them, and they follow Me."*

In biblical culture, sharing a meal represented deep fellowship. Jesus doesn't just visit—He abides! When we invite Him into our lives, we experience His presence, peace, and guidance in a way that transforms us from the inside out.

If you've felt distant from God, He is still knocking. He hasn't left—He's waiting for you to open the door. Welcome Him in, and experience the abundant life found in close fellowship with Him.

Sanctify them by Your truth. Your word is truth.

John 17:17

God's Word is more than just information—it has the power to transform and set us apart for His purposes. In this verse, Jesus is praying for His disciples, asking the Father to sanctify them through His truth. This same prayer extends to every believer today.

The word *sanctify* means to set apart, purify, or make holy. This doesn't mean we become perfect in our own strength, but that through God's truth, we are continually shaped into His image. The process of sanctification is ongoing, refining us and aligning our lives with His will. Ephesians 5:26 confirms this, saying Christ *"sanctifies and cleanses with the washing of water by the word."* The more we engage with God's Word, the more our thoughts, attitudes, and actions reflect His nature.

In a world filled with shifting opinions and cultural confusion, only God's Word remains unchanging and absolute. It is not just a collection of good teachings; it is the foundation of all truth. Psalm 119:160 affirms, *"The entirety of Your word is truth, and every one of Your righteous judgments endures forever."* When we build our lives on His Word, we are anchored, no matter what storms come our way.

Sanctification is not a one-time event but a lifelong journey. As we submit to the truth of God's Word, we are continually strengthened, renewed, and empowered to live in His abundance. If you desire to walk in the fullness of what God has for you, let His Word be your daily guide. It is the truth that sets you free, shapes your destiny, and draws you closer to Him.

*This hope we have as an anchor of the soul,
both sure and steadfast, and which enters
the Presence behind the veil.*

Hebrews 6:19

Hope in God is not wishful thinking—it is a firm, unshakable foundation that holds us steady in every season of life. This verse describes hope as an anchor of the soul, keeping us grounded when storms try to shake us. Unlike the fleeting hopes of the world, which often disappoint, the hope we have in Christ is sure and steadfast.

The imagery of an anchor is powerful. Just as a ship's anchor keeps it from drifting in turbulent waters, hope in God keeps our hearts secure when challenges arise. Life will bring uncertainties, but God's promises do not change. Hope rooted in Him brings lasting peace and joy, even in difficult times.

The phrase *"which enters the Presence behind the veil"* refers to Jesus, our High Priest, who made a way for us to have direct access to God. In the Old Testament, only the high priest could enter the Most Holy Place behind the veil, but through Christ's sacrifice, the veil was torn, granting us unrestricted access to God's presence. Hebrews 4:16 encourages us to *"come boldly to the throne of grace."* This hope is not just about the future—it is an ever-present reality that keeps us connected to the source of all strength.

If life's storms have left you feeling uncertain, hold fast to the anchor of your soul. God's promises will never fail, and His presence is always available to you. Stay rooted in His Word, trust in His faithfulness, and let hope carry you through every challenge.

Blessed is that man who makes the Lord his trust, and does not respect the proud, nor such as turn aside to lies.

Psalm 40:4

Trueblessing is found in placing our complete trust in the Lord. This verse reminds us that those who rely on God, rather than on human strength, pride, or deception, will walk in His favor and experience His faithfulness.

Because it says *"makes the Lord his trust,"* this indicates that trusting the Lord is an intentional choice. Trusting God is not just believing in Him—it is relying on Him as our source, our guide, and our provider. Proverbs 3:5-6 reinforces this truth: *"Trust in the Lord with all your heart, and lean not on your own understanding; in all your ways acknowledge Him, and He shall direct your paths."* It is an instruction to trust in the Lord, therefore, we can choose to do so or choose not to! When we trust God fully, we open ourselves up to His direction and provision.

This world is full of lies—disguised as truth, success, or even wisdom. The verse warns against turning aside to deception, reminding us that we must be intentional about guarding our hearts and minds. It's easy to be pulled in by cultural opinions, half-truths, or even our own feelings, but God calls us to reject those voices and pursue what's real. Trusting Him means choosing truth, even when it's unpopular or inconvenient. The blessing isn't found in blending in with the world—it's found in aligning with what God says is true.

If you've been tempted to rely on your own strength or follow the world's shortcuts, let this verse encourage you to refocus. Those who trust in the Lord will never be put to shame! He is faithful, and when you put your confidence in Him, you position yourself to walk in His blessing, favor, and abundant life.

But when Jesus heard it, He answered him, saying, "Do not be afraid; only believe, and she will be made well."

Luke 8:50

F aith in God silences fear. In this verse, Jesus speaks to Jairus, a desperate father who had just received the devastating news that his daughter had died. But instead of allowing fear to take over, Jesus gives him a powerful command: *"Do not be afraid; only believe."*

Fear is a natural response to difficult circumstances. But Jesus wasn't just telling Jairus to ignore reality—He was calling him to shift his focus from the situation to the power of God. Isaiah 41:10 reassures us, *"Fear not, for I am with you; be not dismayed, for I am your God. I will strengthen you, yes, I will help you."* Fear loses its grip when we trust in God's presence and promises.

"Only believe" reveals the key to overcoming fear—faith. Jesus was asking Jairus to hold onto belief, even when everything looked hopeless. Hebrews 11:1 defines faith as *"the substance of things hoped for, the evidence of things not seen."* Jairus had to *choose* whether to believe the bad report or trust in Jesus' words. When we choose faith over fear, we make room for God's power to work in our lives.

Jesus' words to Jairus were not just for that moment—they are for every believer today. The enemy wants to use fear to rob you of peace, joy, and expectation of God's promises. But faith rejects fear. When you stand on God's Word and believe what He has said, you step into the miraculous.

If you are facing a situation that seems impossible, Jesus' words remain the same: *Do not fear—only believe.* Don't let doubt or circumstances dictate your response. Fix your eyes on God's faithfulness, trust in His promises, and watch as He moves on your behalf.

For the Lord is good; His mercy is everlasting,
and His truth endures to all generations.

Psalm 100:5

God doesn't change with the weather, the headlines, or your circumstances. His nature is unshakable—He is good, He is merciful, and He is always faithful. That kind of consistency is hard to find in a world where everything seems to shift and evolve by the hour. But God is the same yesterday, today, and forever, and that truth brings deep security to our lives.

His goodness isn't based on how we behave or how "smooth" life feels. It's who He is. Even when life feels unfair or uncertain, His goodness hasn't taken a break. He's working behind the scenes in ways we don't always see. His heart toward you is kind, and His plans are still for your good.

His mercy, too, is something you can count on daily. It doesn't wear out or run dry. Scripture tells us His compassions are new every morning—not recycled or rationed out. Whether you've had a great day or one you'd rather forget, His mercy meets you right where you are, offering a clean slate and fresh strength to keep going.

And His truth? That's your anchor. It doesn't shift with cultural trends or lose power over time. What God has said will always stand. His promises still apply today, and they'll still hold true for generations to come. You can build your life on His Word and trust that it won't fail.

So, if things around you feel uncertain, cling to what's unchanging. God is good. His mercy is constant. And His truth will never falter. That's the kind of foundation that can carry you through anything.

Blessing I will bless you, and multiplying I will multiply your descendants as the stars of the heaven and as the sand which is on the seashore; and your descendants shall possess the gate of their enemies.

Genesis 22:17

G od's blessings are not small—they are abundant, immeasurable, and generational. This verse is part of God's covenant with Abraham, where He promises to bless him beyond anything he could imagine. What makes this moment so powerful is that it follows Abraham's greatest test— his willingness to offer Isaac in obedience to God. Because Abraham trusted God, the blessing was set in motion.

The imagery in this verse is striking. *The stars of the heaven* and *the sand on the seashore* symbolize a blessing so vast it cannot be counted. God's plan was not just to bless Abraham but to create a lineage that would impact the world. Galatians 3:29 connects us to this promise: *"And if you are Christ's, then you are Abraham's seed, and heirs according to the promise."* Through Jesus, we are part of this blessing, inheriting God's promises of increase, favor, and victory!

The final part of the verse, *your descendants shall possess the gate of their enemies*, speaks of authority. In ancient times, the city gate represented power and control. God was declaring that Abraham's descendants—including us as believers—would walk in victory over opposition. Jesus reinforced this truth in Matthew 16:18, saying, *"The gates of Hades shall not prevail against it."*

If you've ever doubted God's plans for your life, let this verse remind you that His blessings are bigger than you can comprehend. He is not just adding to your life—He is *multiplying!* Walk in faith, knowing that His promises are for you and for generations to come.

Those who sow in tears shall reap in joy.
He who continually goes forth weeping, bearing seed
for sowing, shall doubtless come again with
rejoicing, bringing his sheaves with him.

Psalm 126:5-6

Seasons of struggle are not the end of your story. This passage paints a picture of sowing with tears but reaping with joy, showing us that perseverance in faith always leads to God's promises being fulfilled. What may seem like a time of loss or hardship is often a preparation for an abundant harvest.

Listen, life does include difficulties. That is just the unfortunate consequence of the fall of humanity, when sin entered into the world. There are times when we invest, serve, pray, and believe, but it feels like nothing is happening. However, just as a farmer sows in expectation of a future harvest, our obedience and faithfulness will yield results in due time. Galatians 6:9 encourages us, *"And let us not grow weary while doing good, for in due season we shall reap if we do not lose heart."*

Regardless of any hardships we may face, God always brings restoration. Difficult season is wasted in His hands. He turns mourning into dancing (Psalm 30:11) and makes beauty from ashes (Isaiah 61:3). If you are walking through a season of tears, trust that joy is ahead.

The imagery of *bringing sheaves with him* speaks of a full harvest—one that exceeds what was sown. God does not just restore; He multiplies! If you have been sowing in faith despite hardship, take heart. The time of reaping is coming, and when it does, your joy will be full. Keep trusting, keep sowing, and know that God's promises never fail.

*And of His fullness we have all received,
and grace for grace.*

John 1:16

God's grace is not limited—it is overflowing, abundant, and ever-increasing. This verse reminds us that through Jesus, we have received the fullness of God's grace, not in small portions, but in continuous waves. His supply never runs out, and He always gives more than enough.

You have received His fullness, therefore you are complete in Him! Everything you need—salvation, righteousness, peace, wisdom, strength, and provision—flows from Him. You lack nothing in Christ because He has already made His fullness available to you (Colossians 2:9-10).

"Grace for grace" describes an ongoing, never-ending supply of God's favor. The original Greek wording implies a continual exchange—one grace replaced by another, like waves in the ocean. Just when you think you've exhausted God's grace, another wave comes. His grace is not a one-time gift but a daily, overflowing supply.

This grace is not only for salvation but for daily living. It strengthens us in weakness, empowers us to walk in righteousness, and enables us to fulfill God's calling. 2 Corinthians 12:9 reminds us, *"My grace is sufficient for you, for My strength is made perfect in weakness."* If you've ever felt unworthy or like you've used up God's patience, let this verse assure you—His grace doesn't run out.

No matter what you face, His grace is sufficient, His strength is made perfect in weakness, and His supply will never fail. Rest in the fullness He has already provided and expect more of His grace to carry you forward.

Rejoice always, pray without ceasing, in everything give thanks; for this is the will of God in Christ Jesus for you.

1 Thessalonians 5:16-18

Living in God's will isn't complicated—it's a lifestyle of joy, prayer, and gratitude. In just a few words, Paul lays out a powerful blueprint for a life of thriving, not just surviving, one that remains steadfast no matter the circumstances.

Always rejoicing doesn't mean pretending everything is perfect. It means choosing joy even in difficult situations, knowing that our hope is in God, not in our surroundings. Philippians 4:4 reminds us, *"Rejoice in the Lord always. Again I will say, rejoice!"* True joy isn't based on what's happening around us but on who God is within us.

Pray without ceasing refers to continual communication with God. This doesn't mean we are always speaking words of prayer but that our hearts remain connected to Him throughout the day. It's an ongoing awareness of His presence, where we invite Him into every decision, struggle, and moment of celebration. Romans 12:12 says, *"Rejoicing in hope, patient in tribulation, continuing steadfastly in prayer."* Prayer is not just a religious act—it's a relationship.

Giving thanks here is a command, not a suggestion. Gratitude shifts our focus from what's wrong to what God is doing. Even in challenges, there is always something to thank Him for. Ephesians 5:20 encourages us to be *"giving thanks always for all things to God the Father in the name of our Lord Jesus Christ."*

If you've been wondering what God's will for your life is, start here. Rejoice, pray, and give thanks. These three habits will transform your heart, strengthen your faith, and align your life with God's best for you.

For thus says the Lord God, the Holy One of Israel: "In returning and rest you shall be saved; in quietness and confidence shall be your strength." But you would not.

Isaiah 30:15

The world tells us that strength comes from striving, working harder, and pushing forward in our own ability. But God's way is different—true strength is found in stillness, trust, and resting in Him. This verse reveals that salvation, security, and strength are not achieved through effort but received through faith.

"Returning" implies turning away from self-sufficiency and back to Him, while *rest* signifies a place of trust. Jesus echoes this in Matthew 11:28-30: *"Come to Me, all you who labor and are heavy laden, and I will give you rest."* Salvation is not earned; it is found in surrendering to His grace.

Quietness represents peace and trust rather than fear or anxiety. Confidence refers to unwavering faith in God's ability rather than our own. Psalm 46:10 declares, *"Be still, and know that I am God."* Strength comes from resting in His power, not from striving in our own.

The last phrase, *"But you would not,"* is a stern warning! Many refuse to trust in God's way, choosing anxiety and self-reliance instead. Yet His invitation remains—when we cease striving and trust Him fully, we find the strength to walk in victory.

If you feel exhausted from trying to control everything, let this verse be your reminder: strength is found in resting in Him. Return to His presence, trust in His goodness, and let His strength sustain you.

Let your conduct be without covetousness; be content with such things as you have. For He Himself has said, "I will never leave you nor forsake you."

Hebrews 13:5

Security in life does not come from possessions, status, or wealth—it comes from knowing that God is always with you. This verse reminds us that contentment is not found in what we have, but in *Who* we have. The greatest promise of all is that God Himself will never leave or forsake us.

Always wanting more is a trap! The world constantly tells us that we need something else to be happy—more money, better opportunities, or greater success. But Jesus said in Luke 12:15, *"One's life does not consist in the abundance of the things he possesses."* True fulfillment comes not from material wealth but from a relationship with God.

"Be content with such things as you have" does not mean we should never desire increase, growth, improvement, or positive change. Rather, it means that our joy and peace should not depend on external circumstances. Philippians 4:11-12 teaches us that contentment is learned through trusting God's provision in every season.

No matter what happens, God's presence remains constant. Deuteronomy 31:8 confirms this: *"And the Lord, He is the One who goes before you. He will be with you, He will not leave you nor forsake you."* Even in trials, uncertainties, or moments of weakness, He is always near.

If you've been feeling alone or struggling with discontentment, let this verse remind you—God is with you. He is your provider, your source of peace, and your ever-present help. Trust in His faithfulness, and rest in the promise that you are never alone.

Let the words of my mouth and the meditation of my heart be acceptable in Your sight, O Lord, my strength and my Redeemer.

Psalm 19:14

What we say and what we dwell on in our hearts matters. This verse is a powerful prayer, asking God to help us align both our words and our thoughts with His will. Living an abundant life isn't just about what we do—it's about what we speak and what we believe in our hearts.

The words of our mouth shape the world around us. Proverbs 18:21 reminds us, *"Death and life are in the power of the tongue."* Our words can build up or tear down, release faith or invite doubt, bring peace or stir up fear. Jesus said in Matthew 12:34, *"For out of the abundance of the heart the mouth speaks."* This means that what fills our hearts will eventually come out of our mouths. If we want our words to be pleasing to God, we must first guard what we allow into our hearts and minds.

The meditation of our hearts includes our thoughts, desires, and even how we talk to ourselves. Philippians 4:8 instructs us to think on things that are true, noble, just, pure, and praiseworthy. When we fill our minds with God's truth, our words will naturally align with His goodness, bringing peace and encouragement not only to ourselves but also to those around us.

The good news is, we don't have to change our words and thoughts in our own effort—He empowers us to walk in righteousness. If you've struggled with negative thoughts or careless words, ask God to help you. Let your speech and your heart reflect His truth, and you will experience the fullness of life He desires for you. The more we focus on Him, the more our words and thoughts will reflect His grace and power.

Return to the stronghold, you prisoners of hope.
Even today I declare that I will restore double to you.

Zechariah 9:12

No matter what you have lost, God is a God of restoration. This verse was originally spoken to Israel in a time of oppression, yet it carries a timeless truth—when we place our hope in God, He not only delivers us but restores far beyond what was taken.

This verse encourages us to see God as our refuge. A stronghold is a place of safety, a fortress where the enemy cannot prevail. Psalm 18:2 declares, *"The Lord is my rock and my fortress and my deliverer; my God, my strength, in whom I will trust."* When life feels uncertain, the answer is not to give in to fear, but to run to God and trust in His faithfulness.

Normally, being a prisoner suggests captivity, but here, it means being *bound* to hope. This hope is not empty optimism—it is an unshakable confidence in God's promises. Romans 5:5 tells us, *"Now hope does not disappoint, because the love of God has been poured out in our hearts by the Holy Spirit."* No matter how things look, hope in God is never in vain!

"I will restore double to you" is a promise of abundance. God doesn't just bring back what was lost—He multiplies it. If you've experienced loss, trust that God is not only able to restore but to increase what was taken.

If you feel like you've been in a season of struggle, don't lose hope. You are not a prisoner of your past or your pain—you are a prisoner of *hope*. God is faithful, and He is already working on your restoration. Run to Him, trust in His promises, and expect to see His goodness in your life.

Cast your burden on the Lord, and He shall sustain you;
He shall never permit the righteous to be moved.

Psalm 55:22

You were never meant to carry the weight of life's struggles alone. This verse is a reminder that God invites us to release our burdens to Him, knowing that He is both willing and able to sustain us. No matter how heavy your load may feel, He promises to uphold you.

The phrase *"Cast your burden on the Lord"* is an instruction, not just a suggestion. To *cast* means to throw or release something entirely. 1 Peter 5:7 echoes this: *"Casting all your care upon Him, for He cares for you."* Many believers carry unnecessary stress because they hold onto problems instead of surrendering them to God. But real peace comes when we fully trust Him to take care of what we can't.

God continuously gives us support, which is what it means when it says He will sustain us. He doesn't just take our burdens—He upholds us in every season. His strength is made perfect in our weakness, and He never tires of carrying us through life's challenges.

"He shall never permit the righteous to be moved" is a promise of divine stability. This does not mean we won't face difficulties, but that we will not be shaken or destroyed by them. Jesus said in Matthew 7:25 that those who build their lives on His Word are like a house built on a rock—storms may come, but the foundation remains firm.

If you've been weighed down by worry, stress, or uncertainty, take this verse to heart. Release your burdens to God, knowing that He will sustain you. Trust in His faithfulness, stand firm in His promises, and rest in the assurance that He will never let you fall.

*For in Him we live and move and have our being,
as also some of your own poets have said,
"For we are also His offspring."*

Acts 17:28

Y our life is not separate from God—everything about who you are is sustained by Him. This verse reminds us that He is not distant or detached but is actively involved in every moment of our existence. True abundance is found in recognizing that our lives are meant to be lived *in Him*.

Our God is the giver and sustainer of life. Colossians 1:17 declares, *"And He is before all things, and in Him all things consist."* Without Him, nothing holds together. When we abide in Him, we experience the fullness of life He designed for us.

"And move" refers to more than simple physical movement—it represents action, purpose, and direction. God is not just the source of life; He is the one who empowers us to walk in our calling. Proverbs 3:6 says, *"In all your ways acknowledge Him, and He shall direct your paths."* When we submit our plans to Him, He leads us into the destiny He has prepared for us, enabling and equipping us for every good work.

Our "being" is not random or accidental; we exist because of His intentional design. Ephesians 2:10 affirms, *"For we are His workmanship, created in Christ Jesus for good works."* Knowing that we are His gives us confidence, security, and a very tangible sense of purpose and design. Without confidence we were created for a reason, we just drift through life!

If you've been searching for meaning or feeling disconnected, this verse is your reminder—your life is rooted in Him. He is your source, your strength, and your purpose. Live every day with the awareness that you are held by His love, empowered by His Spirit, and called to walk in His abundant life.

But thus says the Lord: "Even the captives of the mighty shall be taken away, and the prey of the terrible be delivered; for I will contend with him who contends with you, and I will save your children."

Isaiah 49:25

God is your defender, and He fights for you! No enemy, no stronghold, no situation is beyond His power. Even when things seem impossible, He promises deliverance and restoration for those who trust in Him.

This verse addresses situations that feel inescapable. Whether oppression, bondage, or overwhelming challenges, God's power is greater. Just as He rescued Israel from Egypt and Daniel from the lion's den, He is still setting captives free today. Jesus declared in Luke 4:18, *"He has sent Me to heal the brokenhearted, to proclaim liberty to the captives."* When we trust Him, no chains can keep us bound!

God also promises to stand against those who oppose His people. We are not called to fight in our own strength—He fights on our behalf. Exodus 14:14 reminds us, *"The Lord will fight for you, and you shall hold your peace."* When opposition arises, our response should not be fear or striving but *resting* in the certainty that God is working behind the scenes.

His protection extends beyond us—it reaches our families. If you are believing for a loved one's salvation or restoration, take heart. Proverbs 20:7 says, *"The righteous man walks in his integrity; his children are blessed after him."* God's blessings endure for generations, and He is faithful to those who trust in Him.

No matter the battle, stand firm. God is your defender, working on your behalf, bringing freedom, restoration, and victory. Trust in Him, and watch as He turns every struggle into a testimony of His faithfulness.

So He humbled you, allowed you to hunger, and fed you with manna which you did not know nor did your fathers know, that He might make you know that man shall not live by bread alone; but man lives by every word that proceeds from the mouth of the Lord.

Deuteronomy 8:3

God is the ultimate source of life and provision. This verse reminds us that while physical needs are real, they are not our greatest need. True life is sustained by God's Word, not just by material provision. When we make God's Word our source, everything else we need will follow as a natural result!

In the wilderness, Israel learned firsthand that food alone wasn't enough—they needed God's constant guidance and sustenance. When they had no food, He provided manna, a miraculous *daily* supply that came only from Him. This served as a powerful lesson: dependence on God brings true fulfillment. Jesus repeated this truth in Matthew 4:4 when He declared, *"It is written, 'Man shall not live by bread alone, but by every word that proceeds from the mouth of God.'"* Even in times of lack or uncertainty, His Word remains the source of strength and direction.

God's Word is not just advice—it is life itself. Just as food nourishes the body, His Word nourishes the soul. Also like manna, it is meant to sustain us *daily*—new and fresh as it is needed. When we prioritize His Word, we find wisdom, strength, and provision beyond what the natural world can offer.

If you've been striving to meet your own needs, shift your focus. Provision is important, but it is not your foundation—God is. As you feed on His Word daily, you will experience the abundant life that comes from walking in His truth.

You have caused men to ride over our heads;
we went through fire and through water; but You
brought us out to rich fulfillment.

Psalm 66:12

T rials may come, but they are never the end of the story. This verse acknowledges hardship yet reveals God's ultimate plan—to bring His people into a place of abundance. No matter what challenges you have faced, He is leading you to something greater.

Fire refines, and water overwhelms, but neither can destroy those who trust in the Lord. Isaiah 43:2 echoes this promise: *"When you pass through the waters, I will be with you; and through the rivers, they shall not overflow you. When you walk through the fire, you shall not be burned."* The trials you endure don't need to break you, but they can refine you, preparing you for what's ahead.

God does not leave His people in hardship—He leads them *through* it, out of it, and into something better. Just as He brought Israel out of Egypt and into the Promised Land, He is faithful to bring you out of difficulty and into His blessing!

The Hebrew for "rich fulfillment" means overflow, saturation, abundance, plenty, satisfaction or being completely filled. It's actually the same root word used in Psalm 23:5 where it says, *"My cup runs over."* This isn't just barely getting by—it's about overflowing abundance and more than enough!

If you have been in a season of trials, take heart—God is leading you somewhere better. He specializes in turning struggles into testimonies and ashes into beauty. Keep trusting Him, knowing that He is bringing you into a place of fullness and abundance.

But of Him you are in Christ Jesus, who became for us wisdom from God—and righteousness and sanctification and redemption.

1 Corinthians 1:30

Everything we need is found in Jesus. This verse reminds us that our righteousness, holiness, and even wisdom do not come from our own efforts but from being in Christ. When we accepted Him, we stepped into the fullness of what He has already provided.

We did not earn our place in Christ—God placed us there by His grace. Ephesians 2:8-9 confirms this: *"For by grace you have been saved through faith, and that not of yourselves; it is the gift of God, not of works, lest anyone should boast."* Our identity is secure in Him, not in what we do.

Jesus is the source of true understanding. The world offers knowledge, but wisdom comes from God alone. James 1:5 promises, *"If any of you lacks wisdom, let him ask of God, who gives to all liberally and without reproach."* In Christ, we have access to divine wisdom for every decision we make!

Beyond wisdom, we also don't have to strive for righteousness—it has been given to us. 2 Corinthians 5:21 declares, *"For He made Him who knew no sin to be sin for us, that we might become the righteousness of God in Him."* Sanctification is the ongoing process of becoming more like Him, and redemption is the full deliverance from sin's power.

If you've ever felt unworthy or lacking, remember this: You are in Christ, and He is everything you need. Wisdom, righteousness, holiness, and redemption are already yours. Rest in His provision, knowing that your life is secure in Him.

And Jesus came and spoke to them, saying,
"All authority has been given to Me in heaven and on
earth. Go therefore and make disciples of all the nations,
baptizing them in the name of the Father and of the Son
and of the Holy Spirit, teaching them to observe all things
that I have commanded you; and lo, I am with you
always, even to the end of the age." Amen.

Matthew 28:18-20

J esus gave His followers a clear mission: to go into the world and make disciples. This passage, known as the Great Commission, is not just a command—it is a calling backed by divine authority and the constant presence of Christ.

Before commissioning His disciples, Jesus assured them that He had complete authority over all things. His victory over sin, death, and the grave means He reigns supreme. Because we are in Him, we have the power to stand against the enemy and walk in His strength (Luke 10:19). When we step out in faith, we do so with His backing.

His instruction to make disciples is a call to action. We are not just meant to believe in Him but to share His message with others. Discipleship is more than introducing someone to Christ—it's about helping them grow in their faith so they can teach and encourage others (2 Timothy 2:2).

Jesus' final promise was that His presence would remain with us. Whether sharing the Gospel, mentoring others, or simply living out our faith, He never leaves us. This mission is not a temporary assignment—it is a lifelong calling.

If you've ever wondered about your purpose, remember that you have been commissioned by Christ Himself. Walk in His authority, share His love, and make a lasting impact, knowing that He is always with you.

*Let us therefore come boldly to the throne of grace,
that we may obtain mercy and find grace to help
in time of need.*

Hebrews 4:16

God does not ask us to approach Him with hesitation or fear—He invites us to come boldly. Because of Jesus, we have direct access to the Father, where mercy and grace are always available. No matter what we face, we can confidently bring our needs before Him, knowing He hears and responds.

The word *boldly* implies confidence, not arrogance. We do not come before God based on our own worthiness but on Christ's finished work. Ephesians 3:12 says, *"In whom we have boldness and access with confidence through faith in Him."* Our access to God is not restricted—we are welcomed as His children.

"The throne of grace" reminds us that God's rule is not one of condemnation but of love and unmerited favor. He is a just King, yet His throne is characterized by grace. No matter how many times we fall short, His grace never runs out.

We can always rely on the Lord that no matter what we lack, He provides. Mercy covers our past mistakes, and grace empowers us for the future. His help is not distant or delayed—it is present and personal, meeting us exactly where we are.

If you've been hesitant to approach God, let this verse be your assurance: His throne is open to you. Come boldly, receive His mercy, and walk in the abundant grace He has freely given.

Beloved, let us love one another, for love is of God; and everyone who loves is born of God and knows God. He who does not love does not know God, for God is love.

1 John 4:7-8

L ove is not just an attribute of God—it is His very nature. This passage reminds us that to truly know Him is to walk in love. As His children, we are called to reflect His love in every area of our lives, showing His character to the world.

The instruction to *"love one another"* is not optional—it is evidence of being born of God. Jesus emphasized this in John 13:35: *"By this all will know that you are My disciples, if you have love for one another."* Loving others is how we demonstrate that we belong to Him. It's not always easy, but His Spirit empowers us to extend kindness, patience, and grace, even when it's undeserved.

True love originates from God. The world's version of love is often conditional, based on feelings or personal benefit. But God's love is selfless, sacrificial, and unchanging. Romans 5:8 reminds us, *"But God demonstrates His own love toward us, in that while we were still sinners, Christ died for us."* His love is not dependent on our performance—it is given freely.

Everything God does—everything He has *ever* done—is motivated by love, whether in blessing, correction, or guidance. When we abide in Him, His love flows through us, transforming the way we treat others.

If you struggle with loving others, draw near to God. The more you experience His love, the more you'll be able to extend it. Love is not just what God does—it is who He is. And as His children, we are called to reflect that love in every interaction.

The soul of a lazy man desires, and has nothing;
but the soul of the diligent shall be made rich.

Proverbs 13:4

Desire alone is not enough to bring results—diligence is the key to abundance. This verse highlights the difference between merely wanting something and actively working toward it. Those who put in the effort, with faith in God, will see the fruit of their labor.

The *lazy man* represents someone who longs for success, provision, or spiritual growth but refuses to take action. He wants results without investment, blessing without effort. James 2:17 reinforces this truth: *"Faith by itself, if it does not have works, is dead."* God has given us everything we need, but it requires our participation.

In contrast, *the diligent* are those who take consistent steps toward their goals, whether in work, relationships, or their spiritual walk. Diligence doesn't mean striving in our own strength; it means being faithful with what God has given us. Colossians 3:23 reminds us, *"And whatever you do, do it heartily, as to the Lord and not to men."* When we work with excellence and perseverance, we align ourselves with God's principles of increase.

Being made rich refers to more than simple finances. It refers to a life full of provision, purpose, and fulfillment. Psalm 1:3 describes the diligent believer as *"a tree planted by the rivers of water, that brings forth its fruit in its season."* Those who put in the effort, trusting in God, will experience true prosperity in every area of life.

If you've been waiting for things to change, ask yourself—are you desiring, or are you diligently moving forward? God blesses the work of our hands, so stay faithful, keep pressing on, and expect Him to bring an abundant harvest.

*God is our refuge and strength, a very present help
in trouble. Therefore we will not fear, even though the
earth be removed, and though the mountains be
carried into the midst of the sea.*

Psalm 46:1-2

No matter what chaos surrounds you, God is your safe place. This passage reassures us that He is both our protector and our source of strength. When everything seems unstable, He remains unshaken, always present and ready to help.

The word *refuge* paints the picture of a fortress, a secure place where we can find shelter from life's storms. Proverbs 18:10 declares, *"The name of the Lord is a strong tower; the righteous run to it and are safe."* When trouble comes, we don't have to panic—we can run to Him, knowing He is our ultimate protector.

Not only is God our refuge, but He is also our *strength*. He does not just shield us from difficulty; He empowers us to endure and overcome it. Isaiah 40:29 reminds us, *"He gives power to the weak, and to those who have no might He increases strength."* No matter how weary we feel, His strength is always available.

Verse 2 makes a bold declaration: *"We will not fear."* Even in the most extreme circumstances—when everything seems to be falling apart—we can stand firm, knowing that God is greater than any crisis. Jesus has made us world overcomers, so what do we have to fear?

If life feels overwhelming, take refuge in Him. He is your safe place, your strength, and your ever-present help. Trust in His faithfulness, and fear will have no hold on you.

The young lions lack and suffer hunger; but those who seek the Lord shall not lack any good thing.

Psalm 34:10

God is a faithful provider. This verse contrasts the self-sufficiency of the strong with the dependence of those who seek Him, showing that true provision comes not from our own efforts but from trusting in Him. Even the most capable can experience lack, but those who rely on the Lord will always have what they need.

Young lions are fierce hunters, representing strength and independence. Yet despite their power, they sometimes go hungry. This illustrates that no amount of skill, effort, or worldly resources can guarantee provision. Proverbs 10:22 confirms this: *"The blessing of the Lord makes one rich, and He adds no sorrow with it."* True abundance comes from God, not from our own ability!

The key to experiencing God's provision is *seeking Him*. To seek the Lord means to pursue Him in faith, trusting in His goodness and aligning our lives with His will. Matthew 6:33 reinforces this principle: *"But seek first the kingdom of God and His righteousness, and all these things shall be added to you."* When we put Him first, every need is taken care of.

This verse does not promise that we will never face challenges, but it assures us that God will supply every good thing for us. The trouble is we tend to put more faith in our outward circumstances, or what things look like in the natural realm, than on the promises He has given us in His Word! Yet, He has promised that you will not lack any good thing.

If you've been struggling with lack, shift your focus from your own efforts to seeking Him. He is your source, and when you trust in Him, you will not lack any good thing.

I have set the Lord always before me;
because He is at my right hand I shall not be moved.

Psalm 16:8

When God is your focus, stability follows. This verse reveals the key to living unshaken—keeping your eyes on Him. No matter what comes your way, knowing that He is with you brings confidence, peace, and un-wavering strength.

Making the Lord the priority in every area of your life is what it means to set Him always before you. It's a daily decision to seek Him first, trust His guidance, and rely on His strength. Colossians 3:2 encourages us, *"Set your mind on things above, not on things on the earth."* When our focus is fixed on God instead of circumstances, we can begin to walk in consistent victory.

In biblical times, the right hand represented strength and protection. Isaiah 41:10 echoes this promise: *"Fear not, for I am with you; be not dismayed, for I am your God. I will strengthen you, yes, I will help you, I will uphold you with My righteous right hand."* Knowing He is by our side gives us the courage to face anything.

This verse doesn't guarantee that trials won't come, but "I shall not be moved" establishes that when we set our eyes on Jesus, they won't shake us. Jesus taught in Matthew 7:24-25 that a life built on Him is like a house on solid rock—storms may come, but it will stand firm.

If you've been feeling uncertain or overwhelmed, anchor your heart in this truth: God is with you, strengthening and guiding you. Set Him before you, trust in His presence, and walk forward with confidence, knowing that nothing can move you from His steadfast love!

*But I have prayed for you, that your faith should not fail;
and when you have returned to Me,
strengthen your brethren.*

Luke 22:32

Jesus knew Peter was going to blow it. This wasn't just any follower—Peter was one of His closest friends, the one who swore he'd never walk away. And yet, Jesus wasn't shocked. He wasn't caught off guard. Instead of rebuking Peter, He reassured him: *I've already prayed for you.*

That's who Jesus is. He sees our weaknesses and failures before they ever show up—and He's already made provision for our restoration. He doesn't give up on us when we fall. That's why we needed a Savior in the first place—not because we'd always get it right, but because we wouldn't! His grace doesn't wait for perfection; it meets us in the middle of our mess and walks us forward with love and patience.

Peter went from a fisherman with a temper to a bold apostle who preached to thousands. He denied Jesus in a moment of fear, but he didn't stay in that place. Jesus restored him, and Peter went on to change the world. That's what grace does—it doesn't just forgive you, it reclaims your purpose. It takes the parts of your story you thought disqualified you and turns them into testimonies that help others! What looked like failure became the foundation of Peter's greatest ministry.

If you've messed up, take heart. Jesus isn't surprised. He's not done with you. In fact, He's already been praying for you, just like He did for Peter. Your failure isn't final. His forgiveness is already in place, and your story still matters. Let Him pick you back up—and then use your testimony to encourage someone else. You're not disqualified; you're being prepared. Restoration is just the beginning.

The Lord is my shepherd; I shall not want.
He makes me to lie down in green pastures;
He leads me beside the still waters.

Psalm 23:1-2

This passage paints a beautiful picture of God's provision and peace. As our Shepherd, He is personally invested in our well-being, guiding, protecting, and ensuring that we lack nothing essential. Unlike a hired worker who cares only for his wages, a shepherd is devoted to his flock. Jesus told us this Himself in John 10:11 when He declared, *"I am the good shepherd. The good shepherd gives His life for the sheep."*

A shepherd ensures his flock is fed and cared for, lacking nothing! And sheep don't have to labor and travail in order to have their needs met. He just provides their every need!

Trusting in the care of our Shepherd, Jesus, removes all anxiety. When we rely on Him rather than striving in our own strength, we find true security. His provision extends beyond physical necessities—He meets the needs of our hearts, minds, and spirits.

Sheep only rest when they feel completely safe, and God provides that kind of peace. His presence allows us to pause, breathe, and release our burdens. *"Come to Me, all you who labor and are heavy laden, and I will give you rest"* (Matthew 11:28). Just as still waters bring refreshment, His presence restores and strengthens us, allowing us to move forward with confidence. He even *makes* us lie down in these places of peace!

If life feels overwhelming, take comfort in knowing that He is leading you to a place of peace. His care is constant, His provision is sure, and in Him, you will always find rest.

*He restores my soul; He leads me in the paths of
righteousness for His name's sake. Yea, though I walk
through the valley of the shadow of death,
I will fear no evil; for You are with me;
Your rod and Your staff, they comfort me.*

Psalm 23:3-4

Many times, we try to do the work of soul-restoration on our own. However, when it comes to our minds, wills, and emotions, Jesus is much better at this restoration than we are! For example, if you've been hurt, grieving, or are struggling with addiction, Jesus is more than able to restore your soul. Furthermore, His guidance is not random or uncertain—it is purposeful, leading us in righteousness, shaping us to reflect His character. When we follow His leading, it not only benefits us, but it gives Him glory!

Even when walking through dark and difficult seasons, we do not have to be afraid. The valley of the shadow of death represents life's most challenging moments—times of loss, uncertainty, or hardship. Yet even there, we are never alone. *"For You are with me"* is one of the most powerful promises in Scripture. God's presence does not waver based on circumstances; He remains steadfast. Jesus reassured His followers in Matthew 28:20, *"I am with you always, even to the end of the age."*

A shepherd's rod was used to protect the sheep, and the staff was used to guide them. Likewise, God's correction and direction bring us comfort, not harm. He is both our defender and our guide, ensuring that even in life's darkest moments, we are safe in His hands.

If you're facing a difficult season, hold onto this truth—God is with you. His presence, protection, and guidance will sustain you, leading you into peace and restoration.

You prepare a table before me in the presence of my enemies; You anoint my head with oil; my cup runs over. Surely goodness and mercy shall follow me all the days of my life; and I will dwell in the house of the Lord forever.

Psalm 23:5-6

God's provision is not just enough—it is abundant. He doesn't merely meet our needs; He blesses us beyond measure. Even in the midst of opposition, He prepares a place of blessing, favor, and security. He even rubs it right in the face of the enemy!

A prepared table represents provision and honor. In ancient times, sharing a meal was a sign of acceptance and peace. God not only sustains us, but He does so openly, proving that no enemy, whether spiritual or physical, can stop His blessings. Romans 8:31 declares, *"If God is for us, who can be against us?"* The enemy may surround us, but he is powerless to steal what God has set before us.

Anointing with oil was a sign of favor, healing, and consecration. Just as kings and priests were anointed, God marks us with His presence and empowers us to walk in His purpose. *"Now He who establishes us with you in Christ and has anointed us is God"* (2 Corinthians 1:21). His anointing brings refreshing, guidance, and supernatural ability.

The promise of *goodness and mercy* is not temporary—it lasts a lifetime! God's love actively pursues us, ensuring that His kindness and faithfulness remain constant. And His ultimate blessing is the assurance of eternal life in His presence.

No matter what you face, your Shepherd is leading you into abundance. His goodness is not fleeting—it will follow you all your days, and His presence is your home forever.

Mercy, peace, and love be multiplied to you.

Jude 1:2

God doesn't hold back—He gives generously. In this short greeting, we get a glimpse of just how much He wants us to walk in more than just survival. His heart is for you to live in overflow. Mercy, peace, and love aren't abstract ideas or distant concepts—they're real, tangible expressions of who He is, meant to show up in your everyday life and grow as you walk with Him. He's not offering little sprinkles of blessing here and there. He wants you fully saturated.

Mercy is God's way of meeting you with kindness, even when you've messed up. It's not earned—it's a gift. He sees your shortcomings and still chooses to cover them with grace. His mercy doesn't shame you; it lifts you! It allows you to move forward without being weighed down by guilt or regret.

Peace goes beyond calm circumstances. It's the kind of deep-down rest that holds steady even when life is loud and unpredictable. God's peace keeps your heart anchored and your thoughts clear. You don't have to live on edge or run on fumes—He offers peace that settles your soul from the inside out.

And love? That's the foundation of it all. His love for you isn't based on performance. It's constant, unshakable, and always enough. The more you receive His love, the more it transforms how you see yourself—and how you see others.

If you're feeling empty, anxious, or unworthy, you don't have to stay there. God's desire is to multiply mercy, peace, and love in your life—not just once, but again and again. He's not holding back. So go ahead—open your heart wide and let Him fill it.

The secret of the Lord is with those who fear Him,
and He will show them His covenant.

Psalm 25:14

A relationship with God isn't cold or distant—it's close, personal, and full of depth. He invites us into more than just belief; He invites us into friendship. When you honor and trust Him, He begins to share His heart in ways that go beyond surface-level understanding. That kind of closeness grows as we walk with Him in humility and awe.

Fearing the Lord isn't about being scared of Him—it's about having deep reverence. It's recognizing who He is and choosing to live with a posture of respect and trust. It's a heart that says, "God, I want what You want." That kind of attitude positions you to receive wisdom and insight that doesn't come from the world.

The idea of God sharing His secrets might sound surprising, but that's exactly what He wants to do. Just like a close friend who leans in to confide something special, God shares His thoughts with those who walk closely with Him. Jesus once said to His disciples, *"I call you friends,"* (John 15:15) and that invitation still stands today. You're not just a follower—you're someone He wants to walk and talk with every day.

He also promises to reveal His covenant—His lasting commitment to care for, protect, and bless His people. The more you draw near to Him, the more you'll understand just how faithful He truly is.

So, if you've been longing to go deeper in your relationship with God, know that He's ready and willing. Come with reverence and openness. He's not holding back—He wants to share His heart with you.

The generous soul will be made rich,
and he who waters will also be watered himself.

Proverbs 11:25

God's kingdom operates on the principle of generosity. While the world teaches that holding on to more leads to increase, this verse reveals a deeper truth: those who give freely will be blessed. Generosity is not just about money—it is a heart posture that results in abundance.

It is a spiritual law that when we give, whether in finances, encouragement, or acts of kindness, we position ourselves to receive. Luke 6:38 confirms this: *"Give, and it will be given to you: good measure, pressed down, shaken together, and running over will be put into your bosom."* God's economy works differently than the world's—blessing comes through giving, not hoarding.

"He who waters will also be watered himself" illustrates that as we refresh others, we too are refreshed. Encouraging, supporting, and uplifting others does not deplete us—it *multiplies* the blessing in our own lives! 2 Corinthians 9:6 reminds us, *"He who sows sparingly will also reap sparingly, and he who sows bountifully will also reap bountifully."* The more we give, the more God pours back into our lives.

Generosity is an act of faith. It requires trusting that God is our source and that giving will not leave us lacking. Malachi 3:10 challenges believers to bring their offerings to God, promising that He will open the windows of heaven and pour out blessings too great to contain.

If you've been feeling drained or in lack, consider where you can sow. Are you offering your time, love, and resources freely? God promises that those who give will never run dry. Trust Him, live generously, and watch how He abundantly provides for every need.

He who believes in Me, as the Scripture has said,
out of his heart will flow rivers of living water.

John 7:38

A life connected to Jesus isn't dry or drained—it's overflowing. When you believe in Him, something changes on the inside. You don't just receive life from Him—you become a vessel of life for others. His Spirit fills you up, and that fullness naturally spills out in ways that bring encouragement, hope, and strength to the people around you.

Jesus spoke these words during the Feast of Tabernacles, a joyful celebration that included the pouring out of water in the temple—a reminder of God's provision. Right in the middle of this tradition, Jesus made a bold promise: everyone who believes in Him would be filled with living water. He was talking about the Holy Spirit, who would soon be given to all believers. That same Spirit lives in you today.

Think about what water does—it refreshes, revives, and sustains life. That's exactly what the Holy Spirit does in you. When you feel empty or worn out, it's not about trying harder—it's about coming back to the source. He'll fill you again and again, not just so you can make it through, but so you can thrive and pour out life wherever you go.

And this isn't just about personal renewal—it's about impact. Your life, filled with the Spirit, becomes like a flowing river that brings life wherever it touches. That could be in your home, at work, or in the smallest conversations.

If you've been running on empty, come back to the source. Let Jesus fill you, refresh you, and flow through you with the power and living water of the Holy Spirit!

*Let them shout for joy and be glad, who favor my
righteous cause; and let them say continually,
"Let the Lord be magnified, who has pleasure in
the prosperity of His servant."*

Psalm 35:27

God is not indifferent to your well-being—He delights in seeing you blessed. This verse reveals His heart toward those who walk in His ways. He does not withhold good things from His people; instead, He takes pleasure in their prosperity.

Biblical prosperity is more than financial increase—it includes peace, health, purpose, and every form of well-being. The Hebrew word for *prosperity* here is *shalom*, which means completeness, wholeness, and nothing missing or broken. God's desire is to see His children thrive in every area of life.

This verse also highlights the response of those who love God's ways—joy and continual praise. When we align with His righteousness, we can confidently declare His goodness, knowing He delights in blessing us. Proverbs 10:22 confirms, *"The blessing of the Lord makes one rich, and He adds no sorrow with it."* His blessings bring joy, not burden.

It's important to remember that prosperity is not about selfish gain—it is about being positioned to bless others. 2 Corinthians 9:8 says, *"And God is able to make all grace abound toward you, that you, always having all sufficiency in all things, may have an abundance for every good work."* His desire is for you to walk in abundance so that you can be a blessing to those around you.

If you've ever doubted whether God wants you to prosper, let this verse reassure you. He takes pleasure in seeing you flourish. Trust in His provision, walk in His ways, and declare His goodness, knowing He is faithful to bless His people.

*If any of you lacks wisdom, let him ask of God,
who gives to all liberally and without reproach,
and it will be given to him.*

James 1:5

S eeking wisdom is a demonstration of reliance upon God. He never intended for us to navigate life's challenges alone, which is why He freely offers His wisdom to anyone who asks. Unlike human reasoning, which is limited and often flawed, His wisdom provides insight that leads to peace, success, and clarity.

One of the most comforting aspects of this promise is that He gives *liberally*—without hesitation or limitation! He does not hold back or distribute wisdom sparingly. Proverbs 2:6 affirms, *"For the Lord gives wisdom; from His mouth come knowledge and understanding."* His guidance is always available, and when we seek Him, He will provide the answers we need.

Even better, He gives *without reproach*. Many hesitate to ask for help, fearing judgment, but God never criticizes or shames those who come to Him. Whether we've made mistakes, feel unqualified, or have asked Him before, He welcomes us back again and again. His love is not conditional, and neither is His willingness to give wisdom.

Solomon's story is a perfect example of God's abundant wisdom. When given the opportunity to ask for anything, he chose wisdom. Because of his request, God not only granted him unparalleled understanding but also blessed him in every other area (1 Kings 3:9-13). This shows that wisdom is the foundation for prosperity and success in every aspect of life.

If you need direction, take this verse to heart. God is ready to pour out wisdom, guiding you into the right decisions. All you have to do is ask, and He will provide insight beyond what you could ever gain on your own.

September 25

For even when we were with you, we commanded
you this: If anyone will not work, neither shall he eat.
For we hear that there are some who walk among you
in a disorderly manner, not working at all, but are
busybodies. Now those who are such we command
and exhort through our Lord Jesus Christ that they work
in quietness and eat their own bread.

2 Thessalonians 3:10-12

Diligence is a key principle in God's kingdom. These verses emphasize the importance of hard work, personal responsibility, and living a life of purpose. While God is our provider, He also expects us to actively engage in the opportunities He gives us, rather than idly waiting for our needs to be provided for.

Paul addresses a problem among some believers in Thessalonica who were neglecting their responsibilities, distracted by meddling in the affairs of others. Proverbs 14:23 reinforces this principle: *"In all labor there is profit, but idle chatter leads only to poverty."* God's design is that we work with diligence, trusting that He blesses the work of our hands.

This isn't suggesting that those unable to work are unworthy of support—Scripture is clear about caring for those in genuine need. Rather, it corrects a mindset of laziness and entitlement. God's abundant life includes purpose, and meaningful work is part of that blessing. When we approach our responsibilities with excellence, we honor Him (Colossians 3:23).

A life of diligence leads to provision and fulfillment. When we embrace the work God has given us—whether in a career, ministry, or daily tasks—we position ourselves to thrive. He is faithful to provide, but He also calls us to be faithful with what He has placed in our hands.

*And you are complete in Him, who is the head
of all principality and power.*

Colossians 2:10

Many people spend their lives searching for fulfillment—whether in success, relationships, material
possessions, or personal achievements. Yet true
completeness is only found in Jesus. This verse reminds us that
when we belong to Him, we lack nothing!

To be *complete* means to be whole, fully supplied, and
lacking nothing. The world often tells us we need more—more
accomplishments, more approval, more possessions—to be
truly satisfied. But in Christ, we already have everything we
need. His presence, His love, and His grace provide all that
truly matters.

Jesus is the head of all principality and power, meaning He
has ultimate authority. No force—whether spiritual or earthly—
can override what He has accomplished for us. Because He is
victorious, we stand in victory. Ephesians 1:22-23 says, *"And
He put all things under His feet, and gave Him to be head over
all things to the church, which is His body, the fullness of Him
who fills all in all."* Our identity is rooted in Him, not in our own
abilities or status.

Being complete in Christ also means we don't have to strive
for worth or approval. The love and acceptance we long for are
already ours through Him. Romans 8:38-39 assures us that
nothing can separate us from His love. When we embrace this
truth, we walk in confidence and freedom.

If you've ever felt like you were not enough, let this truth sink
in—you are already complete in Jesus! Nothing the world offers
can add to or take away from what He has done for you. Rest
in His fullness, knowing that in Him, you are whole, loved, and
lacking nothing.

*For it is God who works in you both to will
and to do for His good pleasure.*

Philippians 2:13

L iving an abundant life that honors God is not about striving in our own strength—it is about allowing Him to work in and through us. This verse reveals that God is not only the one who calls us to His purpose, but He also gives us both the desire and the ability to fulfill it!

Many of us struggle with feelings of inadequacy, constantly disappointed in our failures to honor God with our actions. But this verse is a reminder that He is the one working within us. When we yield to Him, He shapes our desires and equips us to carry them out. Ephesians 3:20 affirms this truth: *"Now to Him who is able to do exceedingly abundantly above all that we ask or think, according to the power that works in us."* His power is always at work, guiding and strengthening us for the path ahead.

Not only does God give us the ability to do His will, but He also aligns our hearts with His. He changes our desires so that we want what He wants. Psalm 37:4 says, *"Delight yourself also in the Lord, and He shall give you the desires of your heart."* As we draw near to Him, He transforms us from the inside out, making His purposes our own.

However, before we can fully benefit from this amazing grace at work inside of us, we have to believe! This verse promises that God is actively working in us, but just like any other promise of God, we must receive it by faith.

If you've ever felt like a failure, unable to change yourself, take comfort in knowing that God is actively shaping, strengthening, and equipping you. Confess, "I believe You are working in and changing me, Lord!" Trust Him to complete the good work He has begun in you (Philippians 1:6).

Look at the birds of the air, for they neither sow nor reap nor gather into barns; yet your heavenly Father feeds them. Are you not of more value than they?

Matthew 6:26

Worry is one of the most pervasive ways the enemy can keep us from receiving abundant life. It often creeps in when we focus on our own ability to provide for ourselves. But Jesus reminds us in this verse that God is our source, and if He cares for the birds, how much more will He take care of us?

Birds do not stress over their next meal, yet they are always provided for. They do not store up food the way people accumulate wealth or resources, yet they are sustained daily. This does not mean they sit idle—birds still search for food—but they do so without fear. In the same way, we are called to work diligently but trust that God is the one who ultimately provides.

The key takeaway from this passage is value. Jesus asks a simple but powerful question: *"Are you not of more value than they?"* The answer is an emphatic yes! You are created in the image of God, chosen, and dearly loved. If He ensures that birds never lack what they need, how much more will He ensure His children are cared for?

Worry accomplishes nothing, but trust in God brings peace. He is a faithful provider, and His supply is not limited by economic conditions or circumstances. It doesn't matter where you live, your occupation, or any other natural condition—trusting in God will net the same results!

If anxiety over provision has weighed you down, remember this Word. The same God who provides food for the birds of the air is watching over you. Trust in Him, knowing that He will never fail to meet your needs.

*Through the Lord's mercies we are not consumed,
because His compassions fail not. They are new every
morning; great is Your faithfulness.*

Lamentations 3:22-23

No matter what yesterday looked like, God's mercy is fresh and available today. His love is not based on our perfection, nor does it run out when we make mistakes. This verse reminds us that His compassion is unfailing, and each new day is an opportunity to experience His goodness.

The book of Lamentations was written during a time of deep sorrow for Israel. Yet in the midst of suffering, Jeremiah shifts his focus to the faithfulness of God. Even when everything seemed hopeless, he recognized that it was only by God's mercy that the people were not completely destroyed. His love and grace are what sustain us, even in our darkest moments.

"His compassions fail not" is a powerful truth. People may grow weary of extending kindness, but God's love never grows weaker. Psalm 103:8 confirms, *"The Lord is merciful and gracious, slow to anger, and abounding in mercy."* No matter how many times we fall short, He remains patient and compassionate.

The promise that His mercies are new every morning means that we never have to live in yesterday's failures. Every sunrise is a fresh start, free from guilt and condemnation. Isaiah 43:19 declares, *"Behold, I will do a new thing, now it shall spring forth."* God specializes in renewal, always offering grace for a new beginning.

If you've been carrying regret or discouragement, let this verse remind you—God's mercy is greater than your mistakes. His faithfulness is unshakable, and He is ready to pour out His compassion on you today.

For the eyes of the Lord are on the righteous,
and His ears are open to their prayers; but the face
of the Lord is against those who do evil.

1 Peter 3:12

G od is not distant or indifferent—He is watching over His children with love and attentiveness. This verse is a beautiful reminder that He sees, He listens, and He cares for those who follow Him. His presence is constant, and His ears are open to the prayers of the righteous.

To say *"the eyes of the Lord are on the righteous"* means that He is actively involved in our lives. He is not just observing from afar; He is watching over us with protection, guidance, and favor. Psalm 34:15 affirms this truth: *"The eyes of the Lord are on the righteous, and His ears are open to their cry."* If you ever feel unseen or forgotten, take comfort in knowing that God is paying close attention to you.

Not only does He see you, but He hears you. Your prayers do not go unheard! Even when it feels like there is no immediate answer, He is listening and working on your behalf. 1 John 5:14 says, *"Now this is the confidence that we have in Him, that if we ask anything according to His will, He hears us."*

However, this verse also carries a warning—*"the face of the Lord is against those who do evil."* While God is merciful, He does not ignore wrongdoing. His justice ensures that evil does not go unchecked. But for those who walk in righteousness— and remember, your faith has made you righteous—there is peace in knowing that He is watching over them with love and faithfulness.

If you have ever wondered whether God sees or hears you, be assured—He does. His eyes are on you, His ears are open, and His heart is attentive to your every need. Trust in His faithfulness, knowing that He is always near.

October 1

All Scripture is given by inspiration of God, and is profitable for doctrine, for reproof, for correction, for instruction in righteousness, that the man of God may be complete, thoroughly equipped for every good work.

2 Timothy 3:16-17

G od's Word is more than just ancient writings—it is living, powerful, and essential for every believer. This passage reminds us that Scripture is divinely inspired and serves as our ultimate guide for faith and life.

The phrase *"given by inspiration of God"* literally means "God-breathed." His Word carries His very essence, filled with truth, wisdom, and power. Hebrews 4:12 declares, *"For the word of God is living and powerful, and sharper than any two-edged sword."* It is not just a collection of stories but an active force that transforms lives.

Paul explains that Scripture is beneficial in several ways. It teaches doctrine, revealing truth and establishing a firm foundation of faith. It provides reproof, exposing errors and helping us recognize where we've strayed. It offers correction, guiding us back onto the right path. And it gives instruction in righteousness, training us to live according to God's will. Through these, the Word of God molds and shapes us so that we can walk in His purpose. Psalm 119:105 affirms, *"Your word is a lamp to my feet and a light to my path."* It is not meant to be just read—it is meant to guide our daily lives.

Ultimately, God's Word equips us for every good work. When we study and apply it, we become spiritually strong and prepared for whatever He calls us to do. If you desire to grow, be strengthened, and walk in His purpose, immerse yourself in His Word—it is the key to a life of victory.

October 2

Being confident of this very thing, that He who has begun a good work in you will complete it until the day of Jesus Christ.

Philippians 1:6

Rest assured—God never leaves a work unfinished. If He started something in your life, you can trust that He'll see it through. He's not in a hurry, and He's not giving up. Every part of your journey—every step, every stumble, every stretch—is part of His process to shape you into who He created you to be.

Spiritual growth isn't about striving or trying to be perfect. It's about trusting the One who's doing the work. Isaiah 64:8 says that we are the clay and He is the potter. That means you don't have to have it all together—you just need to stay in His hands. He's shaping you with intention, and nothing about your story is random.

When Paul says this work will continue *"until the day of Jesus Christ,"* it's a reminder that growth is ongoing. You won't always see the results overnight, but that doesn't mean God isn't working. Sometimes the biggest changes happen quietly, behind the scenes, as He uses everyday moments to transform your heart and strengthen your faith.

If you've been feeling stuck or discouraged, remember this: God hasn't left you, and He hasn't changed His mind about you. He's faithful to finish what He started. Keep showing up, keep trusting, and keep your eyes on Him. He's not done yet—and what He's building in you is worth the wait!

He raises the poor from the dust and lifts the beggar from the ash heap, to set them among princes and make them inherit the throne of glory. For the pillars of the earth are the Lord's, and He has set the world upon them.

1 Samuel 2:8

God is in the business of lifting people up. It doesn't matter what your background is, how broken your past has been, or how unqualified you feel—He specializes in taking what the world overlooks and turning it into something beautiful. He's not limited by status or circumstance, and when He raises someone up, it's with purpose.

This verse, part of Hannah's prayer, shows just how far God will go to elevate the humble. Time and again, Scripture tells us that He chooses the weak things of the world to shame the strong and the foolish things to confound the wise (1 Corinthians 1:27). His ways are not like the world's. He sees value where others see failure and calls people into greatness that only He can define.

To be *"set among princes"* and inherit a *"throne of glory"* speaks to more than just outward success. It's about identity and authority in Christ. Ephesians 2:6 says that God has raised us up with Christ and seated us in heavenly places. That means you're not striving for position—you've already been given one in Him.

And this isn't just wishful thinking—God actually has the power to do it. The verse says the foundations of the earth are His. That means He's in charge, fully capable of moving things around to put you right where you need to be. Nothing in your life is too big or too broken for Him to handle. When He lifts you up, it's not by accident—it's on purpose.

Behold what manner of love the Father has bestowed on us, that we should be called children of God! Therefore the world does not know us, because it did not know Him.

1 John 3:1

The love of God is not ordinary—it is extravagant, life-changing, and beyond human comprehension. This verse tells us to *behold*—to pause and take in the magnitude of what it means to be loved by Him. He has not merely shown us kindness; He has given us the highest honor—to be called His children.

To be *"bestowed"* with His love means that it is freely given, not earned. His love is not based on our performance but on His grace. Romans 5:8 affirms this: *"But God demonstrates His own love toward us, in that while we were still sinners, Christ died for us."* Before we ever sought Him, He chose us. He welcomed us into His family, making us sons and daughters through faith in Jesus.

Being called children of God is more than a title—it is an identity. We are not just followers or servants; we belong to Him. Galatians 4:7 declares, *"Therefore you are no longer a slave but a son, and if a son, then an heir of God through Christ."* This means we have full access to His love, His provision, and His inheritance. We are deeply valued, not because of what we do, but because of who He is.

The world may not understand this relationship because it does not know Him. Those who do not recognize God cannot comprehend the depth of His love for His children. But for those who believe, His love is an unshakable reality that transforms everything. If you ever doubt your worth, remember this truth—you are deeply loved, fully accepted, and forever His child. Nothing can change that.

October 5

For I, the Lord your God, will hold your right hand, saying to you, "Fear not, I will help you."

Isaiah 41:13

L ife brings moments of uncertainty, but God offers an unshakable promise—He is holding you. His presence is not distant; it is personal, active, and constant. This verse is a powerful reminder that you are never alone, no matter what challenges arise.

The image of God holding your right hand signifies both guidance and strength. A father holds the hand of his child not only to provide security but also to direct them safely. Psalm 73:23 declares, *"Nevertheless I am continually with You; You hold me by my right hand."* God's grip is firm, ensuring that even when we feel weak, we are never out of His care.

Fear is a natural response to the unknown, but the command *"Fear not"* is repeated throughout Scripture. Jesus Himself often told His disciples not to fear because He knew that fear is a thief of peace. He would never give us a command that we are incapable of doing! When He tells us not to fear, it means He has already provided everything we need to overcome it. Deuteronomy 31:8 affirms, *"And the Lord, He is the One who goes before you. He will be with you, He will not leave you nor forsake you; do not fear nor be dismayed."* Resting in peace through faith in His presence and promise is the antidote to fear.

Beyond simply holding us, God also promises, *"I will help you."* He is not just watching over you—He is actively working in your favor. Whatever you face today, you do not face it alone. Trust in His grip, rest in His promise, and walk forward in confidence, knowing that the One who holds your hand will never let you go.

The steps of a good man are ordered by the Lord, and He delights in his way. Though he fall, he shall not be utterly cast down; for the Lord upholds him with His hand. I have been young, and now am old; yet I have not seen the righteous forsaken, nor his descendants begging bread.

Psalm 37:23-25

Walking with God means knowing that your steps are not random—He is guiding you with purpose. This passage is a beautiful reassurance that He is actively directing your path, delighting in the journey you take with Him. Even when you face difficulties, He is holding you up, ensuring that failure is never final!

To have your steps ordered by the Lord means that He is involved in the details of your life. Proverbs 16:9 confirms this: *"A man's heart plans his way, but the Lord directs his steps."* You are not wandering aimlessly—God is leading you toward His best. When you surrender your plans to Him, you can walk forward with confidence, knowing He is making a way.

This passage also acknowledges that setbacks will come. Life is full of challenges, but God does not abandon you when you stumble. Instead, He upholds you, strengthens you, and helps you rise again. Micah 7:8 declares, *"When I fall, I will arise; when I sit in darkness, the Lord will be a light to me."*

God never forsakes the righteous. He is a faithful provider, ensuring that His children are never left without help. Throughout Scripture there are examples of God providing for His people, miraculously when necessary!

If you ever feel uncertain about your path or weighed down by setbacks, remember this promise: God is guiding you, holding you, and providing for you. Trust His leading, for He delights in every step you take.

October 7

My voice You shall hear in the morning, O Lord; in the morning I will direct it to You, and I will look up.

Psalm 5:3

Prayer is not just a ritual—it is a lifeline, a direct connection with God. This verse reveals the power of starting each day by seeking Him, not just with requests but with expectation. When we bring our prayers before Him, we can trust that He hears, responds, and leads us forward.

David didn't just pray—he prayed *expectantly*. The phrase *"I will look up"* suggests an attitude of faith, anticipating God's response. Too often, people pray out of routine but fail to expect results. Yet Jesus assured us in Matthew 7:7, *"Ask, and it will be given to you; seek, and you will find; knock, and it will be opened to you."* God is faithful to answer, but He desires us to come before Him with confidence, believing that He is working on our behalf.

Morning prayer sets the course for the day, but it should not be the only time we seek Him. While this verse emphasizes beginning the day with God, 1 Thessalonians 5:17 reminds us to *"pray without ceasing."* Prayer is meant to be a continuous conversation with our Father—not just something we do in the morning and forget about. When we remain in constant communication with Him, we invite His wisdom, guidance, and peace into every moment of our day.

James 4:2 tells us that sometimes we don't have simply because we have neglected to ask! That's a powerful reminder to keep our eyes on Jesus. If you've struggled to live out a routine of prayer, just lean into His grace. Ask the Holy Spirit to remind you to come to God in prayer each morning with expectation and to continue seeking Him throughout the day. He listens, He cares, and He is faithful to respond!

But the Lord is with me as a mighty, awesome One.
Therefore my persecutors will stumble,
and will not prevail. They will be greatly ashamed,
for they will not prosper. Their everlasting confusion
will never be forgotten.

Jeremiah 20:11

O pposition is inevitable, but defeat is not. This verse is a bold reminder that no matter what tries to rise against you, God is greater. He doesn't just watch from a distance—He stands beside you as a mighty warrior. With Him on your side, every plan of the enemy is destined to fail.

Jeremiah knew what it meant to face resistance. He was mocked, rejected, and even imprisoned for delivering God's message. And yet, in the middle of all that, he could still declare his confidence in God's power and presence. Like Jeremiah, you're not alone when pressure mounts. *"If God is for us, who can be against us?"* (Romans 8:31). No enemy—spiritual or physical—can undo what God has spoken over your life.

The promise that your enemies will stumble and not prevail is not just about surviving tough times—it's part of your inheritance in the abundant life Jesus came to give you. That life isn't free of challenges, but it is full of victory, peace, purpose, and power in the midst of them! Abundance doesn't mean everything is easy; it means that through it all, you walk in supernatural strength, unshakable peace, and unbreakable hope.

God's presence in your life guarantees more than protection—it guarantees progress. No plan formed against you can succeed when you're walking in step with the One who defends you. So when the pressure rises, don't retreat—stand tall. The Lord is with you, and your life is marked by His abundance, favor, and victory.

The work of righteousness will be peace, and the effect of righteousness, quietness and assurance forever.

Isaiah 32:17

Peace is not found in circumstances, but it comes from righteousness. This verse reveals that when we walk in righteousness, peace is not just a fleeting feeling, but a lasting result of living in His ways.

Righteousness goes beyond right behavior; it is being in right standing with God. Under the New Covenant, we are made righteous not by our own works, but through faith in Jesus. 2 Corinthians 5:21 declares, *"For He made Him who knew no sin to be sin for us, that we might become the righteousness of God in Him."* Because of Jesus, we can live with confidence, knowing we are accepted by God.

The work of righteousness produces peace. This means that peace naturally flows from a life rooted in faith in Jesus, as His righteousness produces good works and aligns us with God's truth. When we put our trust in Him, our hearts are at rest, free from the turmoil that comes with sin, fear, and striving.

The effect of righteousness is quietness and assurance. This is talking about an inner stability—a confidence that remains firm no matter what is happening around us. When we are rooted in God, we do not have to be shaken by life's uncertainties. Psalm 112:6-7 says, *"Surely he will never be shaken.... He will not be afraid of evil tidings; his heart is steadfast, trusting in the Lord."*

If you have been longing for deep, lasting peace, remember that it is the fruit of righteousness. Through Jesus, you have been made right with God, and His peace is yours to walk in every single day.

October 10

And we know that the Son of God has come and has given us an understanding, that we may know Him who is true; and we are in Him who is true, in His Son Jesus Christ. This is the true God and eternal life.

1 John 5:20

J esus didn't just come to show us a better way to live— He came to bring us into a real, personal relationship with the one true God. Through Him, we don't just learn about God; we *know* Him intimately.

Jesus has revealed truth to us and given us understanding of that truth. Without Him, we could never fully grasp who God is. John 14:9 confirms this when Jesus said, *"He who has seen Me has seen the Father."* He is the exact representation of God's nature, and through Him, we have access to divine wisdom and revelation.

This verse also emphasizes our position in Christ. We have security and assurance *"in Him who is true"* as believers. When we accept Jesus, we are united with Him—we are no longer outsiders, but children of God, walking in the fullness of His truth. Colossians 3:3 affirms, *"For you died, and your life is hidden with Christ in God."*

Jesus is not only the way to eternal life—He *is* eternal life. Knowing Him is not about the future; it is about experiencing His life through relationship with Him today. John 17:3 states, *"And this is eternal life, that they may know You, the only true God, and Jesus Christ whom You have sent."*

If you have ever struggled with doubt or uncertainty, take hold of this truth: Jesus has made God known to you. You are in Him, secure in His love, and walking in the reality of eternal life today.

May the Lord give you increase more and more,
you and your children.

Psalm 115:14

G od is a God of increase. His desire is not for you to live in lack, but to grow, flourish, and experience His abundant blessings. This verse is a powerful declaration that His favor is not only for you but for future generations as well.

The word *increase* in this passage is referring to expansion, multiplication, and continual growth. God's blessings are not meant to be stagnant; they are designed to overflow in every area of life. That is abundance! His heart is for you to thrive spiritually, physically, and in every aspect of your calling.

This promise extends beyond individual prosperity—it is generational. God's blessing is meant to be passed down to your children and those who come after you. Proverbs 13:22 says, *"A good man leaves an inheritance to his children's children."* When you walk in God's abundance, you create a legacy of faith, provision, and spiritual strength that impacts those who follow.

It is important to remember that true increase comes from the Lord. While the world chases temporary success, God provides lasting and meaningful growth. 2 Corinthians 9:8 assures, *"And God is able to make all grace abound toward you, that you, always having all sufficiency in all things, may have an abundance for every good work."* His blessings are not just for personal gain but for fulfilling His purposes.

If you've been believing for increase, stand on this promise. Trust that God desires to bless you, to cause you to grow, and to extend His favor beyond your own life. His increase is not just for today—it is a lasting, generational blessing.

That the sharing of your faith may become effective by the acknowledgment of every good thing which is in you in Christ Jesus.

Philemon 1:6

F aith is not dormant or passive—it is active, powerful, and life-changing! This verse reveals that the effectiveness of our faith is directly connected to recognizing what we have in Christ. When we acknowledge the good things He has placed within us, our faith is stirred, strengthened, and able to make an impact.

The word *effective* in this verse comes from the Greek word *energes*, meaning active or powerful. Faith is not just about believing—it is about putting that belief into action. James 2:17 affirms, *"Thus also faith by itself, if it does not have works, is dead."* When we truly understand the riches we have in Christ, our faith naturally becomes more effective, influencing both our lives and the lives of those around us.

Acknowledging *"every good thing"* in us through Christ is key! Many believers struggle with feelings of inadequacy, not realizing that God has already equipped them with everything they need. 2 Peter 1:3 declares, *"His divine power has given to us all things that pertain to life and godliness."* When we focus on His provision, grace, and strength within us, we begin to walk in confidence, expecting His power to manifest in our daily lives.

Sharing our faith is not just about words—it's about living in the fullness of what Christ has done. The more we recognize His work in us, the more our lives reflect His goodness. If you want to see your faith grow, start by acknowledging all He has given you. As you do, your faith will become active, powerful, and effective in everything you do.

For all the promises of God in Him are Yes, and in Him Amen, to the glory of God through us.

2 Corinthians 1:20

God is a promise-keeping God. Every word He has spoken, every covenant He has made, and every blessing He has declared is fulfilled in Jesus. This verse reassures us that we never have to wonder whether God's promises are reliable—His answer is always *Yes* in Christ.

Jesus is the guarantee of God's faithfulness. He is the fulfillment of everything God has promised throughout Scripture. Numbers 23:19 confirms, *"God is not a man, that He should lie, nor a son of man, that He should repent. Has He said, and will He not do?"* If He has spoken it, He will bring it to pass!

God has said "Yes" to all of His promises, and then we are to embrace them. The word *Amen* means *so be it*—a declaration of faith and agreement with what God has already established. When we believe and declare His promises over our lives, we align ourselves with His will and invite His power to work on our behalf.

This verse also reveals that God's promises are not just for our benefit—they bring glory to Him. When we walk in His provision, healing, peace, and victory, our lives become a testimony of His faithfulness. Ephesians 3:20 reminds us that He *"is able to do exceedingly abundantly above all that we ask or think, according to the power that works in us."*

If you've ever doubted whether God's promises apply to you, let this verse be your assurance. In Christ, every promise is already fulfilled. Stand firm in faith, come into agreement with Him and say, "Amen" to His "Yes!"

October 14

Blessed be the Lord, who has given rest to His people Israel, according to all that He promised. There has not failed one word of all His good promise, which He promised through His servant Moses.

1 Kings 8:56

T hroughout history, God has proven His faithfulness time and time again. Every word He has spoken, every covenant He has made, and every promise He has given remains steadfast. God fulfills what He has promised—every time, without exception!

In this verse, Solomon was reflecting on the history of Israel, recognizing that everything God had promised through Moses had come to pass. The Israelites had seen miraculous provision, victories in battle, and the fulfillment of God's Word concerning the land He swore to give them. Joshua 21:45 says, *"Not a word failed of any good thing which the Lord had spoken to the house of Israel. All came to pass."* The same God who kept His word then is the same God who keeps His word today!

God's promises bring peace and security. When we trust in Him, we don't have to strive or stress—there's a place of rest available to us. For example, consider His promise to provide. It's easy to worry about how the bills will get paid or to start scrambling for a backup plan, but instead of giving in to anxiety, we can rely on His faithfulness. He already knows what we need, and He's more than able to take care of it—without us carrying the weight alone.

If you have been waiting for a promise to be fulfilled, take heart—God has never failed, and He won't start now! His Word does not return void (Isaiah 55:11). Stand firm, knowing that not one word of His promises to you will fail.

In all labor there is profit,
but idle chatter leads only to poverty.

Proverbs 14:23

D iligence is a key principle in God's kingdom. This verse highlights the simple yet profound truth that hard work leads to gain, while mere talk produces nothing. Success and abundance don't come from wishful thinking or empty words but from faithful action.

God blesses the work of our hands (Deuteronomy 28:12). When we approach our work with integrity and dedication, we position ourselves for God's provision. He can't reward laziness, because if we have put our hands to nothing, there's nothing for him to bless! However, diligence and hard work, whether in ministry, business, relationships, or personal growth, always bring increase.

On the other hand, *"idle chatter leads only to poverty."* Talking about goals, dreams, or ideas without doing something to move them forward accomplishes nothing. James 2:17 reminds us, *"Faith by itself, if it does not have works, is dead."* While faith is essential, it must be accompanied by corresponding action. Many people desire success or blessings but are unwilling to put in the effort required.

This principle applies not just to finances but to every area of life. If you desire to grow spiritually, you must spend time in the Word and prayer. If you want strong relationships, you must invest in them. If you long to fulfill your purpose, you must step out in obedience.

If you've been waiting for change, ask yourself: Are you taking steps of faith, or just talking about them? Trust that God blesses diligent hands, and as you work with faith and purpose, He will bring increase and reward.

October 16

Those who trust in the Lord are like Mount Zion,
which cannot be moved, but abides forever.

Psalm 125:1

A life rooted in trust in God is a life that stands firm. This verse paints a powerful picture of stability—those who put their faith in the Lord are unshakable, just like Mount Zion, which remains steadfast through every storm.

Mount Zion, often referred to as God's holy mountain, represents His presence, His kingdom, and His unchanging nature. Just as this mountain cannot be moved, those who trust in Him are established on a foundation that cannot be shaken. Jesus echoed this truth in Matthew 7:24-25, saying, *"Whoever hears these sayings of Mine, and does them, I will liken him to a wise man who built his house on the rock... and it did not fall, for it was founded on the rock."* When you anchor your life in God's promises, no storm can uproot you.

Trusting in the Lord doesn't mean you won't face difficulties, but it does mean that you will not be overcome by them. Isaiah 26:3 assures, *"You will keep him in perfect peace, whose mind is stayed on You, because he trusts in You."* Instead of reacting with fear or frustration, you can respond to challenges with faith, prayer, and an expectation of His goodness. The world may be uncertain, but God is unchanging. His faithfulness is the foundation that keeps you steady when everything else is shifting.

If you've been feeling shaken by circumstances, take heart—your trust in God secures you. His promises will never fail, and His presence will never leave you. Stand firm, knowing that just like Mount Zion, you are rooted in something eternal, unmovable, and victorious.

October 17

*And this is the testimony: that God has given
us eternal life, and this life is in His Son.
He who has the Son has life; he who does not
have the Son of God does not have life.*

1 John 5:11-12

E ternal life is not just about the future—it is a present reality for those who have a relationship with Jesus. This verse reminds us that life, in its fullest and most abundant form, is found in Him alone.

Not only is eternal life a present condition, it is a gift, not something we earn. Through Jesus' sacrifice, we are granted access to the kind of life only God can give—a life filled with His presence, His power, and His peace. John 10:10 affirms this truth: *"I have come that they may have life, and that they may have it more abundantly."* Life in Christ is not just about existence—it is about thriving, walking in His joy, and experiencing His fullness.

This passage also makes a clear distinction: *"He who has the Son has life."* Jesus is the source of all true life. Without Him, people may seek fulfillment in temporary things, but nothing apart from Him can provide lasting satisfaction. John 14:6 confirms, *"I am the way, the truth, and the life. No one comes to the Father except through Me."*

To have the Son means to have a relationship with Him—to believe in Him, walk with Him, and receive His grace. It means living with the assurance that you are His, both now and forever. If you have Jesus, you have everything you need. Rest in the truth that your life—both eternal and abundant—is secure in Him.

If you faint in the day of adversity, your strength is small.

Proverbs 24:10

D ifficult times reveal what we rely on for strength. This verse is both a challenge and an encouragement—if adversity causes us to falter, it is not meant to condemn us but to remind us to draw on God's strength rather than our own.

Adversity is inevitable, but how we respond to it makes all the difference. Those who depend on their own ability will struggle, but those who trust in God will stand firm. God never intended for us to rely on our own limited strength—He offers us His supernatural power to endure, overcome, and thrive even in hardship.

When we try to handle adversity on our own, we quickly reach the end of our strength. But His strength within us is limitless. Paul understood this when he wrote in 2 Corinthians 12:9, *"My grace is sufficient for you, for My strength is made perfect in weakness."* Instead of fearing difficult times, we can view them as opportunities for God to display His power in our lives.

We need to evaluate our foundation. Jesus spoke of this in Matthew 7:24-25, comparing those who build on the rock to those who build on the sand. When storms come, only those whose foundation is in God will remain standing. He is our strength and is always there to help (Psalm 46:1).

If adversity has caused you to feel weak, remember—you are not meant to carry it alone. His strength is inside of you, upholding and sustaining you. When you depend on Him, He will renew you and help you stand firm no matter what comes your way.

And those who know Your name will put their trust in You; for You, Lord, have not forsaken those who seek You.

Psalm 9:10

Trust is built on relationship. Those who truly know God—who understand His character, faithfulness, and goodness—will naturally place their trust in Him. When we know who He is, we can be confident that He will never forsake us.

In biblical times, a name represented a person's identity and nature. God's many names—Jehovah Jireh (Provider), Jehovah Rapha (Healer), Jehovah Shalom (Peace)—reveal different aspects of His character. To know His name means to recognize and believe in who He is. Proverbs 18:10 declares, *"The name of the Lord is a strong tower; the righteous run to it and are safe."* His name is a place of protection, provision, and security.

Trusting God is not just about believing He exists—it is about knowing Him personally. The more we seek Him, the more we experience His faithfulness firsthand. A heart that knows God rests in peace, even in uncertain times (Isaiah 26:3).

God is not distant or inattentive—He is near to those who call upon Him. Deuteronomy 31:8 reassures us, *"And the Lord, He is the One who goes before you. He will be with you, He will not leave you nor forsake you."* No matter what you face, you are never alone.

If you struggle with trust, deepen your knowledge of God's character. Seek Him, meditate on His promises, and remind yourself of His faithfulness. The more you know Him, the more you will trust Him—and the more you trust Him, the more you will experience His unfailing presence in your life.

There is no fear in love; but perfect love casts out fear, because fear involves torment. But he who fears has not been made perfect in love.

1 John 4:18

J ohn had a deep revelation of God's love. He repeatedly referred to himself as *"the disciple whom Jesus loved."* This wasn't because Jesus loved him more than the others, but because John had a revelation of that love. His understanding of God's love shaped his life, and it's no coincidence that he was the only one of the twelve disciples who lived to an old age. Though persecutors tried to kill him—even by boiling him in oil—he miraculously survived!

The phrase *"perfect love casts out fear"* does not mean we will never experience fear, but rather that God's love gives us confidence to overcome it. Fear thrives on uncertainty—about the future, our worth, or God's faithfulness. But His love assures us that we are safe in Him. Romans 8:38-39 reminds us, *"For I am persuaded that neither death nor life… nor things present nor things to come… shall be able to separate us from the love of God which is in Christ Jesus our Lord."* When we are deeply rooted in His love, fear loses its grip.

Fear involves torment because it keeps us in bondage, controlling our thoughts and emotions. But God's love frees us. 2 Timothy 1:7 declares, *"For God has not given us a spirit of fear, but of power and of love and of a sound mind."* The more we meditate on His love, the more His peace replaces our fear.

To be *"made perfect in love"* is to fully grasp and trust in God's deep, personal love for us. John walked in this revelation, and it produced confidence, boldness, and even supernatural protection. If fear has been holding you back, follow John's example—know and believe in the love God has for you. His perfect love is powerful enough to cast out every fear.

Your word is a lamp to my feet and a light to my path.

Psalm 119:105

B y this point it should be obvious to you that God's Word is not just a book of instructions—it is a guiding light for every step of life. This verse beautifully illustrates how Scripture illuminates our path, providing clarity, direction, and wisdom in a world filled with uncertainty.

"A lamp to my feet" suggests immediate guidance for the next step, while *"a light to my path"* implies broader direction for the journey ahead. Sometimes, God reveals only the next step rather than the entire road, requiring us to walk by faith. Then other times He shows us a bigger picture of what is to come. Regardless, His Word is our roadmap, ensuring that we do not stumble.

This verse also speaks of the importance of staying in God's Word daily. Just as a traveler in darkness needs a continual source of light, we need the continual illumination of Scripture. Matthew 4:4 says, *"Man shall not live by bread alone, but by every word that proceeds from the mouth of God."* The more we immerse ourselves in His truth, the clearer our path becomes. His Word not only shows us what is right but also helps us make wise decisions, led by the Holy Spirit. When we align our hearts with Scripture, we become more sensitive to His leading and direction in every choice we make.

God's Word doesn't just show us where to go—it also keeps us from straying. Psalm 37:23 says, *"The steps of a good man are ordered by the Lord, and He delights in his way."* If you have been unsure of your next steps, seek His guidance through His Word. His light will never fail to lead you in the right direction, giving you confidence in every step of your journey.

Therefore, if anyone is in Christ, he is a new creation;
old things have passed away;
behold, all things have become new.

2 Corinthians 5:17

L ife in Christ is not about self-improvement—it is about transformation. This verse declares that when we accept Jesus, we don't just get a fresh start; we become completely new creations. Our past no longer defines us, and we are no longer bound by who we used to be.

This promise is for anyone who is "in Christ," meaning anyone who has made Jesus the Lord of their life. No matter your background, mistakes, or past failures, when you place your faith in Jesus, you are made new. Romans 8:1 reassures us, *"There is therefore now no condemnation to those who are in Christ Jesus."* You are no longer guilty, unworthy, or held back by your past—God sees you as righteous and redeemed.

Your former identity, bound by sin, shame, and failure, is gone. Just as a caterpillar is completely transformed into a butterfly, you have been changed at the core of who you are. Ephesians 4:22-24 encourages us to *"put off, concerning your former conduct, the old man which grows corrupt... and be renewed in the spirit of your mind, and... put on the new man which was created according to God."*

In Christ, *"all things have become new!"* Your desires, your mindset, and your future are no longer dictated by your past. You are empowered by His Spirit to walk in righteousness, victory, and purpose. If you ever struggle with feeling unworthy, remember this truth: you are not who you used to be. You are a new creation, set apart for God's glory, walking in the abundant life He has given you.

And let the beauty of the Lord our God be upon us,
and establish the work of our hands for us;
yes, establish the work of our hands.

Psalm 90:17

God desires to bless and establish the work of your hands. This verse is a powerful prayer, asking for His favor to rest upon us and for our efforts to be made firm, lasting, and fruitful.

His grace, favor, and presence covers our lives. When God's favor is on you, everything you do takes on a greater purpose. Psalm 5:12 says, *"For You, O Lord, will bless the righteous; with favor You will surround him as with a shield."* His favor is what sets you apart, causes your work to flourish, and gives you success beyond your own abilities.

Praying that God will establish the work of our hands is a request that we will produce meaningful and lasting fruit. John 15:16 confirms this, *"You did not choose Me, but I chose you and appointed you that you should go and bear fruit, and that your fruit should remain."* Without Him, our efforts are temporary, but when He establishes them, they carry eternal significance.

Success is not about striving in our own strength. Proverbs 16:3 instructs, *"Commit your works to the Lord, and your thoughts will be established."* When we surrender our work, dreams, and efforts to God, He directs our steps and brings lasting impact.

If you've ever wondered whether your work truly matters, take heart—when God's favor is upon you, and He establishes your work, it will not be in vain. Seek His guidance, trust in His blessing, and know that what you do for Him will have lasting purpose.

For if by the one man's offense death reigned through the one, much more those who receive abundance of grace and of the gift of righteousness will reign in life through the One, Jesus Christ.

Romans 5:17

Through Jesus, we are not just saved—we are empowered to reign in life. This verse contrasts the effects of Adam's sin, which brought death, with the overwhelming victory we now have through Christ. Instead of being ruled by sin, fear, or defeat, we are called to walk in dominion, authority, and abundance.

God's grace is not limited—it is overflowing, inexhaustible, and freely given. We can't earn it; we simply receive it by faith as a gift from Him (Ephesians 2:8). Grace is what enables us to live victoriously, free from the power of sin and condemnation.

2 Corinthians 5:21 declares, *"For He made Him who knew no sin to be sin for us, that we might become the righteousness of God in Him."* This means we are no longer trying to earn God's approval or righteousness; we already have it through Jesus. Because we are made righteous in Him, we can approach life with confidence, knowing we have His favor.

In Jesus, we are overcomers, destined and designed to reign! 1 John 5:4 declares, *"For whatever is born of God overcomes the world."* Whether facing trials, temptation, or adversity, His grace and righteousness equip us to live as conquerors.

If you have received Jesus, you are not meant to live in defeat. You have been given the abundance of His grace and the gift of righteousness—walk in them, knowing that in Him, you reign in life.

Blessed is he who reads and those who hear the words of this prophecy, and keep those things which are written in it; for the time is near.

Revelation 1:3

God's Word is not just meant to be read—it is meant to be received, obeyed, and lived out. This verse promises a blessing to those who engage with Scripture, particularly the book of Revelation, but the principle applies to all of God's Word.

The three actions mentioned—*reading, hearing, and keeping*—highlight the methods of how we use and apply Scripture. It is not enough to simply read the Bible; we must truly listen with an open heart, allowing His truth to shape our thoughts and actions. James 1:22 warns, *"But be doers of the word, and not hearers only, deceiving yourselves."* The true blessing comes when we apply God's truth in our daily lives.

This verse also carries a sense of urgency: *"For the time is near."* While no one knows the exact time of Christ's return, we are called to live expectantly, fully prepared, and walking in His ways. Jesus emphasized this in Luke 12:35, saying, *"Let your waist be girded and your lamps burning."* Engaging with His Word keeps us spiritually awake and ready for what He has prepared.

God's blessing is attached to His Word. When we take time to read, hear, and obey, we position ourselves to receive wisdom, direction, and supernatural favor. Psalm 1:1-3 describes the person who delights in God's Word as *"like a tree planted by the rivers of water… whatever he does shall prosper."*

If you desire to walk in God's blessings, make His Word a priority. Read it with expectation, listen with faith, and apply it with obedience. As you do, you will experience the blessing and fulfillment that comes from walking in His truth.

Oh, taste and see that the Lord is good;
blessed is the man who trusts in Him!

Psalm 34:8

Simply knowing about God's goodness isn't enough—He wants us to experience it personally. This verse is an invitation to go beyond head knowledge and step into something deeper: a real, everyday relationship with Him that you can actually feel and see in action.

When David wrote these words, he wasn't speaking from theory. He had faced danger, rejection, and hardship—and through it all, he experienced God's goodness in very real ways. He didn't just hear about God's deliverance; he lived it. That's why he could boldly say, *"Taste and see."* He had tasted, and he had seen!

Tasting implies participation. You can't taste something from a distance. You have to engage with it—try it for yourself. The same is true with God. We experience His goodness by trusting Him in the everyday moments: bringing Him our fears, believing His promises, stepping out in obedience, and watching Him come through.

The second part of this verse reminds us that trusting God is key to walking in blessing. Trust isn't always easy—especially when life feels uncertain—but it's the path to peace, provision, and joy. God doesn't expect us to have it all figured out; He simply invites us to lean on Him and believe that He's faithful.

If you've been holding back, unsure if God will really show up for you, this is your invitation. Don't just observe from the sidelines. Take a step. Try Him. Trust Him. Taste and see—His goodness is better than you imagined. And once you experience it for yourself, you'll never want to go back.

*And Jesus said to them, "I am the bread of life.
He who comes to Me shall never hunger, and he who
believes in Me shall never thirst."*

John 6:35

J esus is the only source of true satisfaction. In this verse, He declares Himself the *"bread of life,"* the One who meets every spiritual need and fills the deepest hunger of the human soul.

Physical hunger and thirst are constant needs—no matter how much we eat or drink, we always need more. But nothing in this world can truly satisfy the longing of the human heart except Him. Many try to fill this void with success, relationships, or material things, but these only provide temporary satisfaction. Jesus alone offers fulfillment that never fades.

To come to Him and believe in Him is to place our full trust in everything He has to offer! This is more than just acknowledging who He is—it is relying on Him daily. Just as physical bread sustains our bodies, Jesus sustains our spirits. Matthew 4:4 declares, *"Man shall not live by bread alone, but by every word that proceeds from the mouth of God."* Feeding on His Word and walking in relationship with Him—Jesus *is* the Word—keeps us spiritually nourished.

This verse also points to Jesus as the ultimate provider. Just as God provided manna in the wilderness to sustain Israel, Jesus is our daily sustenance. He *is* the Bread of Life. When we abide in Him, we find lasting nourishment, peace, and strength.

Jesus promises that those who come to Him will *never* hunger or thirst. This doesn't mean life will be free of challenges, but it does mean that in Him, we will always have everything we need. If you have been searching for something to satisfy your soul, look no further—Jesus is the Bread of Life, and in Him, you will find abundance, fulfillment, and eternal satisfaction.

I will make them and the places all around My hill a blessing; and I will cause showers to come down in their season; there shall be showers of blessing.

Ezekiel 34:26

G od's heart is to bless His people abundantly. This verse paints a vivid picture of His provision and favor, describing His blessings as *showers*—continuous, refreshing, and life-giving.

The phrase *"I will make them… a blessing"* reveals that God's goodness doesn't just flow *to* us but also *through* us. When we walk in His abundance, we become a source of blessing to others. This aligns with His covenant promise to Abraham in Genesis 12:2: *"I will bless you and make your name great; and you shall be a blessing."* God blesses us so that we can impact those around us.

The *"showers"* represent the outpouring of God's provision, favor, and spiritual nourishment. Just as rain is essential for crops to grow, His blessings sustain us and cause us to flourish. Psalm 68:9 says, *"You, O God, sent a plentiful rain, whereby You confirmed Your inheritance, when it was weary."* God knows exactly when and how to send the refreshment we need, whether it be strength, provision, or direction.

This verse also reminds us that God's blessings come *in their season*. Sometimes, we may feel like we are in a dry season, but His timing is perfect. Galatians 6:9 encourages, *"And let us not grow weary while doing good, for in due season we shall reap if we do not lose heart."* His showers of blessing will come exactly when we need them most.

If you've been feeling weary, trust in this promise—God is sending showers of blessing your way. Stay in faith, remain expectant, and know that He is faithful to provide and refresh you in every season.

For the Lord God is a sun and shield; the Lord will give grace and glory; no good thing will He withhold from those who walk uprightly.

Psalm 84:11

G od is both our provider and our protector. This verse reveals His generous nature, promising that He will supply everything we need and guard us as we walk with Him.

The imagery of God as a sun and shield reveals both His guidance and His protection. As the sun, He brings us clarity, direction, and warmth. Just as the sun is essential for life, so is His presence for our growth. As a shield, He is our refuge, our protector against harm. Psalm 3:3 declares, *"But You, O Lord, are a shield for me, my glory and the One who lifts up my head."* No matter what comes against you, He stands as your defense.

The promise that God *"gives grace and glory"* reminds us that He provides both favor and honor. His grace is the divine strength that empowers us, while His glory reflects His presence in our lives. And His blessings are not limited—He pours them out abundantly on those who trust in Him!

One of the most reassuring parts of this verse is the promise that *"no good thing will He withhold from those who walk uprightly."* This does not mean we receive everything we desire on our timeline, but it does mean that God will never keep something from us that will truly bless us. If you are waiting on a promise, trust that His timing and provision are perfect. He is a loving Father who delights in blessing His children!

If you've ever wondered whether God wants good things for you, let this verse be your assurance—He is a sun to guide you, a shield to protect you, and a provider who withholds nothing good from those who seek Him.

It shall come to pass that before they call, I will answer;
and while they are still speaking, I will hear.

Isaiah 65:24

Whenwe pray, we can know beyond any doubt that God hears us. In fact, this verse is a powerful reminder that God's responsiveness to us is immediate and often beyond what we expect!

"Before they call, I will answer" reveals God's intimate knowledge of our lives. He sees every detail and knows what we need before we even ask. Jesus affirmed this truth in Matthew 6:8 when He said, *"For your Father knows the things you have need of before you ask Him."* This doesn't mean we shouldn't pray—it means we can pray with *confidence*, knowing He is already moving on our behalf.

The second part of the verse, *"while they are still speaking, I will hear,"* reassures us that God is never distant or inattentive. He is a loving Father who is always listening. Psalm 34:15 confirms, *"The eyes of the Lord are on the righteous, and His ears are open to their cry."* Even when we feel unheard or unseen, He is actively responding to our prayers.

Sometimes, we may not see immediate results, but that does not mean God is not working. His answers may come in unexpected ways or in His perfect timing. Daniel 10:12 reveals that God sent an answer the moment Daniel prayed, even though the manifestation took time. If you are waiting on an answer, rest assured that He has already heard you, and His response is on the way.

Let this verse encourage you—God is not just aware of your prayers; He is actively responding, even before you call. Trust in His perfect timing, knowing that He is always listening and always at work for your good.

Then He touched their eyes, saying,
"According to your faith let it be to you."

Matthew 9:29

Faith is the key that unlocks God's power in our lives. In this verse, Jesus heals two blind men, but He makes it clear that the miracle is connected to their faith. His ability to heal was never in question—the determining factor was whether they believed.

Many people wait for God to move in their lives, but Jesus consistently emphasized that faith is what activates His promises. Hebrews 11:6 affirms, *"But without faith it is impossible to please Him, for he who comes to God must believe that He is, and that He is a rewarder of those who diligently seek Him."* Faith is not just acknowledging that God *can* do something; it is trusting that He *will.*

This doesn't mean we earn miracles through effort, but that we receive by believing. Mark 11:24 confirms this truth: *"Whatever things you ask when you pray, believe that you receive them, and you will have them."* Faith is a posture of expectation, knowing that God's Word is true.

Faith also requires action. James 2:17 declares, *"Thus also faith by itself, if it does not have works, is dead."* The blind men in this passage actively pursued Jesus, calling out to Him and following Him into the house. Their faith was not passive—it was persistent. Likewise, we must align our actions with our belief, stepping out in faith even before we see the answer.

What are you believing for today? Whether it's healing, provision, or breakthrough, Jesus' words still apply: *"According to your faith let it be to you."* He is willing, He is able, and He is looking for those who will take Him at His word. Step out in faith, trust in His promises, and watch as His power is released in your life.

Not a word failed of any good thing which the Lord had spoken to the house of Israel. All came to pass.

Joshua 21:45

God's Word is unshakable. Every promise He makes is backed by His faithfulness, and not one of them will ever fail. This verse, spoken after Israel had entered the Promised Land, is a powerful testimony that God does exactly what He says He will do.

The Israelites had faced battles, obstacles, and years of waiting, yet in the end, *all* that God had promised them was fulfilled. He did not forget or change His mind. Numbers 23:19 declares, *"God is not a man, that He should lie, nor a son of man, that He should repent. Has He said, and will He not do?"* If He has spoken it, He will bring it to pass.

This same faithfulness extends to every believer today. When you stand on God's promises, you can trust that His Word will not return void (Isaiah 55:11). Whether you are believing for provision, healing, restoration, or guidance, His promises are as certain now as they were for Israel.

Holding onto God's promises requires faith, especially when circumstances seem to say otherwise. Abraham is a great example—he trusted God's promise of a son even when it looked impossible. Romans 4:20-21 says, *"He did not waver at the promise of God through unbelief, but was strengthened in faith, giving glory to God, and being fully convinced that what He had promised He was also able to perform."*

If you have been waiting on a promise, be encouraged—God does not fail! He is faithful to fulfill every word He has spoken. Keep trusting, keep standing, and you will see His promises come to pass in your life.

Ask, and it will be given to you; seek, and you will find; knock, and it will be opened to you. For everyone who asks receives, and he who seeks finds, and to him who knocks it will be opened.

Matthew 7:7-8

God desires for us to come to Him with confidence, knowing that He is ready to respond. In this passage, Jesus reveals a powerful truth: persistence in faith brings results. He is not a distant or reluctant God but a loving Father who delights in answering His children.

The three actions in this verse—*ask, seek, and knock*—represent increasing levels of persistence. Asking is bringing our requests before God. Seeking implies an active pursuit of His will. Knocking suggests perseverance, continuing in faith even when answers are not immediately apparent. Jesus shows that those who persist will see results.

The promise in verse 8 is clear: *"For everyone who asks receives."* This does not mean we get everything exactly how we want, but it does mean God hears and responds. James 1:5-6 reminds us to ask in faith without doubting. Faith-filled prayer is not about begging—it is about trusting in His goodness.

Seeking God goes beyond making requests; it involves pursuing His presence and wisdom. Jeremiah 29:13 assures, *"And you will seek Me and find Me, when you search for Me with all your heart."* When we actively seek Him, He reveals Himself to us.

Knocking requires persistence. Galatians 6:9 reminds us, *"Let us not grow weary while doing good, for in due season we shall reap if we do not lose heart."* If you've been waiting on a breakthrough, keep asking, seeking, and knocking—God's answer is on the way.

Your sandals shall be iron and bronze;
as your days, so shall your strength be.

Deuteronomy 33:25

God equips His people with strength for every season. This verse, originally spoken as a blessing over the tribe of Asher, carries a promise that still applies today to all who trust in Him. It reminds us that no matter what lies ahead, God supplies the endurance and fortitude we need—not just once, but continually.

Iron and bronze represent durability, strength, and stability. In biblical times, the type of sandals someone wore impacted how well they could handle rough and unpredictable terrain. God was essentially saying, "You'll be ready for anything." Spiritually speaking, He outfits us with the kind of strength and peace that carry us through every battle, every challenge, and every phase of life. We're not meant to wear out—we're meant to press on, fully equipped.

The second half of the verse is incredibly encouraging: *"As your days, so shall your strength be."* That means your strength doesn't have to decline with age—God provides exactly what you need for each day. Whether you're young and running with vision or older and walking with wisdom, His strength remains steady and sufficient. Aging doesn't have to mean weakening or wearing out. In Him, you can stay vibrant, fruitful, and full of life all the way to the finish line!

So if you're facing something that feels too big, or if the future looks uncertain, remember this: God hasn't just given you strength for yesterday. He has strength ready for today, tomorrow, and every day after. Walk confidently in that promise— He's already prepared the path and the power to walk it well.

*Now the Lord is the Spirit; and where the Spirit
of the Lord is, there is liberty.*

2 Corinthians 3:17

True freedom is found in God's presence. This verse reminds us that wherever the Spirit of the Lord is, there is liberty—freedom from sin, fear, bondage, and anything else that holds us back from living the abundant life He's promised.

And here's the incredible truth: if you've received Jesus, the Holy Spirit lives inside you. That means freedom isn't something you have to chase—it's already yours! This kind of freedom isn't temporary or situational. It doesn't depend on how you feel or what's happening around you. Because His Spirit is in you, you carry freedom with you into every situation, every decision, and every moment of your life.

This liberty isn't just about being free from sin; it's about being free to thrive. You're free to dream again. Free to step into your calling. Free to walk in confidence, knowing you're fully accepted and deeply loved. The Spirit empowers you to overcome what once held you back and to live boldly in your God-given identity.

He also helps you make wise choices, stay grounded in truth, and walk in peace even when things feel uncertain. That's real liberty—life without chains, shame, or fear. Not a perfect life, but one where God's presence is your constant source of strength and joy.

So, if you're feeling stuck, take a moment to remind yourself: you're not alone, and you're not powerless. The Spirit of the Lord is with you—and in you—and where He is, freedom flows. Embrace it, walk in it, and let His liberty lead the way.

So they said, "Believe on the Lord Jesus Christ, and you will be saved, you and your household."

Acts 16:31

S alvation is a gift that is available to everyone who be-lieves. This verse, spoken by Paul and Silas to the Philippian jailer, reveals the simple yet powerful truth of the Gospel—faith in Jesus Christ brings salvation, not only for the individual but as a promise that extends to their household.

The phrase *"Believe on the Lord Jesus Christ"* emphasizes that salvation is received by faith, not by works or religious effort. Ephesians 2:8 confirms, *"For by grace you have been saved through faith, and that not of yourselves; it is the gift of God."* When we put our trust in Jesus, He redeems, restores, and trans-forms our lives.

The promise *"you and your household"* demonstrates God's heart for families. This does not mean that one person's faith automatically saves others, but it does highlight that God de-sires to work in entire households. We see this pattern throughout Scripture—when one person follows God, it often leads to others in their family coming to faith. Joshua 24:15 de-clares, *"But as for me and my house, we will serve the Lord."* When we live out our faith, we become a witness to those around us, drawing them closer to God.

If you are believing for the salvation of family members, take heart—God's desire is for them to know Him! Keep praying, keep believing, and trust that He is working in their hearts. Your faith has the power to influence and impact those closest to you. Stand firm, knowing that God's grace is not just for you but is available to all who will believe.

My God sent His angel and shut the lions' mouths,
so that they have not hurt me, because I was found
innocent before Him; and also, O king,
I have done no wrong before you.

Daniel 6:22

God is our protector, and He is faithful to deliver those who trust in Him. This verse is Daniel's testimony after being thrown into the lions' den—a miraculous demonstration of God's power to save His people from impossible situations.

Daniel's unwavering faith led him to face persecution, but he never compromised. He continued to pray despite the king's decree, trusting that God was greater than any earthly ruler. His boldness echoes Psalm 34:7: *"The angel of the Lord encamps all around those who fear Him, and delivers them."* God not only protected Daniel but made His power known to an entire kingdom through this miracle.

No matter how fierce the attack, God has the authority to silence the enemy. Now, as New Covenant believers, we have that authority as well! Isaiah 54:17 assures us, *"No weapon formed against you shall prosper."* The same God who delivered Daniel is still delivering His people today.

This verse also highlights the importance of integrity. Daniel was *"found innocent before Him"*—his faithfulness to God kept him secure. Proverbs 2:7 declares, *"He stores up sound wisdom for the upright; He is a shield to those who walk uprightly."* Living in righteousness does not mean we won't face trials, but it does mean that God will be our defender.

If you are facing a situation that feels impossible, remember that God is still shutting the mouths of lions! Trust Him, stand firm in your faith, and know that He is able to deliver you just as He did for Daniel.

But He said, "The things which are impossible with men are possible with God."

Luke 18:27

God specializes in the impossible. While human limitations may exist, God has no limits. What seems unattainable to us is entirely within His power to accomplish. When He does the impossible, it brings Him glory!

The context of this verse is the story of the rich young ruler, who walked away sorrowfully when Jesus told him to give up his wealth and follow Him. The disciples, astonished, asked who could possibly be saved. Jesus responded with this profound truth—salvation, and indeed all things, are possible with God. This applies not only to eternal life but to every area of our lives where we face challenges beyond our control.

When Jesus said, *"impossible with men,"* He was pointing out how limited we are on our own. There are just some things we can't fix, figure out, or make happen no matter how hard we try. But *"possible with God"* changes everything! It shifts the focus from what we can't do to what He absolutely can. As Jeremiah 32:27 reminds us, *"Behold, I am the Lord, the God of all flesh. Is there anything too hard for Me?"* With God, nothing is out of reach.

Faith requires us to trust in God's ability rather than our own. Abraham and Sarah were beyond childbearing years, yet Romans 4:21 says Abraham was *"fully convinced that what He had promised He was also able to perform."* God fulfilled His promise despite human impossibility.

If you're facing a situation that looks hopeless, take heart—God is not bound by earthly limitations. What you cannot do, He can. Trust Him, believe in His promises, and watch as He turns the impossible into reality.

November 8

For He says: "In an acceptable time I have heard you,
and in the day of salvation I have helped you."
Behold, now is the accepted time; behold, now is the day
of salvation.

2 Corinthians 6:2

God's timing is always perfect, and this verse is a powerful reminder that *now* is the time to receive what He
has made available. Paul is quoting from Isaiah 49:8,
emphasizing that today—not some distant future—is the day of
salvation, breakthrough, and God's help.

The phrase *"In an acceptable time I have heard you"* reveals
that God is not ignoring our prayers. He has already heard us,
and He is moving on our behalf. Psalm 34:17 assures, *"The*
righteous cry out, and the Lord hears, and delivers them out of
all their troubles." There is no need to delay in trusting Him—
He is ready and willing to act. His help is not just for emergencies but for daily life. Whether you need strength, wisdom, or
direction, He is present and available.

"Now is the day of salvation" goes beyond just eternal salvation—it speaks to every area of life where we need His
deliverance. Whether it's healing, provision, or restoration,
God's promises are for today. Hebrews 4:16 encourages us,
"Let us therefore come boldly to the throne of grace, that we
may obtain mercy and find grace to help in time of need." We
don't have to wait to access His grace—it is available right now.

If you've been putting off fully trusting God or stepping into
what He has called you to do, don't wait any longer. The time
to believe, to receive, and to walk in His promises is today. His
power is available now—step into it with confidence, knowing
He has already made a way.

But by the grace of God I am what I am, and His grace toward me was not in vain; but I labored more abundantly than they all, yet not I, but the grace of God which was with me.

1 Corinthians 15:10

S uccess in life is not about our own strength and effort— it is about God's grace working in and through us. In this verse, Paul acknowledges that while he worked hard, it was ultimately God's grace that enabled him to accomplish all that he did. Grace is not a substitute for effort, but it empowers us to go beyond our own natural ability.

When Paul said, *"by the grace of God I am what I am,"* he was pointing to the true source of his identity and calling— God's unearned favor. We're not defined by what we've accomplished or by where we've failed, but by what His grace has done in us. His grace not only saves us—it shapes us, empowers us, and equips us to walk in the abundant life He's prepared.

Paul also states, *"His grace toward me was not in vain."* This shows that grace is not an excuse for passivity—it is a divine enablement that calls us to action. Paul labored diligently, but he recognized that God's grace was the true source of his strength and effectiveness. Philippians 2:13 confirms, *"For it is God who works in you both to will and to do for His good pleasure."* When we depend on His grace, we accomplish far more than we could through effort alone.

If you've ever felt like you don't have enough strength, wisdom, or ability, remember that God's grace is always available. You don't have to do it all on your own—His grace empowers, strengthens, and enables you to fulfill the purpose He has for your life.

Then Jesus said to the centurion, "Go your way; and as you have believed, so let it be done for you." And his servant was healed that same hour.

Matthew 8:13

Faith is the key to receiving from God. In this verse, Jesus commends the centurion for his great faith, showing us that belief is directly connected to the results we see in our lives. The centurion, a Roman officer, demonstrated remarkable confidence in Jesus' authority, believing that just a spoken word from Him was enough to heal his servant.

The phrase *"as you have believed, so let it be done for you"* highlights an important truth: our faith plays a role in what we receive. This does not mean we must strive to believe harder or force ourselves into faith—it means trusting fully in the power and willingness of Jesus. Hebrews 11:1 defines faith as *"the substance of things hoped for, the evidence of things not seen."* The centurion had no visible proof that his servant was healed in that moment, yet he believed Jesus' word, and his faith produced immediate results.

Jesus often emphasized the connection between faith and receiving. In Mark 11:24, He said, *"Whatever things you ask when you pray, believe that you receive them, and you will have them."* Faith is not about convincing God to move—it is about trusting that He already has.

If you are believing for healing, provision, or breakthrough, remember the centurion's example. He didn't need to see proof before believing—he simply trusted Jesus' word. That same faith is available to you today. Trust in His promises, believe in His power, and know that He is faithful to bring His word to pass.

In the multitude of my anxieties within me,
Your comforts delight my soul.

Psalm 94:19

Life can often feel overwhelming, but God's presence brings comfort even in the midst of anxiety. This verse acknowledges that troubles and worries may surround us, but God's peace is greater than any fear we face.

When the psalmist talks about *"the multitude of my anxieties,"* it shows that even those who deeply trust God can face seasons of stress, fear, or uncertainty. God never promises a challenge-free life, but He does promise to be with us through it all—bringing comfort when we need it most. Philippians 4:6-7 reminds us not to be anxious, but to bring everything to Him in prayer. As we do, His peace—one that doesn't even make sense in the natural—guards our hearts and minds. That kind of peace doesn't come from perfect circumstances, but from knowing we're held by a faithful, loving Father.

The word *comforts* in this verse refers to God's ability to bring relief, encouragement, and reassurance. His comfort comes through His Word, His presence, and His promises. Isaiah 26:3 declares, *"You will keep him in perfect peace, whose mind is stayed on You, because he trusts in You."* When we shift our focus from our problems to God's faithfulness, we experience His peace in a tangible way.

God's comfort doesn't just remove anxiety—it replaces it with delight. When we turn to Him, we don't just survive difficulties; we find joy in His presence. His peace is not temporary, nor is it fragile—it is steady, unwavering, and always available. No matter how heavy your burdens feel today, God's comfort is waiting for you. He sees every anxious thought and invites you to lay them at His feet. Let His presence delight your soul, bringing rest, strength, and a renewed sense of peace.

Therefore, my beloved brethren, be steadfast, immovable, always abounding in the work of the Lord, knowing that your labor is not in vain in the Lord.

1 Corinthians 15:58

This verse reminds us to stand firm in faith, fully committed to what He has called us to do, because everything done for Him has eternal significance.

Being "steadfast and immovable" points to spiritual stability. In a world full of uncertainty, pressure, and shifting opinions, God calls us to remain anchored in Him. Psalm 125:1 says, *"Those who trust in the Lord are like Mount Zion, which cannot be moved, but abides forever."* When our foundation is Jesus, we can stand strong no matter what comes our way. This kind of steadiness doesn't mean we never feel pressure—it means we refuse to quit, knowing Who we belong to.

Paul also encourages us to overflow in the work of the Lord—not just to show up occasionally, but to give our all with passion and purpose. Whether you're caring for your family, leading a ministry, serving at church, or showing kindness to a neighbor, your obedience matters. The Lord sees what others may overlook, and He values your faithfulness.

And then comes the promise: your labor in the Lord is never in vain. Even if it feels like your prayers are going unanswered or your efforts aren't producing immediate results, God sees it all. Hebrews 6:10 says He won't forget your work and the love you've shown.

So, if you're feeling tired or discouraged, take heart. Keep going, stay grounded, and trust that every step of faith is building something eternal. Your faithfulness is making a difference—more than you may ever know on this side of eternity!

*When you pass through the waters, I will be with you;
and through the rivers, they shall not overflow you. When
you walk through the fire, you shall not be burned, nor
shall the flame scorch you.*

Isaiah 43:2

I t's not a mystery that life will have challenges, but God promises that He will be with us through them all! This verse is a powerful assurance that no matter what trials we face, we are never alone. His presence is our protection, our strength, and our victory.

In life sometimes there *will* be overwhelming circumstances— those moments when we feel like we're in over our heads. But God promises, *"I will be with you."* Just as He parted the Red Sea for Israel and brought them through on dry ground (Exodus 14:21-22), He is faithful to make a way for us. The rivers of difficulty will not sweep us away because He is our anchor. Even when life feels chaotic, His steady hand holds us secure.

Fire represents intense trials, pressures, and attacks from the enemy. Yet, just as God protected Shadrach, Meshach, and Abed-Nego in the fiery furnace (Daniel 3:25-27), He will protect us. The flames may surround us, but they will not consume us. Instead of destroying us, these trials refine our faith and strengthen our trust in Him. James 1:3 reminds us, *"the testing of your faith produces patience."* What the enemy intends for harm, God uses to make us stronger.

No matter what you're facing today—whether deep waters of uncertainty or the heat of trials—God's promise remains the same. You will not be overcome. His presence goes before you, walks beside you, and shields you. Trust in His faithfulness, knowing that He is carrying you through, and victory is already assured.

If you abide in Me, and My words abide in you, you will ask what you desire, and it shall be done for you.

John 15:7

J esus gives a powerful key to answered prayer in this verse—abiding in Him. The word *abide* means to remain, dwell, or stay connected. A branch does not struggle to bear fruit; it simply stays connected to the vine. In the same way, when we remain in Jesus, our lives naturally produce the fruit of His presence, and our prayers align with His will.

Abiding is not a one-time action but an ongoing lifestyle of an deep relationship with Jesus. Psalm 91:1 describes this kind of intimacy, *"He who dwells in the secret place of the Most High shall abide under the shadow of the Almighty."* Staying close to God through prayer, worship, and His Word allows His desires to shape our own.

God's Word is not just a book to read—it must take root in our hearts. When His truth fills our minds and influences our decisions, it transforms how we think, speak, and pray. Romans 12:2 reminds us, *"Do not be conformed to this world, but be transformed by the renewing of your mind."* As we align with His Word, our prayers shift from self-serving to kingdom-minded requests.

This promise does not mean we receive anything we want, although many times it can! However, more importantly, it means our desires become aligned with God's will. 1 John 5:14 confirms, *"If we ask anything according to His will, He hears us."* When we abide in Him, our prayers carry power because they reflect His heart.

Are you abiding in Him today? Stay connected, let His Word shape your desires, and watch as your prayers produce fruit in your life.

They are abundantly satisfied with the fullness
of Your house, and You give them drink from
the river of Your pleasures.

Psalm 36:8

God is not a God of scarcity—He is a God of abundance. This verse beautifully illustrates the overflowing satisfaction found in His presence. He does not merely meet our needs; He fills us to the brim with His goodness, leaving no area of lack in our lives.

True fulfillment comes from dwelling with God. The world offers temporary pleasures that leave us empty, but in His presence, we are completely satisfied. Psalm 16:11 says, *"In Your presence is fullness of joy; at Your right hand are pleasures forevermore."* When we prioritize our relationship with Him, we experience a deep, lasting satisfaction that the world cannot provide.

The second half of the verse, *"You give them drink from the river of Your pleasures,"* paints a picture of an unending flow of God's blessings and goodness. Rivers aren't still—they're constantly moving, always supplying fresh water. In the same way, God continually refreshes and nourishes our spirits.

Jesus echoed this same idea in John 7:38: *"He who believes in Me, as the Scripture has said, out of his heart will flow rivers of living water."* The Holy Spirit is our never-ending source of renewal, pouring into us with peace, strength, and joy.

If you've been feeling drained or empty, remember that God is the source of true satisfaction. Draw near to Him, drink deeply from His goodness, and experience the abundant life He has prepared for you. In His presence, there is always more than enough.

*Then your light shall break forth like the morning,
your healing shall spring forth speedily, and your
righteousness shall go before you; the glory of the
Lord shall be your rear guard.*

Isaiah 58:8

God's blessings aren't reserved only for eternity—they're meant to impact your life right now. This verse shows us what it looks like to walk closely with God: healing, restoration, and protection on every side. When we follow His ways, we experience the kind of transformation that touches every part of our lives.

"Your light shall break forth like the morning" brings to mind the moment the sun rises and everything changes. Darkness disappears, hope is renewed, and a new day begins. That's what it's like when God moves in your life. No matter how long the night has been, He brings light, direction, and joy.

Healing *"springing forth speedily"* reminds us that God doesn't delay out of indifference or trying to teach you a lesson. He is a compassionate healer—ready and willing to restore you in body, mind, and spirit. He wants wholeness for you, not just survival. His healing reaches into the deepest places and brings lasting change.

And how incredible is it to know that His righteousness goes ahead of you, while His glory has your back? You are never exposed or alone. He leads, He guards, and He surrounds you with His presence every step of the way.

If you've been waiting on healing, needing clarity, or just longing for peace, be encouraged—God is moving. Your breakthrough is coming, and His presence is right there with you through it all. Keep walking with Him, and trust that restoration, protection, and new beginnings are already unfolding.

*As each one has received a gift, minister it to one
another, as good stewards of the manifold grace of God.*

1 Peter 4:10

Every believer has been given unique gifts, not just for personal benefit, but to bless and strengthen others. This verse reminds us that our talents, abilities, and resources are entrusted to us by God, and we are called to use them for His glory.

When it says, *"as each one has received a gift,"* it confirms that no one in God's kingdom is without purpose. Romans 12:6 says, *"Having then gifts differing according to the grace that is given to us, let us use them."* Whether your gift is teaching, encouraging, giving, or serving behind the scenes, it has been given to you for a reason. The Body of Christ is designed to work together, with each person contributing something valuable.

Peter then instructs us to *"minister it to one another."* The gifts God gives are meant to be shared. When we serve others, we reflect the heart of Jesus, who said in Mark 10:45, "For even the Son of Man did not come to be served, but to serve." Fulfillment comes not from keeping our gifts to ourselves, but in using them to make an impact. A life poured out in service to God and others is one of true joy and purpose.

This verse also calls us *"good stewards of the manifold grace of God."* A steward manages what belongs to another. Our gifts are not for our own glory but are meant to reflect God's grace to the world. His grace shows up in many ways—meeting every need and transforming lives wherever it flows.

You are equipped with exactly what you need to fulfill your God-given purpose! Step forward in confidence, knowing that as you serve, you are allowing His grace to work through you, making an eternal difference in the lives of others.

For You, Lord, have made me glad through Your work;
I will triumph in the works of Your hands.

Psalm 92:4

J oy is a fruit of the Spirit—something we carry with us—
but it's stirred and strengthened when we reflect on all
God has done. This verse reminds us that true gladness
comes from Him, and when we trust in His power, we can walk
in triumph.

The world offers temporary happiness, but the joy of the Lord
is steady and unshakable. Nehemiah 8:10 declares, *"The joy of
the Lord is your strength."* God's faithfulness, provision, and
love give us a deep, abiding gladness that does not fade, even
in difficult seasons. When we shift our focus from problems to
His goodness, joy takes the place of worry.

The second part of the verse, *"I will triumph in the works of
Your hands,"* reminds us that victory is not achieved by our own
strength—it is found in God's power. When we see His hand
moving, we gain confidence that He is leading us to triumph. 2
Corinthians 2:14 tells us, *"Now thanks be to God who always
leads us in triumph in Christ."* Because of Him, we do not just
endure life—we overcome it. His works in our lives are constant, even when we do not immediately recognize them.

Even in times of uncertainty, we can choose to rejoice, knowing that God is at work. If you've been feeling weary or
discouraged, take a moment to reflect on what He has already
done. The same God who has been faithful before will continue
to be faithful now. As you fix your eyes on His works, your heart
will be filled with gladness, and you will walk forward in victory, knowing He is always working for your good.

But grow in the grace and knowledge of our Lord and Savior Jesus Christ. To Him be the glory both now and forever. Amen.

2 Peter 3:18

Spiritual growth is not automatic—it is intentional. This verse encourages us to actively grow in both grace and knowledge, deepening our relationship with Jesus and experiencing the abundant life He has for us.

Grace is not just something we receive at salvation—it is something we continue to grow in throughout our walk with God. Grace empowers us to live victoriously, strengthening us beyond our own abilities. Paul wrote in 2 Corinthians 12:9, *"My grace is sufficient for you, for My strength is made perfect in weakness."* As we rely on God's grace, we are able to overcome challenges and walk in His strength.

Knowing God personally is vital to victory in this life. It is not just about acquiring information but about deepening our relationship with Him. Jesus said in John 17:3, *"And this is eternal life, that they may know You, the only true God, and Jesus Christ whom You have sent."* The more we seek Him through His Word, prayer, and fellowship, the more we are transformed into His likeness.

Growth in grace and knowledge leads to a life that glorifies God. The verse ends with a declaration of praise: *"To Him be the glory both now and forever."* Everything we do, every step we take in spiritual maturity, ultimately points back to Him.

Are you growing in grace and knowledge? Keep pressing into Him daily. The more you grow in His truth, the more you'll experience the fullness of the life He has prepared for you.

November 20

*Do not remember the former things, nor consider the
things of old. Behold, I will do a new thing, now it shall
spring forth; shall you not know it? I will even make a
road in the wilderness and rivers in the desert.*

Isaiah 43:18-19

U nexpected opportunities and fresh beginnings are part
of God's nature. He is always at work, leading His
people into something greater. This verse is an invitation to stop looking backward and to embrace the new things
He is bringing into our lives.

The command *"Do not remember the former things"* doesn't
mean we should erase the past from our minds, but rather that
we should not allow it to shape our expectations of the future.
Dwelling on past failures can keep us stuck in regret, while
holding onto past successes can prevent us from stepping into
new opportunities. Paul echoes this in Philippians 3:13, *"Forgetting those things which are behind and reaching forward to
those things which are ahead."* God has more in store for us
than what is behind us!

God is not limited by past circumstances or obstacles. No
matter what has happened before, He is always working to
bring fresh provision, new opportunities, and unexpected
breakthroughs. He asks, *"Shall you not know it?"*—a challenge
to open our eyes in faith and recognize His work even when
we cannot yet see the full picture.

Even in barren places, God makes a way. He provides where
provision seems impossible. Just as He made a path through the
Red Sea (Exodus 14:21) and provided water from a rock (Exodus
17:6), He will do the impossible in your life!

Are you holding onto the past, or are you ready for the new
thing God is bringing? Trust Him, let go of what was, and step
forward in faith—because He is already making a way for you.

But this I say: He who sows sparingly will also reap sparingly, and he who sows bountifully will also reap bountifully. So let each one give as he purposes in his heart, not grudgingly or of necessity; for God loves a cheerful giver. And God is able to make all grace abound toward you, that you, always having all sufficiency in all things, may have an abundance for every good work.

2 Corinthians 9:6-8

G enerosity is a principle woven into God's design for abundance. This passage reveals that giving is not about loss—it is about sowing, with the expectation of reaping a harvest. When we give with the right heart, God's grace overflows into our lives, ensuring that we always have more than enough.

The principle of sowing and reaping is evident throughout Scripture. Just as a farmer expects a harvest after planting seeds, we can expect to see fruit from our giving. Proverbs 11:24 states, *"There is one who scatters, yet increases more."* Holding on tightly leads to lack, but generosity leads to increase.

However, God is not looking for reluctant or forced giving. He desires *cheerful* givers—those who give willingly, trusting in His provision. True generosity flows from thankfulness and trust, not obligation. When we give joyfully, we align ourselves with God's heart, knowing that He is our ultimate provider.

The Lord's provision is not limited to finances but includes strength, opportunities, and favor. And the purpose of this abundance is not just for personal gain but so that we can continue to be a blessing to others.

If you've been hesitant to give, trust in God's faithfulness. He will ensure that your generosity leads to an abundant harvest in every area of your life.

And He said to me, "It is done! I am the Alpha and the Omega, the Beginning and the End. I will give of the fountain of the water of life freely to him who thirsts."

Revelation 21:6

Victory has already been declared. In this verse, God speaks with finality—His redemptive plan is complete, and He alone is the source of eternal life and satisfaction. No matter what we face, we can rest in the assurance that His promises are secure.

The phrase *"It is done!"* echoes the words of Jesus on the cross, *"It is finished"* (John 19:30). Just as salvation was accomplished through Christ's sacrifice, this statement in Revelation confirms that all of God's plans will be fulfilled. He is not uncertain or waiting for circumstances to align—He has already secured the victory.

His declaration *"I am the Alpha and the Omega, the Beginning and the End"* reminds us that He is both the author and the finisher of our faith. Everything starts and ends with Him. Colossians 1:17 says, *"And He is before all things, and in Him all things consist."* When we recognize Him as our source, we stop striving and start trusting.

The promise *"I will give of the fountain of the water of life freely to him who thirsts"* reveals God's heart of abundance. He does not withhold His life-giving presence—He gives freely to all who come to Him. Jesus echoed this in John 7:37, *"If anyone thirsts, let him come to Me and drink."* He alone can satisfy the deepest longings of our hearts.

Are you thirsty for more of Him? His supply is endless, and His invitation is open. Come, drink deeply of His grace, knowing that He is the source of all life, now and forever.

But without faith it is impossible to please Him, for he who comes to God must believe that He is, and that He is a rewarder of those who diligently seek Him.

Hebrews 11:6

Trusting in God is not just important—it is essential. This verse reminds us that faith is the foundation of our relationship with Him. It is not about religious rituals or outward actions, but about believing in who He is and trusting in His goodness.

Faith is non-negotiable in our walk with God. It is not enough to simply acknowledge His existence; we must trust Him completely. Hebrews 10:38 says, *"The just shall live by faith."* Faith is not a one-time decision—it is a daily choice to rely on Him, even when circumstances seem uncertain.

Believing that *"He is"* means recognizing God's nature and character. He is faithful, He is loving, and He is always present. Exodus 3:14 reveals His name as *"I AM"*—the eternal, unchanging One. When we trust that He is who He says He is, our faith is strengthened.

The final promise in this verse is powerful: *"He is a rewarder of those who diligently seek Him."* God does not ignore those who pursue Him; He responds! Jeremiah 29:13 says, *"And you will seek Me and find Me, when you search for Me with all your heart."* Seeking Him is not in vain—it leads to deeper revelation, provision, and blessing.

Are you actively seeking God in faith? He is ready to reveal Himself to you, to strengthen you, and to reward your pursuit of Him. Keep pressing in, knowing that He delights in those who trust Him fully.

November 24

For the grace of God that brings salvation has appeared to all men, teaching us that, denying ungodliness and worldly lusts, we should live soberly, righteously, and godly in the present age.

Titus 2:11-12

Salvation is not just about securing eternity with God—it is about transformation here and now. This verse reminds us that God's grace doesn't just save us; it also teaches and empowers us to live in a way that honors Him.

Salvation is available to everyone. Through Jesus, God's grace has been revealed, extending forgiveness, redemption, and new life to all who receive it. Ephesians 2:8 affirms, *"For by grace you have been saved through faith, and that not of yourselves; it is the gift of God."* Grace is not something we earn—it is a free gift that changes everything!

But grace doesn't stop at salvation; it *"teaches us"* how to live. It is not just about what we are saved from, but also what we are saved *into.* The Holy Spirit, working in us, leads us to *"deny ungodliness and worldly lusts."* This doesn't mean we strive in our own strength to be righteous—rather, as we grow in our relationship with God, His grace transforms our desires. Philippians 2:13 declares, *"For it is God who works in you both to will and to do for His good pleasure."*

Living *"soberly, righteously, and godly in the present age"* is possible because grace equips us to do so. It doesn't just forgive; it empowers. As we yield to God's leading, we experience the fullness of the abundant life He has planned.

Are you allowing grace to shape your daily life? God's grace is more than just a safety net—it is the power that enables you to walk in victory, live with purpose, and reflect His goodness to the world.

But the wisdom that is from above is first pure,
then peaceable, gentle, willing to yield, full of mercy
and good fruits, without partiality and without hypocrisy.
Now the fruit of righteousness is sown in peace by
those who make peace.

James 3:17-18

W isdom from God looks different than the world's version. It's not loud or boastful, and it doesn't push its own agenda. Instead, it shows up in how we treat people—with kindness, humility, and peace. Godly wisdom brings calm in chaos, clarity in confusion, and unity where there's division. It doesn't need to prove itself—it simply produces lasting fruit.

James gives us a clear description of what this wisdom looks like: pure, peaceable, gentle, full of mercy, and rich with good fruit. It doesn't play favorites or pretend to be something it's not. This isn't about sounding spiritual or having all the answers— it's about living with integrity and letting God's heart shape how we respond to others.

One phrase that stands out is *"willing to yield."* That doesn't mean backing down from truth—it means being teachable and humble, valuing peace over pride. Wisdom doesn't shout to be heard; it listens, speaks with grace, and chooses what builds others up.

When we live with this kind of wisdom, we become peace-makers. And peacemakers, Jesus said, are blessed. Our words and actions plant seeds—seeds that can either stir up strife or grow a harvest of righteousness.

If you need direction today, ask God for His wisdom—He gives it generously. As you walk it out, you'll experience His peace and become a carrier of it to those around you.

*Let not your heart be troubled; you believe in God,
believe also in Me.*

John 14:1

J esus spoke these words to His disciples on the night before His crucifixion. In just a few hours, they would witness His arrest, trial, and brutal execution. Their world
was about to be shaken in a way they never expected, and fear
and confusion would try to take hold of their hearts. Yet, in the
face of this coming storm, Jesus gave them a command—not a
suggestion—to not let their hearts be troubled.

Jesus acknowledged that fear and distress will try to come, but
we are not powerless against them. He wouldn't tell us to do
something that was impossible to do. This means that, through
His grace, we truly can walk in peace, even in the most over-
whelming circumstances. Isaiah 26:3 confirms this promise:
*"You will keep him in perfect peace, whose mind is stayed on
You, because he trusts in You."* When we fix our thoughts on
Him, worry loses its grip.

The second part of the verse, *"you believe in God, believe
also in Me,"* is a call to unwavering trust. Faith is not just believing that God exists—it is depending on Him completely,
even when nothing makes sense. The disciples didn't understand what was happening, but Jesus was calling them to trust
Him beyond their understanding by faith.

If fear is pressing in on you today, take Jesus at His word. No
matter how uncertain your situation seems, you are not alone.
Choose to trust Him, knowing He is greater than anything you
face. Let your heart rest in His peace, for He is always faithful.

*Oh, how great is Your goodness, which You have
laid up for those who fear You, which You have
prepared for those who trust in You in the
presence of the sons of men!*

Psalm 31:19

God's goodness is not limited—it is abundant, stored up, and prepared for those who trust Him. This verse reminds us that His blessings are not random; they are intentionally set aside for those who walk in faith.

The phrase *"how great is Your goodness"* expresses overwhelming gratitude for God's kindness and faithfulness. His goodness is not occasional or unpredictable—it is a defining part of who He is. James 1:17 confirms this truth: *"Every good gift and every perfect gift is from above, and comes down from the Father of lights."* When we recognize His goodness, our faith grows stronger.

The verse also highlights that this goodness is *"laid up"* and *"prepared"* for those who trust Him. This means that God's blessings are not an afterthought. Just as a loving parent prepares for their child's future, God has already set aside good things for His people. Ephesians 2:10 echoes this, saying we are created for *"good works, which God prepared beforehand."* We do not have to struggle—His provision is already in place!

God's goodness is meant to be seen! When we trust Him, He demonstrates His faithfulness in a way that others notice. Psalm 23:5 declares, *"You prepare a table before me in the presence of my enemies."* His blessings are a testimony that draw others to Him.

Are you trusting in His goodness today? Rest assured that He has already prepared more than enough for you—His goodness is stored up, ready to overflow into your life.

Then I heard a loud voice saying in heaven,
"Now salvation, and strength, and the kingdom of our
God, and the power of His Christ have come, for the
accuser of our brethren, who accused them before our
God day and night, has been cast down."

Revelation 12:10

The enemy's greatest weapon is deception. Jesus called him *"the father of lies"* (John 8:44), and one of his most common tactics is using those lies to accuse and condemn God's people. He whispers reminders of past failures, trying to make us doubt our righteousness in Christ. But this verse declares his defeat! The moment Jesus fulfilled His work on the cross, salvation, strength, and the power of God's kingdom were made available to us, and the accuser lost his authority.

Satan is called *"the accuser of our brethren"* because he relentlessly seeks to condemn God's people. He did this to Job (Job 1:9-11) and to Joshua the high priest (Zechariah 3:1-2). But God does not define us by our past—He defines us by the finished work of Jesus. Romans 8:1 boldly proclaims, *"There is therefore now no condemnation to those who are in Christ Jesus."* No accusation from the enemy can change what Jesus has done.

The phrase *"has been cast down"* is a declaration of victory! The enemy no longer has access to accuse us before God. Instead, Jesus is now our advocate (1 John 2:1), speaking on our behalf. His sacrifice has silenced the enemy's voice, and through Him, we stand blameless before God.

If guilt or condemnation has been weighing on you, remember this truth: The accuser has been defeated, and you are victorious in Christ! Stand firm in the power of His salvation, knowing that no accusation can separate you from God's love and grace.

*From the end of the earth I will cry to You,
when my heart is overwhelmed; lead me to
the rock that is higher than I.*

Psalm 61:2

Life can feel overwhelming at times, but this verse reminds us that we are never alone. When we cry out to
God, He lifts us up, giving us strength, stability, and a
higher perspective.

David wrote, *"From the end of the earth I will cry to You,"*
capturing how distant and overwhelmed he felt in that moment.
He wasn't necessarily far from God physically, but emotionally,
he was at the end of his rope. Still, he knew exactly who to call
on. The same is true for us—no matter how scattered, stuck, or
discouraged we feel, God hears us. Psalm 34:17 says, *"The
righteous cry out, and the Lord hears, and delivers them out of
all their troubles."* Even when we don't feel close, He's never
far.

The request *"lead me to the rock that is higher than I"* is an
acknowledgment that we need something greater than ourselves. A rock represents stability, security, and a firm foundation. Jesus is that rock! 1 Corinthians 10:4 refers to Him as *"that
spiritual Rock that followed them, and that Rock was Christ."*
When we stand on Him, we are unshakable, no matter what
storms come our way. He lifts us above our circumstances, giving us clarity and strength beyond our own abilities.

Feeling overwhelmed does not mean we are failing—it means
we need to shift our focus upward. Instead of trying to carry the
weight on our own, we can surrender it to Him. God is always
ready to lift us higher, above our struggles, and into His presence. If you're feeling burdened today, cry out to Him. He will
lead you to the Rock that never moves, never changes, and
never fails!

November 30

Now faith is the substance of things hoped for,
the evidence of things not seen.

Hebrews 11:1

F aith is having a confidence in God's promises before we see them come to pass. This verse defines faith as both *substance* and *evidence*, showing that what we believe in has real weight, even before it is visible.

Faith actually gives form to our hopes. The word *substance* in Greek (*hypostasis*) refers to something solid and foundational. Faith is not blind optimism; it is built on the certainty of God's Word. Just as a blueprint precedes the construction of a building, faith gives substance to what we believe before it manifests in our lives. Hope by itself is not enough—faith is what turns hope into reality.

The second part of the verse, *"the evidence of things not seen,"* reinforces that faith is proof of unseen realities. Even when circumstances suggest otherwise, faith declares that God's promises are true. 2 Corinthians 5:7 reminds us, *"For we walk by faith, not by sight."* Just because we do not see something immediately does not mean it isn't real—God's promises exist in the spiritual realm before they are revealed in the natural. Faith is what bridges the gap between what God has spoken and what we experience.

Faith is the key to experiencing the abundant life God has prepared for us. It enables us to trust in His goodness, step out in obedience, and hold firm to His promises. If you are believing for something today, know that your faith is not in vain. Stand on His Word, for what He has spoken will surely come to pass. Keep your eyes fixed on Him, knowing that faith makes the unseen a reality.

"Behold, the days are coming," says the Lord, "when the plowman shall overtake the reaper, and the treader of grapes him who sows seed; the mountains shall drip with sweet wine, and all the hills shall flow with it."

Amos 9:13

God's blessings aren't bound by natural timing or our own efforts. Amos 9:13 gives us a vivid picture of supernatural acceleration—where planting and harvesting happen so rapidly that one season's blessings seamlessly flow into the next. It's a promise of divine increase, provision, and restoration that goes beyond what we can achieve on our own.

The line about the plowman overtaking the reaper paints a scene of such abundance that before one harvest is fully gathered, the next planting is already underway. Typically, sowing and reaping occur in separate seasons, but in God's kingdom, He can speed up the process, bringing blessings without the usual delays. What once seemed lost or wasted can be restored in even greater measure.

The imagery of mountains dripping with sweet wine symbolizes joy and overflow. In ancient Israel, wine represented blessing and celebration. This isn't just about having enough—it's about experiencing more than enough. God isn't stingy with His goodness; He's abundantly generous, able to do far more than we can ask or imagine.

If you've been waiting for a breakthrough, don't lose heart. God knows how to accelerate His promises. He can redeem time, restore what's been lost, and bring an overwhelming harvest into your life. Trust His timing, expect His goodness, and get ready—the days of increase are on their way!

December 2

I would have lost heart, unless I had believed that I would see the goodness of the Lord in the land of the living. Wait on the Lord; be of good courage, and He shall strengthen your heart; wait, I say, on the Lord!

Psalm 27:13-14

When circumstances seem overwhelming, it can be easy to lose heart. But David declares that his confidence in God's goodness is what kept him going. This passage reminds us that no matter what we face, we can trust that God's goodness is not just for heaven—it is for *this* life, too.

David was not immune to discouragement, but his belief in God's faithfulness sustained him. The key was not what he saw—it was what he *believed*. Faith is often tested in waiting seasons, but God's goodness is never in question. Isaiah 40:31 echoes this truth: *"But those who wait on the Lord shall renew their strength."* When we trust that God is working, even when we don't see immediate results, we position ourselves to receive His strength.

The instruction to *"wait on the Lord"* is not passive—it is an active trust that expects God to move. Waiting does not mean doing nothing; it means standing in faith, holding onto His promises, and refusing to let go. The phrase *"be of good courage"* reminds us that courage is a choice. When we choose to trust God, He *"shall strengthen your heart."* His strength fills the places where ours fails, giving us endurance to press forward.

If you feel weary, take heart—God's goodness is not just a distant hope. Keep believing, keep expecting, and keep trusting. He is faithful, and He will strengthen you as you wait on Him. You will see His goodness in your life—don't give up before the breakthrough comes!

*So I will restore to you the years that the swarming locust
has eaten.... You shall eat in plenty and be satisfied,
and praise the name of the Lord your God, who has
dealt wondrously with you; and My people shall
never be put to shame.*

Joel 2:25-26

G od is the ultimate restorer. No matter what has been
stolen, broken, or wasted, He can bring it back—even
better than before. This promise was originally given
to Israel after a devastating plague of locusts, but it reveals a
powerful truth that applies to us today: God specializes in
restoring lost time, lost opportunities, and lost blessings.

Time is something we can never recover on our own, yet God
declares that even lost years—seasons of pain, struggle, or
regret—can be redeemed. He does not simply return what was
lost; He restores in a way that brings increase and abundance.

God's restoration is not just about replenishing; it is about
overflowing provision. *"You shall eat in plenty and be satisfied"*
is a picture of abundance and fulfillment. Where there was once
emptiness, God brings satisfaction. Psalm 23:5 echoes this: *"My
cup runs over."* His blessings are more than enough.

God's restoration removes disgrace. The enemy may try to
convince you that your past mistakes define you, but God
replaces shame with joy. His goodness transforms what was lost
into a testimony of His faithfulness.

If you have experienced loss, take heart—your story is not
over. Trust in God's restoring power, and expect to see Him
bring back *more* than you lost.

December 4

*Or do you not know that your body is the temple of the
Holy Spirit who is in you, whom you have from God,
and you are not your own? For you were bought at
a price; therefore glorify God in your body and in
your spirit, which are God's.*

1 Corinthians 6:19-20

Your life is not your own; you belong to God! This verse reminds us that as believers, we are not only saved by Jesus, but we are also indwelt by the Holy Spirit. Our bodies are not just ordinary vessels; they are sacred, designed to house His presence.

Paul calls our bodies *"the temple of the Holy Spirit,"* emphasizing that we are set apart. In the Old Testament, the temple was where God's presence dwelled. Now, under the New Covenant, He lives in *us*. This truth changes how we view ourselves. We are not merely human; we are carriers of God's Spirit. Romans 8:11 affirms, *"But if the Spirit of Him who raised Jesus from the dead dwells in you, He who raised Christ from the dead will also give life to your mortal bodies."* His Spirit empowers us to live victoriously!

Jesus paid the highest price—His own life—so that we could be redeemed. Knowing this should shape how we live. We do not live for ourselves but for the One who saved us. Paul urges, *"therefore glorify God in your body and in your spirit."* Our choices, actions, and even how we treat our bodies should honor God.

You are valuable, not because of what you do, but because of who resides in you! Live with the awareness that you are God's dwelling place, bought with a price, and created to glorify Him in every area of life.

*Yet in all these things we are more than
conquerors through Him who loved us.*

Romans 8:37

Victory in Christ is not in about overwhelming triumph against any adversary in this life. This verse reminds us that no matter what challenges we face, we are not merely enduring—we are *more than conquerors.*

When Paul says, *"all these things,"* he's referring to the trials mentioned earlier in the chapter—tribulation, distress, persecution, famine, danger, and even death. Yet, despite all these hardships, Paul does not say we barely make it through—he declares that we *overcome completely.* The Greek word for *more than conquerors (hypernikaō)* means to have surpassing victory, to overwhelmingly triumph. We do not just win; we win with abundance!

This victory is not through our own strength, but *"through Him who loved us."* It is God's love that gives us the power to overcome. His love is not based on circumstances—it is unshakable and eternal. Paul emphasizes this truth in the following verses, assuring us that nothing can separate us from His love (Romans 8:38-39). When we truly grasp the depth of God's love, we stop fighting from a place of defeat and start living from a place of victory.

Being more than a conqueror does not mean you will never face struggles, but it means that no struggle has the power to defeat you. No matter what opposition arises, the outcome is already settled—through Christ, you have the victory!

If you feel overwhelmed today, remember that you are not just surviving—you are overcoming! Stand firm in the love of God, knowing that He has already made you more than a conqueror.

Do not fear, little flock, for it is your Father's good pleasure to give you the kingdom.

Luke 12:32

God's heart toward us is one of generosity, not reluctance. In this verse, Jesus reassures His followers that they do not need to live in fear, because their Heavenly Father *delights* in blessing them.

"*Do not fear*" is one of the most repeated commands in Scripture. God knows that fear tries to steal our peace, especially when we worry about provision, security, or the future. But Jesus reminds us that we are part of God's "*little flock*"—a term of endearment that reflects His care as our Good Shepherd. Psalm 23:1 declares, "*The Lord is my shepherd; I shall not want.*" When we trust Him, we lack nothing, because He leads, protects, and provides for us.

The promise that "*it is your Father's good pleasure to give you the kingdom*" reveals God's deep love and willingness to bless His children. He does not give grudgingly—He *wants* to provide for us. In fact, Romans 8:32 says, "*He who did not spare His own Son, but delivered Him up for us all, how shall He not with Him also freely give us all things?*" The kingdom is not something we have to beg for—it is our inheritance in Jesus. He desires us to walk in the fullness of His provision, authority, and blessing, just as a loving father delights in caring for his children.

If fear has been holding you back, let this truth sink in: God is not just willing to bless you—He *delights* in it! Trust Him as your Shepherd, knowing He has already prepared good things for you. Step forward in faith, confident that He is leading you into His abundant kingdom.

As for God, His way is perfect; the word of the Lord is proven; He is a shield to all who trust in Him.

2 Samuel 22:31

In a world full of uncertainty, this verse reminds us that God's ways are flawless, His Word is trustworthy, and His protection is sure. When everything around us shifts, He remains steadfast.

God never makes mistakes. His plans are not only good but *perfect.* Even when circumstances seem confusing, we can trust that He sees the full picture. Isaiah 55:9 says, *"For as the heavens are higher than the earth, so are My ways higher than your ways, and My thoughts than your thoughts."* We may not always understand His ways, but we can always trust them.

The statement *"the word of the Lord is proven"* highlights that God's promises have stood the test of time. His Word has been fulfilled over and over again throughout history. Joshua 21:45 confirms this: *"Not a word failed of any good thing which the Lord had spoken to the house of Israel. All came to pass."* What He has promised, He will do.

Finally, *"He is a shield to all who trust in Him"* is a powerful reminder of God's protection. A shield does not remove the battle, but it does defend against the enemy's attacks. Trusting in God does not mean we won't face challenges, but it means we are covered, guarded, and sustained through them.

If you feel uncertain today, take refuge in Him. His ways are perfect, His Word is reliable, and He is your shield—always faithful, always protecting, and always leading you into victory.

December 8

The hand of the diligent will rule,
but the lazy man will be put to forced labor.

Proverbs 12:24

G od designed work to be a blessing, not a burden. This verse highlights the importance of diligence and the consequences of laziness. Those who commit to working with excellence and perseverance will experience leadership, influence, and promotion.

When it says *"the hand of the diligent will rule,"* it means that diligence brings authority. Those who are faithful and consistent in their efforts rise to positions of responsibility. Proverbs 22:29 affirms this principle: *"Do you see a man who excels in his work? He will stand before kings; he will not stand before unknown men."* Diligence positions us for favor and increase, both in the natural and in the kingdom of God.

On the other hand, *"the lazy man will be put to forced labor"* is a warning. Laziness leads to dependency on others, loss of opportunities, and an inability to progress. While the world often looks for shortcuts to success, God's way is through faithfulness. When we work with diligence, we are not just working for human recognition—we are worshiping and honoring God.

Diligence is more than hard work; it is a mindset of stewardship. Whether in business, ministry, or personal growth, consistent effort produces lasting results. If you want to see increase in your life, commit to working with excellence, knowing that God rewards those who are faithful with what they have been given.

Stay diligent, and watch as God opens doors of opportunity, promotion, and blessing in your life.

The Lord will perfect that which concerns me;
Your mercy, O Lord, endures forever; do not forsake the
works of Your hands.

Psalm 138:8

G od's plan for your life is not incomplete or uncertain. He is not figuring things out as He goes—He has already set His purpose in motion, and He promises to bring it to completion.

The phrase *"The Lord will perfect that which concerns me"* is a declaration of confidence. The word *perfect* means to complete, fulfill, or bring to maturity. This means that whatever God has started in your life, He will finish. Philippians 1:6 echoes this truth: *"He who has begun a good work in you will complete it until the day of Jesus Christ."* If He has called you, He has already made provision for everything you need to accomplish it.

The second part of the verse, *"Your mercy, O Lord, endures forever,"* reminds us that His faithfulness never runs out. His plans are not dependent on our perfection but on His unchanging mercy. Even when we fall short, He remains committed to us, to our development and growth, and to our success!

Finally, David prays, *"Do not forsake the works of Your hands."* This is not a plea of doubt but of trust. David knows that God does not abandon what He has created. If He formed you, He will sustain you. If He planted dreams in your heart, He will bring them to pass.

You are not forgotten, and your destiny is not in jeopardy. Trust that God is actively working, shaping, and fulfilling His purpose in your life. He will complete what He has started!

Now may He who supplies seed to the sower, and bread for food, supply and multiply the seed you have sown and increase the fruits of your righteousness, while you are enriched in everything for all liberality, which causes thanksgiving through us to God.

2 Corinthians 9:10-11

G od is both Provider and Multiplier. This passage reminds us that He not only gives us resources but also increases what we sow so that we can be a greater blessing to others.

God's role as our source includes both seed to sow and bread to eat. Everything we have—whether finances, talents, time, or opportunities—originates from Him. But notice that He supplies *seed to the sower.* This means those who are willing to give and invest in His kingdom will always have more to sow. Proverbs 11:25 reinforces this truth: *"The generous soul will be made rich, and he who waters will also be watered himself."*

God doesn't just provide—He multiplies! When we give in faith, He takes what we sow and brings a harvest of supernatural increase. This applies to more than money—it includes every way you sow: through kindness, faithfulness, service, and more.

And what is the purpose of God's blessings? He enriches us so that we can be generous! His provision is never just about us—it is about advancing His kingdom. When we give freely, we reflect His heart and bring thanksgiving to God.

Trust Him as both your supplier and multiplier. When you give, whether through finances, service, or encouragement, know that He is faithful to increase what you have sown.

*You open Your hand and satisfy the desire
of every living thing.*

Psalm 145:16

A bundance flows from God's open hand. He is not withholding good things from His children—He is freely giving, providing more than enough to meet every need. His generosity is not limited or conditional; it is part of His very nature.

The phrase *"You open Your hand"* is a powerful image of God's willingness to bless. He is not reluctant or hesitant—His hands are open, always ready to provide. Jesus reinforced this truth in Matthew 7:11: *"If you then, being evil, know how to give good gifts to your children, how much more will your Father who is in heaven give good things to those who ask Him!"* Earthly parents desire good for their children, but God's love and provision are infinitely greater! He knows exactly what we need and gives freely, without reservation. We never have to beg for His goodness—He is eager to pour it out.

The second part of the verse, *"and satisfy the desire of every living thing,"* shows that God does not just meet needs—He brings fulfillment. He created us with desires, and when our hearts are aligned with Him, He satisfies them in ways beyond our expectations. Psalm 37:4 declares, *"Delight yourself also in the Lord, and He shall give you the desires of your heart."* His blessings are not just material; they include peace, joy, and a deep sense of contentment that cannot be found anywhere else.

If you have been waiting on provision, know that God's hand is open toward you. He sees your needs, hears your prayers, and is ready to satisfy you with His goodness. Trust in His generous heart, receive all that He has in store for you, and live with expectation—His blessings are abundant and always available.

December 12

That your days and the days of your children may be multiplied in the land... like the days of the heavens above the earth.

Deuteronomy 11:21

This verse is tucked into a powerful promise God made to His people about walking in His ways. He told them that if they kept His Word close—talking about it, living by it, and teaching it to their children—their days would be multiplied, and not just theirs, but their children's too.

And not just multiplied in number, but in richness and fullness. *"Like the days of the heavens above the earth"* isn't just poetic—it's a glimpse of the kind of life God wants His people to experience. Long days, yes, but also days filled with peace, joy, and lasting impact. Days marked by divine rhythm, not stress or striving. It's life lived under the blessing of heaven.

This is a generational promise. When we live God's way, we're not only sowing into our own lives—we're planting seeds that affect our children and their children after them. That's legacy. And it comes from staying connected to Him in the everyday moments—choosing His Word, following His voice, and walking in obedience even when it's not popular.

You don't have to settle for days filled with chaos, fear, or regret. God's heart for you is longevity with purpose. It's not about scraping by; it's about thriving, generation after generation, in the land He's given you.

If you've felt rushed, weary, or unsure about the future, let this be a reminder: He's the God who multiplies days. He's the One who brings heaven's peace into our ordinary lives. And as you follow Him, you're making a way for those who come after you to walk in that same blessing.

And this I pray, that your love may abound still more and more in knowledge and all discernment, that you may approve the things that are excellent, that you may be sincere and without offense till the day of Christ.

Philippians 1:9-10

L ove is not meant to be stagnant—it is meant to grow, deepen, and mature. Paul's prayer for the Philippians was not just that they would love, but that their love would *abound* in knowledge and discernment.

Love is not just an emotion; it is a fruit that should continually increase. This love is not blind or shallow—it is rooted in truth. True love is strengthened by *knowledge* and *discernment*. Many assume that love is merely about being kind or accepting, but biblical love is discerning. It understands what is best and aligns with God's wisdom. 1 John 3:18 says, *"Let us not love in word or in tongue, but in deed and in truth."*

Paul continues, *"that you may approve the things that are excellent."* In a world full of distractions and compromises, believers are called to pursue excellence. Godly wisdom helps us distinguish between what is good and what is best. Romans 12:2 reminds us, *"Do not be conformed to this world, but be transformed by the renewing of your mind, that you may prove what is that good and acceptable and perfect will of God."*

Finally, *"that you may be sincere and without offense till the day of Christ"* points to a life of integrity. As we grow in love, knowledge, and discernment, we walk in sincerity, avoiding offense and living in a way that honors Christ.

Ask God to increase your love—not just in feeling, but in wisdom and discernment. When love is guided by truth, it leads to a life that is excellent, sincere, and pleasing to Him.

December 14

*Set your mind on things above,
not on things on the earth.*

Colossians 3:2

W hat we focus on determines the direction of our lives. This verse is a powerful reminder that as believers, our mindset should be shaped by heavenly realities, not earthly distractions.

"Set your mind on things above" implies an intentional decision. It is not a passive suggestion but an active choice to align our thoughts with God's truth. This does not mean we ignore our responsibilities or the world around us, but that we prioritize the eternal over the temporary. When we meditate on God's Word, His promises, and His character, we begin to see life through His perspective. When we do this, our faith grows and the issues of this world seem less troubling.

The second part, *"not on things on the earth,"* does not mean we should neglect our daily lives, but that we should not be consumed by worldly concerns. Earthly things—success, possessions, or even struggles—can easily take up our focus. However, physical things will come to an end, but spiritual things are eternal (2 Corinthians 4:18).

But how do we apply this? When your baby is crying in pain, set your eyes on the cross where Jesus took every sickness. If your bank account is empty, trust in the One who fed thousands with just a few loaves and fish—He is still your provider. When uncertainty arises, fix your mind on God's faithfulness, knowing He has already made a way.

What dominates your thoughts? Are they filled with worry, stress, and distractions, or are they centered on God's truth? Focus on things above, and live with greater faith, hope, and expectation.

This is my comfort in my affliction,
for Your word has given me life.

Psalm 119:50

God's Word is not just a book of history or principles—it is alive, powerful, and able to bring comfort in the hardest times. When we face difficulties, we don't have to be overcome by fear or despair. His promises sustain us, strengthen us, and give us life.

The psalmist declares, *"This is my comfort in my affliction."* He does not deny the presence of hardship, but he acknowledges where his true comfort comes from. Life is full of trials, but God's Word provides stability when everything else feels uncertain. Jesus said in John 16:33, *"In the world you will have tribulation; but be of good cheer, I have overcome the world."* This means that no matter what we face, we can hold onto the victory He has already secured!

The Word of God sustains us when those tribulations hit. When circumstances drain our strength, His Word revives us. Proverbs 4:20-22 reminds us that God's Word is *"life to those who find them, and health to all their flesh."* His truth not only brings spiritual renewal but also impacts our physical and emotional well-being. Just as our bodies need food to survive, our spirits need the nourishment of God's truth. Without it, we can grow weary, but with it, we find renewed hope and endurance.

When you feel overwhelmed, don't let discouragement have the final say. Turn to the promises of God. His Word is your source of comfort, strength, and renewal—it breathes life into every weary soul and reminds you that He is always faithful.

December 16

Hope deferred makes the heart sick,
But when the desire comes, it is a tree of life.

Proverbs 13:12

Waiting can be tough—especially when the thing you're believing for feels far off. Whether it's healing, provision, breakthrough, or a deeply personal dream, hope that feels delayed can wear you down. God understands that kind of weariness. Scripture doesn't ignore it—it acknowledges that deferred hope can make the heart ache.

But that's not where the verse stops. It goes on to remind us of the beauty of fulfillment: *when the desire comes, it is a tree of life.* That's more than just relief—it's refreshing, restorative, and deeply satisfying. Just like a tree brings shade, fruit, and stability, fulfilled hope brings joy that strengthens and sustains.

It's important to know that delay is not denial. Just because something hasn't happened yet doesn't mean it's not coming. God's timing may not match ours, but His faithfulness is unwavering. He sees the full picture, and He's working behind the scenes—even when we don't see it. Psalm 27:14 encourages us to *"wait on the Lord; be of good courage, and He shall strengthen your heart."* The waiting may feel long, but it's not empty. God is present in it.

If you're in a season of waiting, take heart. Don't let go of your hope. Keep trusting in the One who planted that desire in you. He hasn't forgotten, and He never fails. When the promise is fulfilled, it will bring more than just an answer—it will breathe life into every part of you. And it'll be worth every moment you spent holding on.

Call to Me, and I will answer you, and show you great and mighty things, which you do not know.

Jeremiah 33:3

Reaching out to God is not a one-sided conversation—He promises to answer! He is not distant, indifferent, or too busy. Instead, He invites us into a relationship where He responds, reveals, and guides us into His plans.

"*Call to Me*" is not just an offer; it is a command. God wants us to seek Him, to ask, and to expect an answer. Prayer is not a last resort; it is the way we connect with the One who knows everything and holds all wisdom. Jesus said this in Matthew 7:7: "*Ask, and it will be given to you; seek, and you will find; knock, and it will be opened to you.*" When we call on God, He hears us—not with reluctance, but with love and eagerness to respond. Even when we do not see immediate answers, we can trust that He is working behind the scenes for our good.

God promises not only to answer but to "*show you great and mighty things, which you do not know.*" His wisdom goes beyond human understanding, and He reveals things we could never figure out on our own. Sometimes, the answers He gives are unexpected, leading us into deeper trust. Ephesians 3:20 reminds us that He "*is able to do exceedingly abundantly above all that we ask or think.*" His plans are often bigger than our requests, unfolding in ways we never anticipated.

Are you facing uncertainty, a big decision, or a situation where you need direction? Call on God with confidence, knowing that He is eager to reveal His plans. He longs to show you great and mighty things—things beyond what you could ever imagine! All you have to do is ask and trust in His perfect timing.

On the last day, that great day of the feast, Jesus stood and cried out, saying, "If anyone thirsts, let him come to Me and drink. He who believes in Me, as the Scripture has said, out of his heart will flow rivers of living water."

John 7:37-38

Spiritual thirst is real. The world offers many things that give a hollow promise of satisfaction, yet nothing truly fulfills the longing of the human heart except Jesus. In this passage, He offers not just a temporary refreshment, but an ongoing, overflowing source of life.

The invitation is clear: *"If anyone thirsts, let him come to Me and drink."* This is an open call to all who recognize their need for something more. Just as our bodies cannot survive without water, our spirits cannot thrive without Christ. When we come to Him, He does not give just a small portion—He fills us to overflowing!

Jesus continues, *"He who believes in Me, as the Scripture has said, out of his heart will flow rivers of living water."* This *"living water"* represents the Holy Spirit, whom Jesus gives to those who believe (John 7:39). This means His presence within us is not stagnant but continually refreshing and renewing. Just as a river brings life wherever it flows, the Spirit of God within us overflows into every area of our lives, impacting not only us but those around us as well.

Are you feeling spiritually dry? Come to Jesus! Drink deeply of His presence. He will not only satisfy your thirst but will make you a source of life and encouragement to others. His Spirit in you is an endless river—flowing with joy, peace, and power.

If you then, being evil, know how to give good gifts to your children, how much more will your Father who is in heaven give good things to those who ask Him!

Matthew 7:11

Every loving parent desires to give good things to their children. They provide food, shelter, protection, and affection, not out of obligation, but out of love. In this verse, Jesus uses that natural parental instinct to illustrate an even greater truth—if flawed human parents know how to give good gifts, how much more does our perfect Heavenly Father delight in blessing His children?

God is not just a little better than earthly parents—His goodness surpasses all human love! Unlike human love, which can be limited or conditional, God's love is unwavering. He gives, not reluctantly, but joyfully. He knows exactly what we need and when we need it. His timing and His gifts are always perfect.

However, Jesus also emphasizes *"to those who ask Him."* God is a generous giver, but He also wants us to come to Him in faith. He is not withholding good things; He is inviting us to trust Him, ask Him, and believe in His provision. Psalm 84:11 reminds us, *"No good thing will He withhold from those who walk uprightly."* Just as a child confidently asks a loving parent for help, we can approach God boldly, knowing He delights in responding to our needs.

Are you hesitant to ask God for what you need? Know that He delights in blessing you. Approach Him with confidence, knowing that He is a loving Father who desires to give you every good thing that aligns with His perfect plan for your life. When you trust Him fully, you can live in joyful expectation of His goodness.

Now hope does not disappoint, because the love of God has been poured out in our hearts by the Holy Spirit who was given to us.

Romans 5:5

Hope in God is never in vain. Unlike worldly hope, which is uncertain, biblical hope is a confident expectation of His goodness based on our trust in His faithfulness. This verse assures us that when we place our hope in Him, we will never be disappointed because His love has already been poured into our hearts.

The phrase *"hope does not disappoint"* is a powerful declaration. In a world where people experience broken promises and unfulfilled expectations, God's promises stand firm. He does not tease us with empty words—His Word is true and unfailing. Numbers 23:19 reminds us, *"God is not a man, that He should lie, nor a son of man, that He should repent. Has He said, and will He not do?"* Because He is faithful, we can trust that our hope in Him is secure.

Paul explains why this hope is so certain: *"Because the love of God has been poured out in our hearts by the Holy Spirit."* God does not give us a small portion of His love—He pours it out abundantly. This love is not based on our performance or circumstances but is a gift from the Holy Spirit. Just as a downpour of rain soaks the earth, God's love completely fills our hearts, leaving no room for fear or doubt.

If you've ever felt let down, know that God's love is unshakable. His Spirit within you is a constant reminder of His presence and faithfulness. Let this truth anchor your heart—hope in Him will never leave you disappointed!

The plans of the diligent lead surely to plenty, but those of everyone who is hasty, surely to poverty.

Proverbs 21:5

S uccess is rarely the result of luck—it is the fruit of diligence, wisdom, and consistency. This verse highlights the contrast between those who carefully plan and work diligently versus those who rush ahead without thought.

Prosperity and increase are the result of steady, intentional effort. God is not against abundance—He desires for His people to walk in blessing. However, He does not reward laziness or reckless decision-making. Proverbs 10:4 confirms, *"He who has a slack hand becomes poor, but the hand of the diligent makes rich."* Diligence is about more than working hard; it includes seeking God's wisdom, stewarding resources well, and making choices that align with His principles.

On the other hand, *"everyone who is hasty"* refers to those who act impulsively, chasing quick fixes or shortcuts. A lack of patience often leads to poor decisions and unnecessary struggles. Proverbs 28:22 warns, *"A man with an evil eye hastens after riches, and does not consider that poverty will come upon him."* God's way is not about instant gratification—it is about steady, faithful progress.

Are you making decisions with diligence and wisdom, or are you rushing ahead without seeking God's guidance? True success comes from planning with Him, working with integrity, and trusting that He will bring increase in due time. Be patient, stay diligent, and watch as He blesses the work of your hands.

Jesus said to her, "I am the resurrection and the life.
He who believes in Me, though he may die, he shall live.
And whoever lives and believes in Me shall never die.
Do you believe this?"

John 11:25-26

Death is not the end for those who believe in Jesus. When He spoke to Martha after Lazarus died, He wasn't just offering comfort—He was revealing something deeper. He is the resurrection and the life, and that truth changes everything. Eternal life doesn't start when we die; it begins the moment we believe!

Jesus wasn't simply pointing to a future resurrection. He was declaring that resurrection power was standing right in front of her. Life in Him isn't just about someday—it's for right now. His Spirit brings strength, healing, and restoration in the middle of our current reality. What once felt final or hopeless can be revived when touched by the life of God. Nothing is beyond His reach.

And then Jesus asked her a simple but profound question: *"Do you believe this?"* It's a question He still asks us today. Do we truly believe that He's more powerful than death, loss, or fear? Do we believe His life in us is greater than anything trying to come against us? Do we really believe that what He has for us is an abundant life here on earth?

If you're facing something that feels overwhelming or final, remember this: His life in you is stronger. His resurrection power is active right now—not just to save your soul, but to revive your hope, strengthen your heart, breathe life into dreams you thought were gone, and bring breakthrough. There is no situation too far gone when Jesus is present. He is life itself—and that life is already at work in you.

For whatever things were written before were written for our learning, that we through the patience and comfort of the Scriptures might have hope.

Romans 15:4

God's Word was given not just for instruction, but for encouragement, strength, and hope. Every promise, every historical account, and every lesson in Scripture was written to equip us for life and remind us that no matter what we face, there is always hope in Him.

The phrase *"whatever things were written before were written for our learning"* points to the entire Word of God. The Bible is not just an old book filled with stories—it is living, relevant, and full of wisdom for today. From Genesis to Revelation, we see God's faithfulness, His power, and His love for His people. 2 Timothy 3:16 confirms, *"All Scripture is given by inspiration of God, and is profitable for doctrine, for reproof, for correction, for instruction in righteousness."* Every passage serves a purpose, guiding us to grow in faith and trust Him more. Even the difficult stories in the Bible serve as examples, showing us God's mercy and the power of His redemption.

Paul continues, *"that we through the patience and comfort of the Scriptures might have hope."* Life is filled with challenges, but God's Word strengthens us to endure. When we see how He delivered, healed, and provided for those before us, it builds our confidence that He will do the same today. His promises are not just for those in the past—they are for you, right now.

Are you feeling discouraged? Dive into the Word. Let the Scriptures fill you with patience, comfort, and unshakable hope. The same God who was faithful then is faithful now, and His promises for you will never fail.

*The steps of a good man are ordered by the Lord,
and He delights in his way.*

Psalm 37:23

L ife is full of choices, and sometimes it's difficult to know if we're on the right path. This verse assures us that when we trust God, He directs our steps, ensuring that we walk in His perfect plan—right in the middle of His will for our lives.

God isn't distantly observing our lives without getting involved. He is actively working in our circumstances, arranging divine appointments, opening doors, and guiding us, step by step. He cares about the little decisions just as much as the big ones. Even when we don't see the full picture, we can trust that He is leading us in the right direction with perfect timing, wisdom, and care.

The second part of the verse, *"and He delights in his way,"* is a beautiful reminder of God's love for us. He doesn't just tolerate us—He takes joy in watching us walk in His purpose. Just as a loving parent delights in seeing their child grow and learn, God rejoices in our obedience and trust. Even when we stumble, He doesn't pull away. Psalm 37:24 continues, *"Though he fall, he shall not be utterly cast down; for the Lord upholds him with His hand."*

His guidance isn't just about arriving—it's about growing along the way. Are you unsure about your next step? Trust that God is guiding you. Seek Him in prayer, lean on His Word, and move forward with confidence. You're not walking alone—He's with you, ordering your steps, strengthening your heart, and delighting in your journey.

*Blessed is she who believed, for there will be a fulfillment
of those things which were told her from the Lord.*

Luke 1:45

Faith unlocks what God has already spoken into your
life. The moment you take Him at His Word, you step
into the blessing that He always meant for you to have.
When He speaks, and you receive it by faith, it will be fulfilled!

Mary didn't see the fulfillment of God's promise to her
immediately, but she *believed* it. That's what made her
blessed—her faith, not her circumstances. She didn't wait for
everything to make sense or for outward signs of confirmation.
She simply trusted that if God said it, it was as good as done.

This kind of trust goes beyond feelings or logic. It's not blind—
it's anchored in the character of a God who never lies and never
fails. Faith says, "Even if I can't see it yet, I believe You're
working." And that belief positions you to receive.

God has already spoken His promises over you. His Word is
full of declarations of healing, provision, peace, and purpose.
They're not vague hopes—they are guaranteed by His
faithfulness. But like Mary, we have a part to play: we believe.
And when we do, we are counted among the blessed!

It's easy to let delay make us doubt. Hope deferred can try to
wear us down. But the moment you choose to believe again,
hope springs to life. Faith is the hand that reaches out and grabs
hold of what grace has already made available.

Don't wait for the perfect moment to believe—start now.
Rejoice before you see it. Speak His promises out loud. Let your
faith rise and push past every doubt. There will be a fulfillment.
God always finishes what He starts. Just like Mary, you are
blessed because you believe!

December 26

I will instruct you and teach you in the way you should go; I will guide you with My eye.

Psalm 32:8

Decisions shape our lives, and knowing which path to take is not always easy. But we are not left to navigate life alone—God Himself promises to instruct, teach, and guide us. He is not a distant observer; He is a loving Father who actively leads us in the right direction.

The phrase *"I will instruct you and teach you"* highlights God's personal involvement in our growth. His guidance is not vague or impersonal—it is specific and tailored to our journey. James 1:5 assures us, *"If any of you lacks wisdom, let him ask of God, who gives to all liberally and without reproach, and it will be given to him."* He does not withhold wisdom from those who seek Him, nor does He expect us to figure everything out on our own. He delights in revealing His will to His kids!

The next part, *"I will guide you with My eye,"* speaks of His attentive care. It is a picture of a loving parent watching over a child, directing them with a simple look or nudge. Unlike worldly advice, which often leads to confusion, God's guidance is perfect. Proverbs 3:6 promises, *"In all your ways acknowledge Him, and He shall direct your paths."* His leading is not forceful, but gentle—He shows us the way and gives us the choice to follow. His direction brings peace, confidence, and security, even when the future seems uncertain.

Are you facing uncertainty? Instead of relying on your own understanding, seek His instruction. God's wisdom will never lead you astray, and His presence will never leave you to figure things out alone. Trust Him to guide your steps—His way is always best, and He will never lead you where His grace cannot sustain you.

The Lord will guide you continually, and satisfy your soul in drought, and strengthen your bones; you shall be like a watered garden, and like a spring of water, whose waters do not fail.

Isaiah 58:11

God never intended for His people to live in survival mode—in a constant stake of lack, weakness, or uncertainty. On the contrary, this verse offers a beautiful promise of how He leads, sustains, and strengthens us every step of the way in a life of abundant supply.

It begins with the assurance that God's guidance isn't occasional—it's constant. He's not just available during crises or major crossroads. He is with you daily, offering wisdom, direction, and peace as you walk with Him. Even when the path ahead seems unclear, His presence brings clarity.

Then we're reminded that He satisfies our soul in dry seasons. Life isn't always easy. There are times we face pressure, lack, or disappointment. But even in those moments, God provides what no one else can. He nourishes the soul. He fills the empty places. His presence becomes the refreshment that carries us through drought.

The final part of this verse paints a picture of steady, overflowing strength. A watered garden thrives, and a spring never runs dry. That's the kind of life God promises—one rooted in Him, flourishing even when circumstances don't look ideal. His Spirit refreshes us from the inside out, producing peace, joy, and vitality that cannot be shaken.

If you've been feeling worn out or uncertain, let this verse remind you: God is your guide, your strength, and your source. Stay connected to Him, and you'll never run dry. He is faithful to refresh and restore you daily.

He who did not spare His own Son,
but delivered Him up for us all, how shall He
not with Him also freely give us all things?

Romans 8:32

G od doesn't bless reluctantly—He blesses freely. If He didn't hold back His own Son, the most precious gift imaginable, why would He hesitate to provide anything else you need?

The word *freely* here is translated from the Greek word *charizomai*, which comes from the root *charis*, meaning grace. It carries the idea of giving generously, out of favor—not based on merit, but out of love. This isn't about God paying you back for good behavior. This is about His heart to bless, simply because you're His.

He already gave the greatest gift—Jesus. That gift cost Him everything. So, it only makes sense that He would also provide everything else needed for the life He's called you to live. That includes spiritual gifts like wisdom and peace, but it also includes practical needs like healing, strength, and financial provision.

When you understand the magnitude of what He's already given, it puts everything else into perspective. Need provision for your bills? Direction for a big decision? Comfort in grief? Strength for your body? He's not just willing—He's eager to provide. And He does it *freely*.

If you've been wondering whether God really wants to take care of you, let this verse settle it once and for all. Look at Jesus. He gave His best for you already. What makes you think He'd stop now?

You don't have to beg. You don't have to earn. Just believe and receive. His generosity flows from grace—and He delights in blessing His children.

But the path of the just is like the shining sun,
that shines ever brighter unto the perfect day.

Proverbs 4:18

L ife with God is not stagnant. It is a journey of continual growth, transformation, and increasing clarity. This verse beautifully illustrates how those who walk with Him experience an ever-brightening path, filled with His guidance, wisdom, and abundant life.

The *"path of the just"* refers to those who have been made righteous through faith in Christ. As we follow Him, our journey becomes brighter—filled with growing clarity, purpose, and maturity. Psalm 119:105 reminds us, *"Your word is a lamp to my feet and a light to my path."* God's Word lights the way, guiding each step so we never have to walk in confusion or darkness.

The imagery of *"the shining sun"* reminds us that our journey with God is progressive. Just as the sun rises gradually, bringing more light with each passing moment, so does our understanding, faith, and spiritual growth increase over time. We don't receive all wisdom at once, but as we walk with God, He continually reveals more of Himself and His plans for us. 2 Corinthians 3:18 describes this process: *"But we all, with unveiled face, beholding as in a mirror the glory of the Lord, are being transformed into the same image from glory to glory."*

This verse also offers hope. If you feel like you're in a season of uncertainty, remember that your path is not meant to grow dim but to shine ever brighter. God is leading you forward, and His light will continue to grow in your life. Keep walking with Him, knowing that He is bringing you into greater revelation, victory, and fulfillment.

Therefore I remind you to stir up the gift of God which is in you through the laying on of my hands.

2 Timothy 1:6

God has placed gifts, callings, and abilities inside each of us, but it's our responsibility to stir them up and put them to use. Paul wrote this encouragement to Timothy, a young leader who needed a reminder to actively engage with the gifts God had given him. The same applies to us today—what God has placed in you is powerful, but it must be cultivated and developed.

A fire left unattended can die down, but stirring the embers reignites the flames. In the same way, spiritual gifts can grow dormant if we neglect them. Romans 12:6 says, *"Having then gifts differing according to the grace that is given to us, let us use them."* Whether it's a gift of teaching, encouragement, leadership, or serving, God's intent is that we stir up and use what He has given us to bless others and advance His kingdom.

Fear, doubt, or complacency can cause us to hesitate, but the next verse reminds us, *"For God has not given us a spirit of fear, but of power and of love and of a sound mind"* (2 Timothy 1:7). The enemy wants to keep us timid, but God calls us to boldness. When we step out in faith, He provides the strength and confidence we need.

Have you been neglecting a gift God has given you? It's time to stir it up! Step out in faith, use what He has placed inside you, and trust that He will empower you. You are equipped for His purpose, and as you take action, your gifts will grow stronger and impact those around you.

But seek first the kingdom of God and His righteousness, and all these things shall be added to you.

Matthew 6:33

What you prioritize determines the direction of your life. In this verse, Jesus gives us a simple but powerful principle: when we put God first, everything else falls into place. Whether it's at work, school, business, or as a parent, when you place God as the top priority in your life, you won't have to worry about the rest.

To seek first the kingdom of God means to pursue His ways, His will, and His purposes above all else. It's not about adding God to our plans—it's about aligning our lives with His. Proverbs 3:6 reinforces this, saying, *"In all your ways acknowledge Him, and He shall direct your paths."* When we seek Him first, He leads us in the right direction.

Jesus spoke this verse in the context of worry. Just before this, He told His followers not to stress about food, clothing, or the cares of life because their Heavenly Father knows what they need (Matthew 6:31-32). The world chases after material things, but Jesus calls us to a different focus. When we put God first, He takes care of our needs. Philippians 4:19 assures us, *"And my God shall supply all your need according to His riches in glory by Christ Jesus."*

This promise doesn't mean we sit back and do nothing. Seeking first the kingdom means following God's voice, walking in faith, and trusting God's provision. When we put Him above our ambitions, relationships, and desires, He ensures that everything we truly need is provided.

If you've been feeling overwhelmed by life's demands, shift your focus. Instead of chasing after things, chase after God! When you seek Him first, you'll find that His blessings, provision, and direction will follow.

OTHER BOOKS
BY TERRADEZ MINISTRIES

All Is Not Lost: *Your Path from Trauma to Victory*

Fearless: *Breaking the Habit of Fear*

Miracles and Healing Made Easy: *Inspiring Stories of Faith*

Thorns, Barns, & Oil Jars: *Uproot Financial Misconsceptions*

God Wants You Rich: *The Scandalous Truth*

Exposing the Spirit of Mammon: *Make God Not Money Your Master*

Your Life with God: *What It Means to Be Born Again and Receive the Baptism of the Holy Spirit*

39 Reasons Healing is Yours: *Healing Scriptures That Beat Sickness to Death*

Hannah and the Beanstalk! *A True Story of Faith*

Hannah and the Lost Jelly Shoe *A True Story of Faith*

Hearing God: *31 Daily Devotions That Tune You in to God's Frequency*

AVAILABLE ON OUR WEBSITE
TERRADEZMINISTRIES.COM/SHOP

EMPOWERING BELIEVERS
IN THE PROMISES OF GOD

Ashley and Carlie Terradez have a mandate to empower believers in God's prooises, exercising Luke 4:18 by proclaiming and providing an example of God's promises and provision through Christ Jesus. With a special emphasis on relationship with God, supernatural healing, and financial provision, we empower people to access everything that Jesus has already provided for us through His death, burial, and resurrection.

On our website, you will find many free ministry resources and discipleship programs made available by our generous partners.

TerradezMinistries.com

Connect with Us

YOUR HOUSE OF
FAITH

Sign up for a **FREE** subscription to the Harrison House digital magazine and get excellent content delivered directly to your inbox!

harrisonhouse.com/signup

Sign up for Messages that Equip You to Walk in the Abundant Life

• Receive biblically sound and Spirit-filled encouragement to focus on and maintain your faith
• Grow in faith through biblical teachings, prayers, and other spiritual insights
• Connect with a community of believers who share your values and beliefs

Experience Fresh Teachings and Inspiration to Build Your Faith

Deepen your understanding of God's purpose for your life
Stay connected and inspired on your faith journey
Learn how to grow spiritually in your walk with God

In the Right Hands, This Book Will Change Lives!

Most of the people who need this message will not be looking for this book. To change their lives, you need to **put a copy of this book in their hands.**

Our ministry is constantly seeking methods to find the people who need this anointed message to change their lives. **Will you help us reach these people?**

Extend this ministry by sowing three, five, ten, or *even more* books today and change people's lives for the better! Your generosity will be part of catalyzing the Great Awakening that many have been prophesying and praying for.

www.ingramcontent.com/pod-product-compliance
Lightning Source LLC
Chambersburg PA
CBHW070403100426
42812CB00005B/1624